"By turns lyrical, sassy, witty, and reverent, Debra Rienstra reclaims the spiritual power of a woman's body, mind, and soul."

· BONNI GOLDBERG, author of *Beyond the Words* and *The Spirit of Pregnancy*

"Celebratory, reflective, and gloriously true, *Great with Child* is the thinking woman's companion to pregnancy."

· LORILEE CRAKER, author of *When the Belly Button Pops, the Baby's Done*

"A polished meditation on the body, on creativity and change, on the relations between men and women, and on our relationship to God."

· TRUDY BUSH, *The Christian Century*

"Combines a richly informed feminism with an equally informed faith."

· JILL LIGHTNER, amazon.com

"By about page ten, most readers will wish they could sit down with Rienstra and have a heart-to-heart. . . ."

· LAUREN WINNER, *Books & Culture*

D1468833

great with child

ON BECOMING A MOTHER

Debra Rienstra

WordFarm
LA PORTE, INDIANA

WordFarm
2010 Michigan Avenue
La Porte, IN 46350
www.wordfarm.net
info@wordfarm.net

Cover Image: iStockPhoto
Cover Design: Andrew Craft
USA ISBN-13: 978-1-60226-003-0
USA ISBN-10: 1-60226-003-6

Printed in the United States of America

Library of Congress Cataloging-in-Publication Data

Data applied for.

P 10 9 8 7 6 5 4 3 2
Y 19 18 17 16 15 14 13

contents

Thus great with child to speak, and helpless in my throes,
Biting my truant pen, beating myself for spite,
"Fool," said my muse to me; "look in thy heart, and write."

SIR PHILIP SIDNEY, *Astrophil and Stella,* SONNET 1

1) *longing*

Not so much a thought as a pinpoint on the horizon of thought; not so much appearing as the
world slowly rolling to reveal it; not so much
the world but a breath of eternity, releasing this
infinitesimal Yes. Between meetings and paper-
work and meal plans and financial decisions and
the seemingly more substantial everything of life,
it drifts quietly toward resolution, takes hold in a
little crevice of mind, and begins. There is time
now in the cluttered shuffle of things for only this
tiny Yes.

We have been speaking of it, my husband and I, with few and care-ful words, as it has a kind of sacred piquance. To speak of it aloud too much might flatten or dishonor it. But this slip of assent will grow.

For me, this Yes arises from within the kind of human hunger that memory forms and feeds. Five years after Miriam was born, three after Jacob, I remember their babyhoods with a mute, heart-clutching nostalgia. This is a fresh longing now for an experience (or the pre-served portion of it) I have lived before: first, the deep attentiveness of pregnancy, then the harrowing intensity of birth, then that surren-der of the self to demands that press the boundaries of endurance and to a small person who, once here, will make any previous life seem impossibly incomplete.

There are other strands of hunger tangled up in this, too, spindly little shabby ones: a weary desire to escape the routine, the inconve-nient, the tedious difficulties of getting up, going to work, coming home. I half know I'm looking for change and variety, excitement, risk, for an escape.

But deeper than all that is the peculiar hunger of the body itself. Not for sexual union, although of course that human longing for inti-macy is caught up, masterfully, with the desire to create. The body-hunger I feel is low in the gut, a kind of emptiness repeatedly reaching out to be filled. It is ancient, archetypal.

I came across a strangely unembroidered, uncontextualized oracle in the biblical book of Proverbs that tells me I'm not the only one to feel the womb itself seem to cry out in this hunger:

> *There are three things that are never satisfied,*
> *four that never say, "Enough!":*
> *the grave, the barren womb,*

land, which is never satisfied with water,
and fire, which never says, "Enough!"

The longing to create life is elemental, on the level of fire, earth, and death. The steadily humming tissues and organs, as they play out their unconscious patterns, long to serve something spiritual, to touch the eternal. Perhaps the mortal body snatches out toward the immortal body. I believe that immortality is not a matter of disembodied spirits floating about in some cloudy afterlife, but of flesh, the carnal, renewed and perfected beyond our imaginings, reborn with all of creation. It does not seem strange to me, then, that our physical bodies lean hard, with our souls, toward the eternal.

Laughter

I've been taught since childhood that the Bible is an instructive place for exploring elementally human things, and no part of it is more elemental than the book of Genesis, with its ancient stories telling us like vivid and persistent dreams the deep truths of humanity, God, and ourselves. Womb-hunger, I find, is a deep current in the familiar stories of the matriarchs. Sarah, Rebekah, and Rachel are all "barren" for a time until the Lord "remembers" or "listens to" their pleas. For Sarah and Abraham, barrenness is an especially wrenching and puzzling problem, as God promises early in their story to make Abraham the father of a great nation. But chapters go by and no conception occurs. Some commentators, particularly feminist ones, see the pattern of barrenness, delay, and joyful fulfillment in these stories as one important way in which ancient Hebrew writers as-

serted the superior power of their one, true, and, not incidentally, masculine God over the fertility-goddess religions among which Hebrew
monotheism arose. Fertility, these ancient writers wished to emphasize, comes not from goddess-idols or the earth's cycles, but from
God alone. This erasure of the power of feminine divinity by a superior, masculine divine power follows the pattern of many Near
Eastern civilizations, in fact. The matriarchal gives way to the patriarchal, and a world of woes for women ensues.

But the delay between desire and physical conception in the Genesis narratives is more than a compositional device in service of religious orthodoxy. It is a basic matter of human experience. Perhaps
the barren times in these stories, and later, in a more detailed and
poignant version in the story of Hannah, emphasize the power of
God over the womb, but they also offer a pattern of longing to participate with the creator in the creation of something greater than
oneself. Cultural historians might suggest that these women wanted
children because a son was their only avenue to status and a remembered name. Barrenness, in their culture, would make them a
shamed nothing, a cipher. But their longing, and that of their husbands,
spreads outward into the symbolic, signifying all our longings to defy
death. It is located not just in their own time and place, but in the
human soul.

Moreover, in the songs of joy they sing when the babies finally
do come, these ancient mothers recognize the power of God let loose
within them. Rather than being silent vessels of the masculine God's
power, they are given voices; they express longing and anger and
frustration and then triumph when their longings are fulfilled. Biblical scholar Phyllis Trible shows that the God of these narratives is
consistently described throughout the Hebrew scriptures as the God
of compassion, and the Hebrew verb to express having compassion

(*racham*) is directly related to the word for womb (*rechem*). The woman's womb is the physical metaphor for the abundant love of God.
Thus the power of God over fertility remains a feminine power, and
the experience of the mother in bringing forth life parallels the power
of the Creator to bring forth all things. The words of the First Mother,
Eve, on the birth of her first son echo this relationship of co-creation:
"With the help of the Lord I have brought forth a man." (The name
Cain is a pun on the Hebrew for "brought forth" or "gotten.") The
"getting" of a new person is a source of joy and delight, just as the
creation of the world is depicted as a source of delight to the Creator,
a delight emphasized not only by the declarations of "very good," but
also by the earthy wordplay of the Hebrew account. Sarah's response
to her son Isaac's birth best expresses this joy. When Isaac is finally
born in her old age, she acknowledges both her earlier disbelief at
this possibility as well as her joy at the reality of it by naming her son
"he laughs"—a cleverly honest name—and she remarks: "God has
brought me laughter, and everyone who hears about this will laugh
with me." God has done this, and it is marvelous in her weary, shining
eyes.

   This is the laughter Ron and I hunger and wait for now, the
laughter of participating in creation, of letting our flawed, sometimes
doubtful, foolish, cynical, selfish, but ultimately loved and glorious
selves experience in our bodies the delight and power of God.

A w a k e n i n g

   I had experienced the hunger and its fulfillment twice before, and
it lay dormant for a time. But it was reawakened the spring my daughter was four, my son was two, and I thought I had become pregnant

without planning to. It began with queer feelings in the stomach and tingling in the breasts. Long before my period was due, I started obsessing: *What if . . . ?* I was rather alarmed; this was no time for a new baby. My job was far too demanding and I was too unsettled in it. And yet, feeling that hunger awakened, I was secretly glad. I began to think of a new baby as an escape. This would spare me the difficulty of fighting that daily battle to do my job well and prove to others that I could do it.

A weird obsession took over. I started composing possible speeches to my department chair. Perhaps I should try the cavalier approach: "Well, you know, these things happen!" Or maybe the detailed, scientific explanation: "It must have been those antibiotics that suppressed the effect of the pill." Or perhaps the blunt approach would be best: "You know what? I'm glad, as this will give me an excuse for a graceful exit from this good-for-nothing job!" Meanwhile, I obsessively noted subtle changes in my body, clandestinely inspecting my breasts about 25 times a day, wondering if it could be true, hoping it was, wanting the inescapable complications of it all. In a spasm of breathless irrationality, I even went out and bought a pregnancy test. It was negative. Well, maybe I took it too early, I thought.

But then, my period came, right on time. And I felt relieved. It was not yet, I concluded in calm and dignified mental tones, the Right Time. I really did have to give my professional work more of a chance. I wanted my son to grow up a little bit more before having a sibling. Yes, this was best. But still I puzzled over why I had experienced what seemed like convincing symptoms. Could it have been psychosomatic? My body's way of fulfilling a semiconscious wish to just give up and get out of my job? A cowardly reaction on my part, if true. But finally I concluded that my body was probably not doing anything unusual at all; I was simply paying attention for once to a hormonal routine I usually ignored.

Once I had finished marveling at my own silliness, one thing remained: where before I hadn't been absolutely sure, now I knew that I definitely wanted another child. Making an emergency space for one in my addled mind convinced me that I deeply desired to make a real space for one soon. When I told Ron about this, he needed no convincing at all. "You know I want more kids!" was his matter-of-fact reaction. Perhaps, then, this little practice run was a matter of body wisdom more than psychic foolishness, a hunger cry from within.

The Reckless Yes

So the fitting number of months have passed, and now we permit ourselves to speak the Yes, with words and with our bodies, deliberately and surely.

When I went off the pill I started listening to my body again. I attended to its rhythms and subtle shifts. On the third day of my first non-chemically controlled period, I had a horrible headache all day, the kind of headache that feels as if some tank of brain chemicals had bottomed out and my brain was shriveling up inside my skull. I took Ron's old college textbook for human biology off the shelf and found a helpful chart showing that this is not too far from what actually happens: the levels of both estrogen and progesterone plummet just before the onset of menstruation. This explains the terrible upheaval some women feel in their bodies at this time. The "progesterone plummet" can be fast and severe, making it tough for the body's systems to cope gracefully. Then, the levels of both hormones bottom out during the bleeding stage of the cycle. The resulting headache for me on that bottom-out day was a rotten distraction, but it occurred to me that I might better think of it as a kind of ritual emptying, a low point on a curve that could now rise to buoy something completely new and uncontrolled, something outside myself and my ability to direct.

This is why I am fond of this moment of the Yes: it is reckless.

Recklessness and fertility go together. The ancient Greeks knew this in the person of the crazy party god Dionysus. Recklessness is not, of course, always a good thing. Dionysus is also the god of drunkenness, excess, even violence. For some people, the act that engenders conception is most unfortunately reckless, as one or both partners say "yes" only to heated flesh in the moment, or to some confused desire for acceptance and love, and not to the potential consequences. And when there is violence, then there is no Yes at all, but only a male assent to misogynistic violence and evil, and the life that results seems a cruelly ironic backlash at the destructive forces that initiated it. God have mercy.

But even when the decision to have a child is a fully conscious one, it is not without recklessness. Ron and I know very well that another child is laughably impractical. We are both semicompetent professionals, with enough investment in education to strongly motivate us both toward career-minded decisions. Since our two children will both be in school in a couple of years, the careerist thing to do would be to wait out these two years with our current one-main-income arrangement (mine) and then move ahead full steam on parallel career tracks. Moreover, since we are committed to religious education for our children—a soberingly expensive prospect—another child would increase our financial burden for education alone by 50 percent. Combined with the longer "wait" time until the kids are in school and the reduced income during that time, another child is, financially speaking, a mistake.

And it's not just money. The slow track is hard not because we're so ambitious for career advancement, but because there are so many things we love to do that we have set aside for a season because our children need our time and energy. When I think of all the music I can't play, all the books I can't read, all the exercise I'm definitely not getting, I often drift toward self-pity and sometimes despair. I would never make a different choice. I never resent what I give to Miriam and Jacob. But I do keenly feel the loss of what I give up. Another child will mean more of this, for a longer time.

And besides all that, our house isn't quite big enough, either. We're filling up the bedrooms now. Where would we put a nursery?

Well, one can duly note these contingencies, listing them off in late-evening sessions with pencils and yellow legal pads. But pragmatism hardly captures my fancy. Instead, I find the recklessness irresistibly alluring. I greet it with a sense of rebellion against all that is practical and sensible, about me, about anything. My usual taste for control and closure makes this recklessness all the more delicious. It is a relief from myself. I take pleasure now in surrendering to the unknown.

Human beings must begin in recklessness. Even the most carefully planned and intensely wanted baby must begin with the parents saying Yes to something they cannot control. I wonder if creation is always like this. I wonder if God felt reckless when he spoke the first creative word. The Judeo-Christian notion of divine creation through fiat and the majestically ordered poem of creation in Genesis hardly suggest recklessness, but I like to think of God covering his eyes with one hand, cringing with the wildness of it all, and saying "Let there be . . ." Then, the cautious parting of the fingers, the divine eye peeping through, a reverberant whisper declaring, almost in surprise: "That's good!"

This giving over of the self to whatever happens, this poising of the self for possibility—I could not relish it if it weren't for the ultimate trust I have in the sense of this universe, in the compassion and power of the Creator, in God's sharing of hunger and promise of joy, somehow, sometime. This is not, for me, recklessness in a void. The giving over of my tiny helm is a chance to drift on something larger than myself. So I say now: Streams and patterns of cosmic flow, chance and chaos, Providence and Divine Love—now *you* decide. I merely open myself, and wait.

2) possible futures

Counting

So now, the marking of the calendar, the counting of days, the wrestling with what might be and what is not yet.

During the first cycle, I manage to shrug off most of the twinges and snortles of my internal operations until about day 21. For several days in the middle of the month we were busy "working on the project"—Ron and I are readier to joke a bit now. But then comes that dreadfully slow week of waiting and wondering. Do I feel anything? Is that a new twinge? Or just premenstrual? *Well, who can know?* I casually chirp to myself. I pretend to be very cool and controlled.

I didn't know this the last two times we set out to conceive, but apparently at the moment when egg meets sperm, no particular signals radiate jubilantly throughout the woman's body. Oh, there are little chemical perturbations right at the site of the new cell, but nothing gets into the bloodstream. Not until touchdown occurs, and the tiny entity (called a blastocyst by the time it reaches the uterus) actually picks a spot on the uterine wall. Then it files for a building permit, so to speak, by notifying its presence to the gigantic host organism it is planning to overhaul with its wildly expanding arrival. But here's the frustrating part: from ovulation to touchdown can take anywhere from six to twelve days. That means, for those waiting and wondering, at least a whole week of complete blankness, when a little life-altering being may—or may not—be taking a microscopic joyride through your insides, and you know nothing either way about it. This little free-floating bounce of independence will conclude, if successful, with a deeply embedded attachment that will continue biologically, then emotionally, for about eighteen years or maybe forever.

On day 22 I think maybe we are coming out of the week of blankness and I am feeling this or that twinge, and my casual shrugging turns to . . . fear. Recklessness takes on its usual threatening sneer. My body is giving me just enough of a reminder of what I knew about pregnancy: the weariness, the feeling of vulnerability, and I start thinking about the academic year ahead that needs lots of preparation and Ron starting a new part-time job and the extra hours and stress . . . and excitement fades into anxiety. For a few minutes anyway. Then I go back to hoping.

On day 23 a headache sends me to bed in the afternoon for one of those naps that feels as if you've gone to another planet and back in twenty minutes. I had vowed to wait until the next day, when my period would normally come, and see what happened before resorting to chemical diagnostics. But Ron gets all excited and convinces me to use the second of the two test-strips that I had saved from last spring's false alarm. I am easy to convince.

Three minutes later: negative. Definitely, undoubtedly, negative.

Disappointment. And relief. We throw the box and strip away and I think, Well, that's the end of my impatience. Next time, I'll know to believe nothing, to remain steadfastly unimpressed with whatever signals my body sends to tease me. I will accept nothing but a clear day number 29. Or maybe 42.

And I remember, now, what I'm asking for. The soberness of this undertaking comes back to me. Ron is disappointed, too. Now he could not boast about being "a young ram," as we joked when we succeeded in the first month with our daughter. But I can see the gleam in his eye.

~

That we can imagine the future is one of those crazy abilities, like blowing bubblegum bubbles or playing violin concertos, that makes us unique as humans. But sometimes we'd prefer to turn off this little feature, at least temporarily.

Another cycle, another blank week of holding two possibilities before me, one in each hand. The first few days of "blank week," I absolutely bore myself trying to read my body's faintest of signals. Why can't I just forget about it for a few days, for heaven's sake?

Another morning, I expect my period, nothing happens, the future-imagining program automatically kicks in. Well, if it happens this month, I muse, then we would have a baby in the spring, and this is how I could arrange things with work, and blah, blah, blah. I keep trying to shut that program down, but it's stubbornly persistent.

The whole day passes, I start to think about those subtle tugging sensations I had felt for a week in the lowest abdomen, that stomach-ache in the middle of a few nights ago, and didn't my breasts look a little weird? Too late—the mind flies down that future path.

Despite my vows, another test, and another negative. So much for that future. Now I swing my mind around again and aim for an alternative one, one with more trying, a later arrival date. I think of my two darlings and decide maybe we should stop there. We are being foolish, after all, and who needs all this emotional turmoil in the flow of things anyway?

Blood

So blood comes. How easily it slips out of our bodies, and we must somehow catch it, manage it, this messiness of life. In a lovely poem by Deborah Harding called "Late," a woman describes her silent thoughts one early morning when she wonders if she is pregnant or if her period will finally come. And then:

Stepping into a steaming shower
I think I feel something, that inevitable red
sloughed in my hand, a prayer
stripped from my lips, and in those first
drops, the egg is lost—in the wet
curve of my palm

a tiny shard of her, glistening,
translucent as the beginning of a tear.

Blood is powerful and dreadful, life and death, a sign of vitality and grave danger, of purity and defilement. Its symbolic weight has made it the center of rituals demonic and holy from ancient times. In her commentary on the Torah, scholar Ellen Frankel observes that these seemingly contradictory meanings make blood "uncanny." And women's close association with blood makes them mysterious by association. As a result, the Jewish purity codes hardly know what to do with menstrual blood. It lands in a category of ritual impurity even though, unlike other bodily discharges, the appearance of menstrual blood is "the only condition that is *ongoing, predictable, and a sign of bodily health.*" Ancient Jewish menstrual taboos confuse us and madden contemporary scholars because they seem at once to honor women and stigmatize them.

Today, we're very matter-of-fact about blood. Health-care workers have their own purity rituals in the age of AIDS, but these are science-based rituals, lacking in spiritual content. As for menstrual blood, we seem to regard it merely as an occasion for the purchase of products designed to manage it. A consumer prompt.

Recently, I've noticed attempts in literature and medical/psychological writing to appreciate rather than despise, denigrate, or pathologize women's menstrual cycles. This represents a very long uphill climb, I'm afraid, out of a long history of puzzlement and revulsion toward the monthly cycle. Freud, for instance, followed the ancient Greeks and Egyptians in thinking that women were more prone to mental illness and hysteria because of disturbances in the uterus—the Greek word for womb is *hysteron.* But Freud didn't know much about women, it turns out. His famous question, What do women want? was easily answered by the cartoonist who depicted Mrs. Freud with a thought balloon above her head containing an image of her husband doing a little vacuuming.

I have tried, although usually not in my most irritable moments, to see the monthly cycle as a gift, despite its discomforts. After all, it makes women resilient. Life's uncertainties and surprises jolt us a little less because we are used to adjusting; our very bodies are constantly changing. And the hormonal shifts that bring on sadness and irritability *can* make us more sympathetic. I know that the sorrows of the world hit me harder during those days—news photos of hungry children, a friend's mother dying of cancer. I brood on them more, I "weep with those who weep" in my prayers a little more attentively. Those are my few noble moments, though. Usually I turn these hormonally induced impulses toward self-pity, irritation, and petty resentments. Oh, and how delicious it can feel to let loose with a few sharp words. But perhaps irritability is redeemable as compassion. After all, we bleed because the world bleeds. Life is always paid for with suffering and blood. That is the way of the fallen world. Women know this in their flesh.

Dr. Joan Borysenko proposes that this greater sympathy and perceptiveness have an actual biological basis. Women are in fact more empathetic during the premenstrual and menstrual phases of their cycle, she argues: "Things that may be bothering us, but that we are unwilling to confront, tend to come to light as if they are being flushed from the unconscious to the conscious so that we can attend to them." Attending to these signals and dealing with them honestly, then, is the key to turning premenstrual crabbiness into a healthy kind of psychic "housecleaning." She continues:

This emotional housecleaning is wrongly viewed as bitchiness or complaining, but when seen rightly and heeded, it may be a valuable stress reducer and guide to what we need to change or pay attention to so that our lives will run more smoothly. This is the benefit to feeling down. Additionally, since intuitive capacity, empathy, and interdependent perception are also right-brain functions [which are enhanced in the premenstrual/menstrual part of the cycle], it follows that the premenstrual and menstrual phases of our cycle are indeed times of enhanced wisdom.

"Yeah, right," many sisters will scoff as they clutch their cramping middles and aching heads. These days, some doctors are proposing that women might take oral contraceptives in longer cycles so that they do not menstruate every month. After all, modern women menstruate many more times in their lives than our great-grandmothers and women before them did, since these days women are waiting longer to have children and having fewer of them. A modern woman menstruates about 350 to 400 times compared to the 100 times estimated for women of previous generations. And there's some evidence that reducing the number of ovulations reduces breast cancer risk. So which is healthier for our bodies? Taking pills to alter our cycles? Having more children, as in the old days? Or letting our bodies do what they do, even if it makes us moody? There is not currently enough long-term research to know, and it may be a complex enough question that it can't be answered definitively.

Well, Borysenko's efforts to find value in mood cycles at least offers a counterpoint to a culture that is terribly afraid of sadness and dark ruminations. Cheerful happiness is the desired norm and anything other is viewed as unstable, distressing, dangerous, and in need of pharmaceutical intervention. But what if cycling in and out of dark times is actually the healthiest approach to life?

I went on a retreat once whose theme was "Leading Ordered Lives." On the first evening, the pastor leading devotions used a beautiful prayer from St. Thomas Aquinas to focus our thoughts. One of the phrases from this prayer, though, dropped me into a bit of an angry reverie: "May I not be saddened by anything unless it turns me from You." In his comments on this phrase, the pastor suggested that Aquinas was pointing to a kind of "general blueness" that people of faith should eschew as inappropriate. Wait a minute. Sadness is a sin?

Well, *that's* obviously the pious thinking of men, I internally protested. *They've* never experienced the natural, uncontrollable, emotional results of menstrual cycles. Sometimes, we women feel sad *for no reason.* In fact, anyone with a tendency toward depression knows about this. Chalk it up to chemical imbalances if you wish, but please don't call that sadness a sin. When I feel this way, I suppose it would be sinful to let my mind focus on all the dreadful inconveniences and disappointments I suffer in my piteously difficult life. But there is much in the world around me to be sad about, many people who live their days in lament and darkness. Can't my random sadness be a kind of solidarity with them? Can't it hum, low and quiet, along with the great mourning of all humanity, all creation? Listen here, Mr. Aquinas: Sadness can turn one *toward* God.

I have learned through decades of churchgoing (and no doubt Aquinas knew this, too) that spiritual health depends on repeating a cycle of downward and upward spiritual movement, sinking and rising, across a lifetime. The pattern of Christian worship—the "worship parabola" as my liturgy-wonk husband likes to call it—properly embodies this movement so that we practice it every week and know it in the shape of our souls. We confess, repent, receive forgiveness, then attend to God, praise God, and give thanks. We can't have all one or all the other; we need both sadness and rejoicing. So if one must cycle through the sad and dark in order to perceive and receive the light, and if women's bodies are designed to model this same kind of cyclical movement, is that design a pain or a power?

And furthermore, of all people, Christians ought to have the most appreciation for menstrual cycles if for no other reason than that Christianity has a highly redemptive view of blood: Christ's blood washes us clean from sin, goes the old proclamation. And the less squeamish among the Christian faithful can actually sing with gusto some of those hymns, especially popular early in the twentieth century, that ooze and flow all over the place:

There is a fountain filled with blood
flowing from Emmanuel's veins.
And sinners washed beneath that flood
Lose all their guilty stains!

or

There is power, power, wonder-working power
in the blood (in the blood) of the lamb (of the lamb)!

or

Oh, precious is the flow
That makes me white as snow!
No other fount I know,
Nothing but the blood of Jesus.

When I was a teenager, I went to church twice every Sunday (this was the custom of my Dutch immigrant community), and the Sunday evening services would begin with several songs like these. I used to cringe at these paean-to-blood hymns; they were embarrassing, beneath us. I wanted a sophisticated, clean, intellectual religiosity. Strangely enough, though, the old folks loved these hymns and sang out those swinging rhythms with eager passion. Having been bruised and knocked around by life a little more, I think, they wanted their religion to have some guts. Some blood and guts, even. I'm beginning to understand this now, to enjoy these weirdly gruesome, cheerful old chants and to recognize as well the solemn beauty of the words spoken each week in my current church as we pass the sacramental cup to one another: "This is the blood of Christ, shed for your sins." These days I squirm when I hear people speaking of the Christian faith as pretty much amounting to following in the footsteps of a hardworking ancient Near Eastern social activist, or to counterbalancing the myriad unpleasantnesses of life with the winsomeness of love. I want to yell out, "But what about *blood!*" Take the elemental rigor out of the faith and what's left is a self-help bestseller—nice, but not tough enough to stand and give answer to the ravages of human suffering and evil.

Is there power in the blood? We women don't shed our blood for sins, ours or other people's. But we do shed it, typically, amid some sadness, and we do shed it for the possibility of new life. Does this not give us a kind of connection to Jesus that has been very little discussed or appreciated, a kind of automatic stigmata? Because I see Christ's bleeding at the center of redemptive history, can I also see women's bleeding resonate outward from this, across all ages of history and races of women? Peasant farmers and student protesters, wealthy landowners and corporate managers, refugees and homesteaders, tribal matriarchs and factory workers—wherever women have participated in the world and suffered its blows, our bleeding testifies to pain and hope, uncannily combined.

Normally, I think very little about my own bleeding times. They come, they go. Whatever. I cope with any emotional effects that ensue and manage the actual flow easily enough. I cheer myself right now with this little frenzy of appreciation for womanly bleeding and its deep spiritual resonances. Not that I don't believe it. But these days, frankly, I'm sick of blood. It appears as the rival of my longing, the disappointment, the unwelcome. The not-this-time.

3) *l o s s*

This time, I wait until a few days past my regular cycle and still get a negative test. But I know something is different, and I resist the result with mental protests: Maybe that test was wrong. It wasn't a national brand, after all; it was a cheapo, generic version. It said it was accurate the first day of your missed period, but I have a short cycle. It probably isn't sensitive enough. Stupid thing. I go to the office that day thinking about how my woman-wisdom will surely triumph over modern consumer science. I also feel weirdly woozy, like something is flooding my brain and floating my concentration away.

When the next day comes and goes, I am sure. I wait two more days and use the second (cheapo) test, indifferent to what it says, because I *know*. When the second test comes back with barely the faintest little line, if you hold it up to the light and squint your eyes just right, I get mad. That thing doesn't know what it's talking about! I order poor Ron to go to the store for the real thing, the most expensive brand. Of course, if I really believed my so-called woman-wisdom, I wouldn't need to do this, but I have enough confidence in chemical truth—and enough worry about being wrong again—to need a definite yes.

The next day with the "real" test, we get our yes. I had stretched my hands out to the future, holding a different possibility in each. Now one hand releases one possible future for good, and the fingers of the other wrap tightly around the possibility chosen for us. Now the rejoicing as we step into this future, now the songs of thanks, the joyous secret, the plans for letting the news be told, when the time is right.

Letting Go

Blood! No, please—not blood!

I come home from the office, visit the bathroom, and find drops of blood on my underwear. My heart beats hard, my face flushes. Tension crawls up my shoulders and grips the back of my neck. We go to some friends' for supper and I'm distracted. Every smile is strained, every visit to the bathroom a matter of dread. What's happening? I've had bleeding during pregnancy before. Maybe this is just a brief episode.

But no. When I get home, there's more. Too much.

The next morning, I call the doctor and then the waiting begins. The nurse is reassuring, though realistic. This could be a rare episode of significant bleeding, or it could be the end. I will have two blood tests done, one today, one in two days. The readings will show for sure.

I stay in bed and read, but my mind is back to the two futures. How quickly our imaginations hurtle ahead of our bodies. The mind is not at all resigned to the "linear nature of the time-space continuum." The imagination can reconstruct a life scenario in seconds, tracing events and making plans, then zip back and trace out an entirely different scenario. Worse, it can hold more than one in tension, torturing the emotions as they ignite like electrical current between the different charges of each future. This way? Grief. That way? Anxiety. And I must hang between now, for days.

Meanwhile, the body plods along, heartbeat by heartbeat. The tissues absorb and secrete, move and rest, contract and expand, all things slowly, steadily working to the pulsing rhythm of the system. Time does not contract and expand. It merely paces along, relentlessly inflexible. It passes. That's all.

Blood, blood, lots of blood. There is no pain, but there is too much bright red blood. I read the relevant sections over and over in the pregnancy reference book. As usual with these things, my experience falls exactly between two possibilities. On the one hand, lots of bleeding without pain is listed as a symptom of possible miscarriage. On the other hand, the book helpfully points out, "An occasional woman experiences what seems like a regular period." So am I, or am I not, "the occasional woman"? I try to search for woman-wisdom. What is my body telling me? But I'm only sure for moments at a time. I don't trust it. I'm grateful for empirical evidence, for science, for chemistry, for the whole megalith of modern medicine. I want facts.

As I wait and wonder and try to read my body, I realize that all that wise reflection on how this decision means gathering a readiness to meet whatever comes—that was a sham. The truth is, I was looking for a particular experience, something that fell within certain parameters. What I feel now, what my body is doing, is not what I wanted. I'm dismayed by my desire to start over, to reject this whole attempt. If this is a pregnancy desperately trying to hang on, I don't want it. I want a sure, secure pregnancy. What if I must stay in bed while I drip drip drip my way through this?

I wonder what I will do if I'm given a choice. "Well, Debra," I imagine my doctor saying, frowning while perched on his little padded scooter chair, "if you want to hang on to this one, you're going to have to stay in bed for weeks, and then there's no guarantee. Or we can just take care of it right now." What would I do? I don't believe abortion is morally permissable. I would have to attempt to save the life. But how I would resent it! What moral good is there in doing the right thing with great resentment?

I go to church alone on Sunday. Ron is preaching at another church; and mercifully, we had arranged before any of this that the children would have a little sleepover at Ron's parents'. At the end of the service, when the last row comes forward for communion, every third person is carrying a beautiful, perfect infant. I decide I will leave right after the service. I don't want to talk to the young parents or the college students or (help me) my colleagues who go to my church. I don't want to smile and answer, "I'm fine, how are you," when they greet me. I don't want to see all those beautiful babies. Not today.

The next day, I wait for the phone call with the results of the test.

I have had moments I was sure it was over, but the other symptoms of pregnancy persist and these make me wonder and even hope. But as I shower in the morning, I pray suddenly, and a little frantically, that this pregnancy is over.

The call comes, the nurse is kind. "We have the results. You've had an early miscarriage. The first test showed a low level of HcG, and the second was negative." I assure her that I'm fine, I'm even glad. Now I know what's happening. It's a clear resolution, and it happened early. It could have been much worse. I reflect after I hang up that I only had this future in my mind for about a week. I can set it aside with only a little grief.

Ron and I talk quietly about trying again later, about how grateful we are that we have two beautiful children, that this would be so hard if we were trying for the first time at our age. We have learned about waiting. We can do it. My mother was 39 when she had me. We'll be all right. We're a little sad that our children will be spaced farther apart than we had hoped, but that is our only sadness—a luxurious one indeed.

A few hours later, in the bathroom, I find on the tissue a small, dark glob. Before this, there has only been blood. I marvel at its simple, homely materiality. It's not disgusting to me, or even sad. Knowing the truth the lab results provided, it seems, allowed my body finally to release hold of something that several days before had shut off. I say aloud, weirdly, "I'm sorry," and that's all. After this moment, the bleeding diminishes quickly over the next 24 hours, and I feel my body returning to normal.

~

Children will defy the places, plans, and schemes we make for them in our lives. Sometimes they do this, apparently, even when they are only shadow children. I wanted a March baby; I thought it was neat that the pregnancy would officially date from June 21, the summer solstice. But this is not the sort of thing one can plan on or even ask for. Those who believe birth control is permissible have the ability to say, "Not now." I believe this is a good thing, because we can genuinely cultivate the openness. But once we open ourselves to what comes, the child's story takes over. Whatever child we may someday have will come and become according to her or his own story, not mine. I must simply wait for and welcome that story.

Still, when I think about this experience, I can see why some people find the moral uproar over early abortions so unnecessary. The physical facts of the matter seem far too inconsequential to support all the fuss. And yet, morality cannot be only about physical facts, but about principles broad and elastic enough to acknowledge that there is more to human life even than myriads of physical facts. If we do not recognize in our physicality, however tiny, unattractive, unnoticeable, some kind of holiness, respect, meaning—then what are we? Our humanness depends on this.

One of the most profound and far-reaching implications of the Christian belief that God both created the world and entered it personally, is that matter *matters;* it has inherent meaning. It is not simply neutral, empty and waiting for us to grant whatever meaning or value we choose at any given point. We strain to touch the meaning of the physical world, to find words for it; but the source of its profundity is beyond us.

Desire and Grief

After this disappointment, I've been thinking more about the truth that, at bottom, I have a quite particular idea of what I want—a healthy child, soon—and I am not truly open to whatever comes. Modern health care and birth control give us much higher and stronger expectations about our fertility than past women could afford. But when we have better control over our fertility, does this make us think of babies as a commodity, a *thing* we want to *get*? The longer Ron and I try, the less this feels like an openness to possibility and the more it becomes a desire for something. I want this. That determination is what keeps me going. I want this, but when it comes, it may not be the exact *thing* I want. If I do not get it, I'll be indignant, angry.

Is this wrong? How can I be expected, in the name of openness, to receive grief as calmly as joy? Is it wrong to desire something very particular? What of those other people who are struggling with this particular desire with much greater desperation than I? My small disappointment uncovers for me the intensely quiet griefs of so many around me.

Our friends Karen and Mark, I've recently learned, have been trying a long time for another baby, since their second child, Carolyn, was one year old. They tried for a whole year before she happened, and since Carolyn's birth, Karen has had two miscarriages. Paul and Betsy, nearing the age of 40, are trying for their second child. She, too, has suffered two serious miscarriages, the second exactly one year after the first—a nightmarish anniversary. Then there's Trevor and Linda, hoping to start their family. It's been a year for them and no results. Then there's my brother- and sister-in-law, having planned so carefully to prepare for children, finishing their education, traveling overseas, returning to the United States, buying a home, and acquiring jobs with good medical insurance. Now, the biological window is beginning to close, and months go by with no success. Where is God's response to their desires? To their grief?

One study I read about found that women trying unsuccessfully to become pregnant have stress levels, registered in terms of anxiety and depression, equal to women with cancer, HIV, or heart disease. Even today, when women have abundant avenues to status, meaning, and fulfillment other than childbearing, barrenness still causes powerful feelings of inadequacy and isolation. I've seen it in the grim faces, the grayed and tired voices of the women I know who live with absence, month after month. Not all women long to enter the madonna archetype, but for the many who do, the waiting can be agony. It is a kind of little death.

At these times, I would guess, the Bible's pictures of barrenness are comforting, but only like a blanket on a hard, rough ground. The stories of the matriarchs—Sarah, Rebekah, and Rachel—picture their longing and agony and remind us that barrenness and fertility are in the hands of God. They vividly dramatize how the fertility of other women (Leah, especially) serves to torture the waiting ones, and how sometimes the taunts of the "successful" mothers are deliberate. The modern analogues for Leah's taunts are probably the thoughtless remarks of other people, whether family or strangers, with unintentional cruelties such as "Don't you think it's time you two start a family?" or "That child needs a little brother or sister!" In Hannah's story, in I Samuel, we enter the most intimate and desperate moments of the waiting woman in the presence of God, overhearing the words of her prayer in the temple: "Look upon your servant's misery and remember me!"

God eventually remembers all these biblical women, and they and their children become links in the covenant promise. So that's comforting. For them the waiting is swallowed up in joy. But what if this never happens to my patient, longing friends? Is God taunting them, holding out on them? Should they conclude that their grief is "the will of God" and move stoically on, guiltily concluding that their desires are against the will of God? Are they spending way too much psychic prayer energy asking for something too selfish, too extravagant?

Well, yes. Of course it's a selfish and extravagant desire. How could it not have some selfishness to it, considering the kind of people we all are? And extravagant? Those are the only desires worth pummeling the heavens for. But so what if the longing for a child isn't an utterly pure spiritual aspiration? So what if it's part narcissism, part needing to be needed, a thirst for adventure, curiosity, boredom, a pinch of jealousy of others, a thousand little dreams of cute and cuddly tiny people hugging stuffed bunnies and whooshing down slides. It's not as if the biblical Rachel's desire for a child isn't tangled up with less-than-neutral motives, namely rivalry with her sister, Leah. God "remembers" Rachel anyway and she becomes a Mother in Israel. Clearly, purity of motivation is not the prerequisite. Nevertheless, women search their souls for fault during the barren times: "See if there is any wicked way in me."

When I study the *Bhagavad Gita* with my students, they are surprised to learn from this ancient Indic writing just how enthusiastic Christianity is, by comparison, about desire. The hero of the *Gita*, Arjuna, is instructed by Krishna to "put away desire" as the root of all suffering: "Thus awaking to Him who is above understanding, establishing thy soul on the Soul, slay the enemy, O mighty armed one, whose form is Desire, who is hard to overcome." In the *Gita*, desire is the enemy. The advocated alternative is not stoicism, exactly, but a state of perfect equilibrium no matter what happens. To desire is to fall into *maya*, illusion.

But my students and I, comparing several passages from the Bible, find that, while there are many injunctions against desires for sinful things (they know all about these), and while we are encouraged to put aside worry and anxiety out of trust for God's care, desire itself is quite a different thing. One of my favorite parables is the story of the "importunate widow." Jesus tells of a woman who repeatedly importunes a judge to get him to rule in her favor; she gets him out of bed at night, bugs him constantly, until he finally gives her justice. Not, Jesus points out, because he is a particularly upstanding judge who believes in the perfect rightness of her cause, or because he was a social-justice-minded person who sought to relieve the law's bias against single women. No, the judge gave the woman her desire because he wanted her off his back. This is presented as a parable about prayer, which means that Jesus is holding out a subtle invitation here to bother and pester God.

Desire is the psychic engine that powers us toward God. It is not wrong to desire something good, to desire it deeply, earnestly, tenaciously. It is not wrong to grieve when this good thing is delayed, or when it never comes. I believe God understands and honors desire, even when that desire will finally be answered with a "No." One of my colleagues, now the mother of three adopted children, suffered the grief of infertility for many years. She says that the word "barren" still pains her. And she tells me that the hardest spiritual lesson she had to learn during those years was that sometimes God says, "Not that, but this." Even in desire there must be an openness that is not exactly a welcoming of grief, but a sober acknowledgment of the possibilities, a willed acceptance of the risks.

Those people I know who are mature in their faith, older people who have hung on in the presence of God and been bumped and batted around a little—they're not beyond desire. They still desire this or that circumstance or event or good outcome. But through many years of seeking friendship with God, receiving many of their hearts' desires, and facing the disappointment of living without many of them, these saints have found a kind of peace. I see it in my father-in-law, whose living-room windows frame a ravishing view of Lake Michigan. We bring friends to his house sometimes to drink in this view and sun themselves on the beach that spreads out at the foot of the wooden steps like a sugar-sand quilt fringed with beach grass. And when our friends politely thank Dad for having them over and remark on his beautiful house, he says, "Well, it's just a hunk of wood." This is the same man who wants his obituary to read: "He did surgery. He played golf. He had fun." I guess you could say he wears the world lightly. This lightness is born of experience that God's apparent withholdings are never permanent, or at least never without some merciful recompense, and often preparatory for something better than we could have first imagined. In that trust, there is great freedom to receive what comes, to be in all things content.

This is hard to see while we wait and long, however. It is the hard-won prize of many years, not readily available to the eager, clamoring desirousness of youth.

I wonder, if the desire for a child could be perfectly pure, what would it look like? Sometimes, when that longing presses on my heart, I feel a strange kind of love for a person, an Other, who could be, but who is not yet. This is the part of desire that seems most crazy, most foolish, but also, somehow, divine.

4) life

Cycles pass, the blood comes, and each time, it tears out the footings of another possible future.

Each month, during the week of blankness, I obsess about another symptom, thinking maybe this is the indicator, this is what I should attend to. One month, it's a queasy stomach. Then, swollen breasts, then a weird craving (mu shu pork, for heaven's sake), then dizziness. But humor is built into women's bodies: every early symptom of pregnancy mimics a symptom of imminent menstruation. Fooled you again!

I feel at odds with my body. It's trying to keep up with my imaginings and desires, but it seems to falter and fail. Or maybe—probably— it's going about its business with an unconscious wisdom my arrogant but fuddled mind simply can't follow. Either way, I'm frustrated that my mind can't perceive the mysteries of the rest of me. I wonder if something is wrong, if my body is trying to tell me something that I'm too busily deluded to see: this is not the time for a baby; you have some silent, serious illness and you need to get better first; you're neglecting your current children, what makes you think you can attend to a third?

Our perceptions are so tentative, confused, ephemeral anyway. It's a wonder we ever have moments of clarity or understanding with other people when we are so often clueless about ourselves. John Milton, the great poet who is often these days dismissed as a classic dead white male, actually knew quite a bit about feeling lonely and misunderstood. He attributed this condition directly to the Fall. In *Paradise Lost,* his depiction of the biblical story, Adam and Eve are distinct individuals before the Fall, but they understand each other perfectly. After they each eat of the forbidden fruit, they argue ferociously, misperceive one another's intentions, and, worst of all, find that their inner lives are as stormy and nasty as Eden's weather has suddenly become. And in the last lines of the poem, we see them leaving Eden behind as they, "with wandering steps and slow, through Eden took their solitary way." They are alone with each other, but they are alone *from* each other as well, alienated even from themselves.

We are trapped in the confusion of our subjectivity. These days, on the most rarefied intellectual levels as well as on the levels of pop culture, we are taught to "acknowledge perspectivalism" or "celebrate diversity." This is a pleasant and useful balancing imperative to "totalizing discourses" that attempt to impose the same story on everyone, squashing our differences into abstracts of normality. But multiple perspectives and diversity do leave us with loneliness. We are creatures who long deeply for the intimacy of understanding. We need to hear, "You and I are alike; I understand you." So much of our frantic seeking after the right partner or job or church is the desire for that simple connection. Acknowledging our differences is really the easy part; communing with another heart, truly and lastingly—*that's* difficult, especially when we are often such strangers to ourselves.

I want to be friends again with my own body. It does not need to obey my whims, I guess, but if only it could speak to me and tell me what's happening!

S u r p r i s e

Day 27 and no blood yet. Just a major breakout. I can't believe I'm 33 years old, my hair is gray enough to justify using hair color (I think so, anyway), and I still get pimples! Good grief.

Could it be? A few days ago I felt depressed, thinking surely this month again, nothing. I felt that strange, vaguely wild irrationality you know is not based on real outside circumstances, but on the body's internal chemical churnings. Chemically stimulated or not, you question everything, lash out internally at everything. I'm tired of my husband; he annoys me. I'm tired of my job; it's a big pain. I don't feel like doing anything. Who cares, anyway?

The sadness passed the next day, but still I felt sure that this was another cycle that would turn over into the next. I prepared myself for the marking of another *one* on the calendar to show where the next cycle started, the bolstering of my determination for another round of effort. The initial excitement of "the project" has worn off some, the gleam in the eye just a tiny bit dimmed.

But day 27 now, and nothing. No headache from the "progesterone plunge." No cramps, really. Weird stomachaches, though. And no blood. Could it be? I'm trying to stay skeptical this time. Maybe the lack of weird feelings around day 22 is a sign that this is a normal month. Then again, maybe it's a tiny blessing to get me through that rotten week of waiting without getting all excited too early.

I'll wait till Friday, day 29, before doing any lab experiments. Tomorrow could bring disappointment.

Friday morning, five A.M. I get up to go to the bathroom. The test is there on the counter, since I put it within reach the night before. I decide to do the test in the predawn quiet, alone. I want this moment to myself. My heart pounds as I wait the two minutes, though I know what the answer will be. And there it is, simple and unambiguous, a strong blue line. I crawl back into bed, placing the test strip on the headboard. Ron stirs. "Turn the light on a minute," I whisper. "Why?" he moans. "Just do it," I say. He turns on the light, I show him. We kiss, hold each other, go back to sleep wearing smiles subtle as the first light of dawn.

When morning comes, I feel more joyful than I have felt in a long time. I asked; God said yes. An exchange of assent, reaching across the cosmos, near as heart within heart. I was at odds with myself, but now I feel enveloped in God, as if I have stumbled, after much seeking, into a place that vibrates with beauty and life, and I merely stand and feel the hum surround me and pulse through me.

I have learned how precious are these moments of pure joy in life, the moments of deep understanding that even in this old world, sometimes a longing is answered with a Yes. All the complexities of pain and redemption, loss and salvage, grief and healing, destruction and hope, make us perhaps tougher or perhaps more fragile, perhaps more grateful for small treasures as well as great mercies. But the complexity of this good-but-fallen world makes us smaller, too, diminished in our capacity for pure joy. Adams and Eves on the other side of the gates, we forget what the garden was like, then begin to wonder if it was even ever real. We become skittish, waiting for the other foot to fall, shaking our heads cynically and muttering about the way things work, or just pattering cautiously around every good gift, as if it might suddenly be swiped away. Because it might.

And I trace now a thin thread of worry somewhere in my mind, about miscarriage or genetic defects or teenage rebellion or early, tragic death—my mind fast-forwarding through the child's life before the child amounts to more than a few thousand cells. But I feel a profound sense of calm. Something seems right and secure and uncomplicated about this. I decide to resist worry and second-guessing, to let myself be lifted on the updrafts of this dovetailing assent, to admit that ultimately the complexities collapse into a fundamental simplicity: that of one Being giving to another, out of love and the pleasure of giving.

For the next few days, the feeling of calm continues. It's as if my body has passed the rapids of the usual days of menstruation, and now it sails through calm waters. I feel good; the symptoms are there, but subtle. I indulge in my usual weekend afternoon sleepiness and nap luxuriously.

~

Something has begun. Since I've done this before, I know rationally and with some confidence of experience that what has begun now will, by God's grace, bring into this world a new person. But at this

moment, as these days pass rather normally, all I know is the sensation, in my body, of slight swollenness, a subtle preparatory flush of
notification that something is on its way.

A marvelous mystery. A person has taken root inside me, but I
do not know who this will be. I know nothing about the genetic
permutations already thrown together (except whose bodies they
came from), nothing about the character of soul this person might be
given. When my imagination tries eagerly to fill in the mystery, I curb
it. We must not "rush into the silent spots," one of my professors
used to say about the beautiful and often cryptic Old Testament narratives. I do not want to rush into this new person's silence before he
or she has a chance to become. Some women feel mysterious connec-
tions to their unborn children before they even qualify medically as
fetuses. Some poets write in direct address to these cell-children:
"and you, like the powerful muscle/we call heart, grow stronger
within me." But I can't get that far, can't make that kind of second-
person construction. My parental tasks are to nurture, to love, to understand, and to teach. Eventually. For now my job is simply a kind of
loving waiting, a surprisingly passive patience while the automatic,
relentless power of life will grow this tiny mustard seed into the very
obvious, present, and sheltering little sapling of someone entirely
new.

There are preparations to be made. But they are mostly from the
point of view of the world, not of the child. I must make a place in my
life, in my family, and in this world for a new person. Part the seas,
make the rough places plain, make the crooked straight, because this
person will change the terrain, as surely and persistently as tree roots
burst a sidewalk apart.

5) *w e a k n e s s*

When I was pregnant with my daughter, my mother-in-law gave me an icon of the Virgin Mary, a small copy of an early-fourteenth-century Byzantine image. We Protestants typically have little use for saints and icons—our loss, in my opinion—but my mother-in-law is a wise and sympathetic curator for the treasures of all realms of faith, and as a result I sometimes end up with some booty. The icon depicts the moment of the Annunciation. The angel Gabriel strides toward the seated Virgin, one wing still raised—from the flight, presumably—and one arm reaching toward her, almost as if he is about to grab her. Mary greets the angel, but not in the humble, open pose one might expect from the woman who is supposed to exemplify perfect obedience. Instead, one arm hangs at her side, almost as if she is groping for something with which to brace herself. The hand nearest the angel is raised, palm outward, in a gesture of . . . surprise? Greeting? Or is it . . . hesitation?

I think the iconographers understood the complexity of obedience; Mary's gesture is purposely ambiguous. In the famous account of the story in the Gospel of Luke, the young girl whom the angel greets is at first afraid. "Fear not," the angel must assure her. This is the standard line whenever angels appear in the Bible, probably because surprised terror is the usual response when God comes to call. Once Gabriel has explained God's plan to Mary, she apparently has pulled herself together enough to be curious about God's particular methodology in bringing this about: "How will this be, since I am a virgin?" Once the angel reminds her that "nothing is impossible with God," and points to her very old, very pregnant cousin Elizabeth as a case in point, Mary responds with her famous proclamation of trust and obedience: "I am the Lord's servant. May it be to me as you have said."

Mary's raised hand in the icon seems to me a profound symbol of all the fears and confusions that come with a momentous, God-directed change. If there is hesitation in that hand, it is the iconographer's way of suggesting that fear is to be expected, and that this does not diminish Mary's ultimate surrender to God's will for her. In fact, it makes her obedience more human, and therefore more plausible a model for us.

Capturing the Virgin in this moment also insists that every call has a cost. Mary, at this point, could only have a vague premonition of what the cost for her might be. Her song of rejoicing, as recorded in Luke, is full of thanksgiving for God's fulfillment of his ancient promise to her people. But Simeon, a wise old fellow at the temple, later warns her that her son has a difficult destiny and because of him, he tells her, "a sword will pierce your own soul, too."

Mary's task was the bearing and raising of a child, which can operate as a symbol of all things that require great effort and bear fruit far beyond the personal rewards involved. But the literal bearing and raising of a child is indeed a calling, a mission, and moments of joyous surprise and expectation have the shadow of a cost. I think this is why the first several weeks of pregnancy typically feature an assortment of discomforts: we need reminding, and this is especially true in our self-indulgent culture, that if we foolishly imagine for a minute that parenthood is an accomplishment or achievement or right, sooner or later something will smack us with the realization that it is, above all, a surrender.

The Basics

These first few weeks, my body insists on reminding me of this. Every cell is undergoing a slight alteration, as if I were lying on one of those ultra-high-tech infirmary beds in a *Star Trek* episode and the doctor is informing the captain in urgent, low tones that "the alien has invaded her body and is altering her physiology at the cellular level!"

My body is fussing over this tiny new creature by manufacturing an entirely new organ in its honor (the placenta) and meanwhile, the rest of me is left weak, tired, and vulnerable. My weakness forces me to shed every task but what absolutely must be done. Even the prospect of going up a flight of stairs prompts a cost-benefit analysis. I have to push preparation for class or housecleaning (what little I do already) further aside in order to fit in a nap, or I will be in deep hibernation by 7:30 at night. Already this child is claiming a place in our lives, rejecting the frivolousness of anything not committed to itself, claiming energy and time before it even has a face. All of us are affected, not just me. Ron is doing far more than his share of cooking and laundry and cleanup. And the children, too, have to learn more independence while I rest or nap, and more patience while I eat first before I have the strength to fix their breakfasts.

And speaking of food, the hunger of these weeks is not the pleasant, food-sounds-yummy-now feeling familiar to well-fed people. This is an urgent, desperate emptiness in the gut. It hurts. I have had to learn to recognize a feeling of queasiness and stomach pain as the signal for hunger. Then comes the task of figuring out what I can eat, "searching my cravings." Most things sound horrible. Usually only one particular item sounds good: an egg, pizza, wheat toast, a bagel with peanut butter. Once the food radar has zeroed in on its target, I *must* have it. Nothing will stand in my way. One afternoon I dreamed of apricots during my nap. I wanted them, I *needed* them, right that minute. I went straight from my bed to the cupboard and opened a can of peaches—the closest approximation my pantry could offer in less than two minutes. At least they were orange.

This kind of primitive lunging for food, combined with inexplicable revulsions, makes certain pregnancy books seem obsessively prissy. Far be it from our culture to just let a woman eat when she needs to! Oh, no: there must be *guilt!* One popular pregnancy book righteously insists that every bite counts, and we have to be even more virtuous during pregnancy than ever before—watch your fat, eat lots of green leafies, consider anything sweet your mortal enemy, and avoid any food with any sort of chemical on it or in it or having been anywhere near it during any time in its existence. My response to this is: "Whatever." If I followed the diet instructions in some books, I would spend the entire day planning and sorting and shopping and chopping and putting wheat germ on everything. But this cramp in my gut doesn't leave room for mental calculations about food groups or grams of protein. My friend Jennifer used to say that during the first trimester, the "construction workers" are down there furiously building around the clock, and when they call up for food, you had better provide. It's in their union contract.

Keeping those workers happy day and night means spending a lot of time hunting and gathering in the kitchen. As a result, I have discovered, as many animal species probably already know, that constant grazing is a fairly boring lifestyle. Fortunately, the volatility of my cravings provides a little humor. For instance, an archaeological dig through my freezer yields evidence of cravings that thrived briefly in an earlier age and are now extinct. There's a very large bag of frozen corn in there, and a box of a dozen burritos with only two missing. Cravings also make meal planning especially challenging. We have to plan at least three extra meals for each week, because chances are good that when bean-soup-and-bread night arrives, I won't be able to endure even the thought of a bean. Then there was the guacamole project. I had guacamole at a friend's house one night, and it tasted so yummy to me that I planned to serve it at our annual Christmas party. I bought all the ingredients, and the day of the party I eagerly mashed the stupid avocadoes, mixed it all up, put it in a pretty dish—I couldn't touch it. Yuck.

Maybe all this is a way of preparing the mother for meeting the constant demands of an infant's hunger. If I had never experienced this painful, primitive hunger, would I have any sympathy for baby's hunger in the middle of the night for the third time? And the weird revulsions and cravings may be good training for older children. When my three-year-old Jacob gags up his broccoli but wants cheese on his applesauce, who am I to complain?

~

Preoccupied as I am with my turbulent physical functioning, I feel off-kilter, skewed, when trying to deal with anything more complicated, like social graces. My moods won't stay within civilized bounds; they keep spilling all over, as if I'm a clumsy person who is always knocking her purse open and dropping its embarrassing private contents on the floor.

When the day of our annual Christmas party arrived, for instance, and all the housecleaning had yet to get done, I got a little stressed. In fact, I got so stressed I completely froze. I couldn't even lift a dust cloth. After much tearful palavering with Ron, I finally admitted that the only course of action was to go upstairs and take a nice, long nap while Ron did all the cleaning. He did it all in two hours, which really made me feel like a slug. (Granted, he's not quite as particular as I am about the definition of "clean.") But there was no other option. It was exactly like having a "system hang" on your computer, when the thing just seizes up completely and the only thing to do is turn everything off, let the electrons settle, and then reboot.

The Squeeze

Frustrations that I could normally handle with a combination of annoyance and strategic aplomb take on looming proportions and threaten to devour me like midnight monsters. In the tenth week, I wake up in the middle of the night, hungry. In the dark kitchen, I pour myself a bowl of Cheerios and sit down to munch sleepily. On the kitchen table I notice a pink "while you were out" note. It's a message for Ron from a college administrator, telling him about a meeting at eleven o'clock on Friday morning. Ron has not yet mentioned this little fact to me. Suddenly, I'm angry, not at Ron but at this other man. Friday is supposed to be *my* day to finish my grades and close the book on the semester. But of course, I fume silently, it never occurred to *this* man that calling Ron to a meeting on that day might throw Ron's whole family into a major schedule reshuffling. He's probably one of those men who always had Someone Else caring for his children while he dashed off on business trips.

I start thinking through how we can adjust to this stupid meeting. A babysitter? Not on a weekday. Ask a favor from my mom? Why should she wreck her day for some petty meeting? Finally I decide I just have to skip that whole day and finish my work next week, the week I was supposed to save as family time at home. That would involve no one's inconvenience but mine—and Ron's when he has to be on kid-duty next week so I can go into the office and finish.

So that's obviously the best choice. But I'm angry. How many times this semester have I tried to fit the same amount of work into a yet smaller amount of time? I like staying home on Fridays so Ron can have a day in the office and I can have a weekday home with the children. Of course, there's a price. I have to make up for the lost office time by doing a great deal of reading preparation on the weekends—which means that Ron has to keep the kids busy during the day or be without me in the evenings so that I can work then. And lately, when I've been feeling lousy from the pregnancy, I simply am not capable of working whole days anymore. So I've been squeezing the work into shorter days and trying to work an hour or two at night if I have the energy, which I don't always have. Now, at the very end of the semester, just as I'm about to drag across the finish line, panting and wheezing, my final piece of time is squashed. It's the last maddening straw that's breaking my will to keep going.

Maybe under normal circumstances I could have figured this out in five minutes, but here in the hormone zone, it takes me about two hours to think it all through in the middle of the night. And of course it doesn't occur to me that maybe Ron is just being *invited* to the meeting and is not absolutely *required* to come (which turns out to be the case). When morning comes, I'm not at all rested and have to sleep in a little longer to be able to get out of bed—which, of course, shortens my workday. It's the squeeze.

≈

Maybe if I were saintlier, I would appreciate weakness more. I know very well that famous passage from the letter to the Corinthians in which St. Paul writes about his "thorn in the flesh" and then about delighting in his weakness because, he says, "When I am weak, then I am strong." The idea is that his weakness allows space for God to fill him with divine strength. In my experience, weakness is just really terrific after it's all over with and you're back to full strength. Then those lovely benefits might accrue of expanded compassion for others, tougher will to handle the next round of difficulty, more secure trust in God since, after all, you got pulled through the last one. But the weakness itself stinks. When I am weak, then I am bewildered. When I am weak, then I relinquish the power and pleasure of pulling my weight, managing the household, doing my job, being an all-around capable person. When I am weak, then I have to depend on others, and they never do things quite the way I like them, and besides, they might need me someday when it's not convenient. Nothing attractive about it, as far as I can see.

Paul estimates that the whole point of weakness is to keep him from becoming conceited. Is this a danger for pregnant women? I suppose pride in her own amazing personal powers could be a danger for a woman manufacturing a new person inside her body. But I'm not feeling too triumphant at the moment. And pleased as I am to be pregnant, the weakness is not the source of my delight. Instead I'm using one hand to brace myself, and raising the other as a shield against a divine strength that overshadows.

6) waiting

We had planned to announce the news to my
family at our Thanksgiving get-together at my
brother's house in Detroit. At the last minute,
my parents got the flu and couldn't drive over
from the other side of the state, so we had to make
a long-distance announcement to them. When we
informed them they were going to have grandbaby
number seven, my mother's response was: "Are
you sure?" Now there's one I hadn't anticipated.
Was I sure, she wants to know. What does she
take me for, a nervous teenager?

I have to remember that back in the 1950s and 60s, when my mom was having babies, there was no such thing as a home pregnancy test. So women were never "sure" until they visited the doctor for the first time. Until the official sanction of the medical profession had been bestowed upon it, a baby's existence remained somewhat uncertain. At least, from the parents' point of view. Presumably it was just as certain as ever from the baby's.

So now that all the family members and friends and church people and acquaintances and colleagues have gotten over the surprise (shock, in some cases) and all the hands have been shaken and congratulations offered, we can all settle down to the rather anticlimactic process of waiting.

For me the waiting has a distinct shape, different from the cyclical waiting of conception time. This waiting is linear, with a beginning, middle, and—God willing—joyful culmination. At this stage, though, the culmination seems a very long way off, a destination well beyond the visible horizon. For now, I stroll along, grateful that the ground has stopped lurching but wondering about this still-quiet companion traveling inside me. I wait attentively for tiny movements, for some way of connecting with this person. I begin to long to meet this individual, to see and hold and know. This is a joyful time, but it requires patience. There are many months still to go, and I must wait.

The Work of Waiting

Nothing in our culture speaks approvingly of waiting. Waiting in line is an inconvenience that merchants apologize for and attempt to ease with rows of point-of-purchase merchandise. Waiting to purchase something until one can afford it is an act of old-fashioned fiscal piety that credit cards and payment plans have made obsolete. No need to wait for the mail (there's overnight delivery or fax machines) or for the library to open (there's the Internet) or for a meal to get prepared (there's takeout). Americans don't believe in waiting for any pleasure or satisfaction or relief. Waiting is what we do when things aren't right; it's a state of things that should be avoided, fixed, escaped. A passive failure in a world that desires action. Meanwhile, our insistence on instant gratification keeps the economy humming; there's always an opportunity to earn some bucks by delivering the goods faster.

So I suppose the waiting of pregnancy can be considered a radical, countercultural act. Not that I have any choice about it. I'm merely trying to think of a way to settle into a long wait when everything around me seems geared to instant results.

Fortunately, the waiting of pregnancy is not exactly passive. I am doing work to create this person. It is a different kind of work, however, from anything else I know. I do not have to contribute mental effort to make it happen. My body adapts and the baby grows according to a wisdom designed into it—decidedly not in response to whatever clever brainstorms and willful effort I can muster. I do this work unconsciously while I sleep or while I'm thinking about other things, just as much as when I focus my thoughts on my belly. All the conscious effort I can contribute, really, is to feed and rest my body. This does require arrangement, preparation, and follow-up, it's true. Sometimes getting a nap in the afternoon requires an entire morning of careful planning. But eating broccoli and going to bed by ten still amounts merely to a curiously simple support system for the real work, the mysterious cell-by-cell knitting of delicate tissues and rubbery little bones, miniature eye-jellies and blossoming ears.

Lacking conscious control like this feels strange and a little uncomfortable, like speaking a foreign language. Everything else I have ever done, it seems, came through persistent force of will and disciplined effort. Apparently, other pregnant women feel like me, restless in the midst of this weirdly automatic, womanly work. This might explain why during pregnancy some women suddenly acquire near-military discipline when it comes to exercise and diet. They feel they have to *do something*: "No, no. I can't have a cookie. Chocolate chips have caffeine in them. Besides, it's 4:03 and I'm scheduled to go power walking." This might also explain why I am compelled to write: this is my way of refusing to accept waiting-in-grace. I'll make this a matter of works and merit in whatever way I can.

But let me just enjoy it, this effortless work! Nothing is so uncomplicatedly wholesome and holy as this. And how rarely in history has it been acknowledged as women's good work. Labor and delivery, obviously work because of the pain and danger, have received sympathy and concern through the ages, but too often, as the cursed analogue to Adam's sweaty toil in the soil, childbirth pain is celebrated in misogynist writing and talk as exactly what those vile women deserve. (How often have women written gleefully about how men deserve every weed they pull?) Nevertheless, the quieter work of pregnancy is part of women's massive and profoundly beautiful contribution to human history, and while its archetypal image is imprinted in human culture, the inner experience of it, the soul-work of it from the woman's point of view, has been passed over mostly in silence. Perhaps this, too, is why I write: to speak from out of that silent place.

Adulthood Secrets

Waiting, it seems, is characteristic of women's lives, even apart from the months of pregnancy. I wonder if other young mothers feel as I do, that nothing else is quite so hard in this season of life as waiting. Now, in my thirties, I find it harder than ever to keep out of my mind what I'm *not* doing. I'm ready to stop learning new things all the time, stop being the apprentice, the novice. I would like to get into that phase of life where I exercise skills, day in, day out, toward the satisfaction of mastery. Instead, my current main occupation, parenthood, is truly an adventure in improvisation and learning every day. And it pushes so much else aside. I must wait until tomorrow, when Ron is home with the children and I am free to work, before I can read this book, or finish that stack of grading, or even think a coherent thought. I must wait until some other year, some other season, before I have the time and energy to work more steadily and effectively in my professional field. I must wait till some other time in my life before Ron and I can go to movies or plays or concerts or take off for a weekend without the complexity and expense of arranging for sitters. I must wait until my children are older and more independent before I can make more ambitious contributions to church committees or activities, and simply be grateful now for all those people at different stages who are doing much of the work.

Harder even than all these things for me has been putting aside music, something I always thought of, since my early teen years, as my extra, my delicious side dish. Now that I have muddled along without playing my viola in an orchestra or even singing in a church choir for a few years, I realize how deeply I love music, how deeply it has nourished my soul. But even serious amateur music takes buckets of time, and I can't bear to work my day job and then troop out the door for a rehearsal in the evening, that many more hours away from my little ones. Not to mention trying to arrange for practice time—no way. I might be able to squeeze in an hour a week of practice time, but at that rate I would still sound so bad my heart would sink, not soar. The pleasure comes (for me anyway) only with assiduous, sustained effort. Better to spend my meager energies a little at a time, late at night, writing. I've made my choices. So I wait.

Setting aside desires and ambitions, both lofty and mundane, is a difficult part of being a mother. Did women from other times and places feel this, too? Did American pioneer women wait eagerly for the day when they could really go to town on that quilting? What might my grandmother, a Dutch immigrant who bore seven children after the age of 30, have daydreamed about while she made beds and boiled potatoes for her brood and got on her hands and knees to dust the baseboards? Maybe women like her didn't think much about lovely things they were missing. They were just glad to keep body and soul together. Maybe. But I bet they had their longings, too. And what about the whole men's side of this?

I'm beginning to suspect that waiting is a secret about adulthood no one ever bothers to tell you while you're growing up. My college students are full of anxieties about waiting, but they figure it's part of the deal at their stage. They're waiting for the right life companion to show up; waiting for an angel to please visit in the night and tell them flat out what career path to pursue; waiting to move out of shared apartments and get their own space, have an income, buy a car. They don't like it, but they figure it will be over eventually. I can't bear to tell them that it gets worse. You wait for longer periods of time and you care even more deeply.

When Ron and I were talking with some of our grad-school friends about the little griefs of putting loved things away for a time, our friends Andrew and Dawn said, "Yeah, you have to put down the ducky." The *ducky*? They went on to describe an old *Sesame Street* sequence in which Ernie comes to Hoot the Owl complaining that he can't get his saxophone to sound right; it always squeaks. Hoot points out that Ernie is trying to hold on to his beloved rubber ducky while he plays, and that this will never work. The two then launch into a jazzy song and dance expounding a very grown-up lesson: "Ya gotta put down the ducky if ya wanna play the saxophoooooo-oooone."

The only reason I can stand this waiting at all without lapsing into constant frustration, resentment, or despair (rather than just occasional) is that I have a husband who is doing it with me. I can understand the women of the 60s who rebelled against staying home with children, deploring the stifling loneliness and feeling of entrapment while their husbands carried on as if having a family were a weekend amusement. I would be like a boiling kettle if I had to work with those old assumptions. But thankfully for my sanity and our marriage's health, Ron is giving up his share of things, too. We're trying to share fairly the pleasures, responsibilities, and little griefs of parenthood. He would love to exercise his preaching skills every week, but instead of taking a 60-hour-a-week pastor job at a church, he has a part-time job doing worship with college students. It's a good job and he enjoys it, and with my reduced-load teaching job we get by fine. He feels the unease of waiting differently than I do: he says he sometimes feels he's not a grown-up yet. I suppose this reflects our cultural habit of measuring manhood by social position. At any rate, he's also waiting for the day when he can put it in high gear and cruise.

Pouring Slowly

Why didn't anyone explain to me that waiting is a necessary part of life? Sure, I've read about it in the Bible: "Wait for the Lord; be strong and take heart and wait for the Lord," implores Psalm 27. But biblical waiting always seems to be about peoples and nations and covenants and redemption, addressed to people in circumstances of true suffering. Does it have anything to do with the tiny private patiences of the spoiled, like, for instance, viola playing? Waiting is not a hugely dominant literary topos, either. How much dramatic potential is there in waiting? That's the part the writers skip, marking the next scene "three years later" or beginning the next chapter with "the next day." I suppose *Waiting for Godot* is about waiting, but absurdist futility offers me little wisdom right now. And there's Penelope in *The Odyssey*—now there's a patient woman. But she doesn't get interesting until Book 21, when she comes up with the idea (at Athena's prompting) to test the suitors with Odysseus's old bow; until then the narrator pops in to visit her long enough only to show her weeping profusely. Then it's right back to monsters and Sirens.

My friend Milton has a few words to offer, though. An ambitious soul who had astonishingly high expectations for himself, he also was taken by surprise by a season of waiting. Many things delayed his poetic ambitions, including a minor political inconvenience known as the English Civil War, but he also faced the onset of blindness in middle age. In his wrenching poem lamenting this blindness, the poet attempts to ease his frustrated desire to serve God with his poetic talents. In answer to the speaker's anguished question about what God requires when "light" is "denied," Patience speaks:

> God doth not need
> Either man's work or his own gifts; who best
> Bear his mild yoke, they serve him best; his State
> Is Kingly. Thousands at his bidding speed
> And post o'er Land and Ocean without rest:
> They also serve who only stand and wait.

This provides a not unwelcome theological assurance, but it does not satisfy the longing. Milton must have felt this, because the rhyme scheme here does not provide the clamp-shut closure often featured in sonnets. The matching rhyme for that last line is three lines up, buried in an enjambed sentence. The poem doesn't seal off, but rather opens out, because the longing lingers on.

Apparently, God is working hard on me these days in the patience department. I must trust that God will not forget, that these things I love are not gone forever, only for a time. The Dean of the Chapel at my college was a pretty fine violinist in his day, but he set his fiddling aside for seminary and grad school and a distinguished career in teaching and scholarship. He tells me he deals with the longings by applying a thick salve of faith in the afterlife. "If I really believe in heaven," he wrote me in an e-mail once, "then I can trust that those joys will come back to me. Plenty of time to work out those Carl Flesch études later, there." Well, he's a person of more vivid faith than I, because I can't seem to bend my hopeful imagination around heavenly jam sessions. I believe fervently in life beyond this life, but that's all too far away. I want some more of that good stuff now, or at least soon. I want it to cheer my way here, in this valley.

I take more comfort from the mature women I know, particularly a retired professor in my department who got her Ph.D. at 45 after raising two sons, became a well-respected scholar, then started writing poetry in her sixties. She continues, in her mid-seventies, to come into her small, "emerita" office on campus almost every day, dressed as elegantly as a Supreme Court Justice. She is still one of the most prolific scholars and writers in our department. When she spoke to a group of new professors one time, one of the young women asked her how she did it all. "Oh," she replied, "I could never have managed it when I was younger and my children were young. I had much more energy later." The young women profs in the room looked at each other wide-eyed, astonished and relieved.

The words of the wise women remind me, too, that what I have now, once it's gone, will not come back. "Your children are only little once!" I tuck this away for safekeeping and try to attend to Miriam and Jacob wholeheartedly, hang out with them in the yard, read every book by their favorite authors with them, laugh with them at our family's inside jokes. Meanwhile, I resign myself to doing only a little at a time of those "other things." I came across a helpful image from a wildly different context, a biography of Queen Elizabeth I. One of her advisers reportedly suggested to her, when discussing the speed of religious reform, to think of the English populace as a bottle with a very small neck; they can only take in a little at a time. I try to think of my nonmotherly life right now as a narrow-necked bottle. I can only pour into it slowly, and a little at a time. Later, the neck will open wider again, and the other things of life will flow in faster. And then, of course, I'll lament with aching nostalgia my younger days and Jacob's little voice asking for juice and the screen door slamming and Miriam's Duplo creations on every flat surface.

The book of Proverbs says: "Hope deferred makes the heart sick, but a longing fulfilled is a tree of life." I admit with sadness that part of my heart, the part in which music swelled and flourished, is dry now, dormant. But the beautifully fulfilled longings of this time keep the deferred hopes from their withering effects, and instead reshape my heart. It's possible that it's getting roomier and softer, losing its stony parts and slowly becoming flesh.

Unfolding

Perhaps we should consider the special, holy work of pregnancy as the truer picture of all that human beings do, all our actions in this world. We fuss and flurry about anxiously to build and achieve and secure, thinking that the successful results redound credit to us. But all that we are and are capable of is a gift, ultimately. Whatever is blessed about one's birthplace, education, family, health, all this is a gift. The encouraging words of a teacher, a job opportunity proffered by a friend, a gorgeous sunset that appears just when life seems entirely gray and hopeless, all these are gifts. Even nasty or frightening or difficult circumstances sometimes get salvaged and lead to something surprising and beautiful. How then can we claim any accomplishment as truly our own? All things are brought into being by God. I do not mean to imply that free will is an illusion; our individual wills are real. But our actions are caught up in God's patient and elastic plan. To paraphrase Proverbs: "A woman's mind plans her way, but the Lord directs her steps." We can damage and destroy God's direction, or we can participate willingly and attentively. But the outcome does not belong to us. Pregnancy, then, with its disconcertingly unconscious progress, may be the truer picture of our histories, individual and cosmic. Ultimately, we simply watch in wonder for God's work to unfold into its vast and intricate completion.

The symbolic resonance of pregnancy with the spiritual life is beautifully described by Henri Nouwen in an article that appeared years ago in the journal *Weavings*. I discovered the article by accident (another gift), poking in the nooks and crannies of my mother-in-law's many bookshelves one weekend. Nouwen observes that all those who trust in God are waiting for the completion of God's work in themselves and in the world. This understanding allows us to wait with an active attentiveness and trust that "the seed has been planted, that something has begun." We do not need to think of waiting as the world does—as a bad state to get out of as soon as possible—but as a condition of life filled with hope and joyful expectation. Nouwen writes:

> The spiritual life is a life in which we wait, actively present to the moment, trusting that new things will happen to us, new things that are far beyond our own imagination, fantasy, or prediction. That, indeed, is a very radical stance toward life in a world preoccupied with control.

One important element of this kind of open-ended waiting is to let go of wishes—this is the hard part. Nouwen admits, "It was only when I was willing to let go of wishes that something really new, something beyond my own expectations, could happen to me." God is waiting, too, concludes the article. Waiting, as the book of Romans has it, for the birth of the New Creation, for the full revelation of the sons—and daughters—of God.

7) fear

The tiniest bit of slightly darkened discharge sends me into a quiet panic. Maybe this pregnancy isn't going to hang on, and I will have to deal with grief. After all (spasm of Calvinist guilt), I don't deserve another joy anyway. I've got two healthy children already, I live in a rich country, I have a pretty happy family: who do I think I am, asking for another healthy baby?

Of course, one consultation in a pregnancy book is enough to confirm any horrible suspicion. Let's see . . . slightly brownish discharge . . . intermittent . . . here it is! Trophoblastic disease! There's probably no baby in there at all—just a weird growth that imitates the signs of pregnancy but turns out to be nothing but icky, overgrown vesicles! Well, now I have something scientific to obsess about for a couple days.

Pregnancy is very much like the old science-fiction premise in which a person enters a creepy subspace dimension or electromagnetic field and suddenly every horrid mental picture materializes into "reality." Whatever frightening, disgusting, or tragic possibility a pregnant woman can devise in her hormone-enhanced imagination, there is no doubt a rare condition that actually produces such an effect. What if the baby were to have bones so weak they just crumpled?! Fact: that's called *osteogenesis imperfecta* and it occurs with varying severities in about 1 in 200,000 live births. What if my baby were to have no brain? Fact: that's called *anencephaly* and it occurs in between 1 and 5 out of every 1,000 live births. What if my baby were to have no abdominal wall, so that his intestines were held in by a slim membrane, or by nothing at all? Fact: those conditions are called *omphalocele* and *gastroschisis,* and they occur, respectively, in 1 of 5,000 live births and 4 in 10,000 pregnancies.

Our friends Karen and Mark, finally pregnant again after months of trying and that heartbreaking miscarriage at ten weeks, said that when they express only cautious excitement about the new pregnancy, people think they're strangely dark and pessimistic. "No," they insist, "we're only being realistic. We know very well that we can take nothing for granted."

The cultural stereotype of the pregnant woman involves happy smiles, glowing skin, a beautifully rounded middle. Rarely do we speak of the fears and worries involved in being pregnant, at least not without quick reassurances that abnormalities are rare and chances are excellent that all will be normal. I'm finding again, though, that

fear is as much a part of pregnancy as joy. Maybe for many the balance tips toward fear. Even besides miscarriage—which is, in fact,
very common—a pregnant woman has plenty of reasons to take nothing for granted about her baby's health or safe arrival. Statistics are
in your favor, true, but statistics are abstractions, not personal promises. Nothing guarantees *you* will *not* be that 1 in 5,000.

People can be ridiculously insensitive to a pregnant woman's state
of fearfulness. At a party one evening, in the context of a how-are-
you-dealing-with-the-discomforts conversation, I was relating the
story of a woman I know who carried twins to term and then gave
birth to two seven-pounders. This prompted an older woman to top
that story with the tale of someone she knows who gave birth to
eight-pound twins. Not only that, but these two babies, though they
seemed perfectly fine for the first six months, later turned out to have
a rare genetic spinal defect that killed them both before the age of
two.

Why must people insist on impressing pregnant women with the
most bizarre child-defect story they know? Why must we use the
unspeakable heartbreak of other people to make our little maneuvers
in conversational competition? Later, when I mentioned this incident
to Ron, he suggested that I should have returned with a story of a
woman in her sixties who one minute was merrily chatting at a party
and the next minute dropped dead of a heart attack. Or who slipped
on the ice on the way out of the party and knocked her noggin and
never regained consciousness. Or who encountered a vicious dog on
her way home and then got into a tangle with a speeding SUV. Or
maybe her demise involved a falling chandelier . . . at this point, we
dissolved into wicked mirth.

I struggle to "control my thoughts" lest the Pregnancy Dimension
drive me to madness. But I wonder if I should explore this state of

heightened fearfulness. These early months of pregnancy seem to ease open emotional pores. I'm more sensitive, more paranoid about everything, more emotionally permeable. Not just about my own baby's health and well-being, but about everything. Annoyances and troubles bother me more quickly and stick with me longer. Does this mean I'm a little closer to madness, or hysteria, to use the etymologically appropriate word? Enduring a hormone-induced state of delusion? Or is this a state of clearer vision, of seeing things as they are? Life and death, "weal and woe" as the great medieval English writers put it, so intimately related, so firmly pressed against each other?

Dreams

Almost every night I awaken at about four in the morning, usually from a frightening dream. These are bigger, more vivid dreams than usual, dreams that bubble up from below and keep all of my sleep at a low, uneasy simmer. They are strong enough to break out into consciousness, especially at that time when consciousness is most susceptible to fear—in the dead quiet of the night.

Understandably, some of my nightmares focus on the baby. I dreamed of the baby born with the cord around its neck, blue and lifeless. I dreamed that the baby was born with a deformed face. The eyes were misshapen and the walls of the cheek and tongue were weirdly thick. But, horribly, the baby wanted to nurse vigorously, almost violently. The worst part of it was my own revulsion toward the baby and its neediness. I suppose such dreams force me to face my fears of a baby's constant demands, and closely related to this, my fears of not liking my own baby, of there turning out to be something less than appealing or even revolting about him or her.

But my fearful dreams sometimes seem to have nothing to do with the baby. In one dream Ron and I were in bed, near morning, and I asked him to get up and close the door to the upstairs porch, which we keep open sometimes for fresh air. He got up to do so, but discovered a burglar on the porch, a tall white man with longish brown hair, stealing Ron's guitar amp, of all things. The man laughed and threatened Ron with a knife, then disappeared down the stairs (there aren't really any stairs from our porch). Then, still in the dream, I got out of bed and found myself naked, so I pulled a towel in front of me and went to the phone to call the police. Then we went downstairs and discovered our living room ransacked and our stereo gone.

Another night I dreamed that our family was on a bus tour in a large city, and my daughter got separated from me and went with another group of adults. I thought it was all right, but then I saw her from the bus window, stepping out into a busy street while the supposedly responsible adults chatted casually on the curb. I woke up in terror. Another night I dreamed that she knocked on our bedroom door. I opened the door to find her, looking as she did when she was about two—except that she had no legs.

Even the mundane little dangers I routinely watch for seem, in these dream states, huge and threatening. As I begin to fall asleep, I can feel the darkness of my imagination swirling into large and threatening shapes. I picture my son walking right off the edge of the little second-floor porch, I see my daughter running into the street. I suppose it all has to do with the greater vulnerability of pregnancy, with the major life change it represents for all of us, and my inability to control completely what the world will hand to me and those I love. The "black box" of my own belly becomes the black box of all the world.

When I awaken from the more elaborate nightmare versions of these storied fears, all I can do is pray fervently through the terror and helplessness, pray that God will protect my precious ones from all harm. The usual reassurances of my faith—God's many blessings, the many occasions of protection in the past, the belief that nothing can separate us from the love of Christ—these have power in the quiet terror-times only to nudge forward meek little protests against the implacable truth that in this world there is simply no guarantee against suffering. I pray and pray instinctively, probably with little sense, until the weakness of the flesh—thanks to God for that—drags me back to sleep. When morning comes, the images sometimes remain, but the gut-twisting fear is gone.

I can make sense of this overflow of fear psychologically, but I don't know what to make of it spiritually. It's natural and normal to have such fears, the pregnancy books reassure, and it does make sense to have anxieties on the brink of a major life change. But they seem unreasonably, senselessly powerful. Are my fears abnormal? Are they . . . sinful? If I had greater faith, would the dreams not come? Would I awaken to stronger feelings of comfort and reassurance, like the people who say that angels come to them and embrace them gently in the night? If this is all a matter of hormone levels, then does that mean that hormones influence the state of our souls, tipping the delicate balances of fear and trust? As far as I know, this question represents completely unexplored theological territory.

While I'm waiting for theology to catch up to women's reality, what should I *do* with my fears? Should I pray to be freed from them? Or should I stand to face them? After all, "normal, healthy" humans survive their days, to tell truth, by papering over the real threats of this precarious world with comforting, half-conscious lies, like "That can't happen to me." Perhaps my dream fears are like looking at the world in a freshly cleaned mirror, so sharply reflective it hurts your eyes.

Real-World Fears

The light of day brings only limited relief. I find it harder to cope with real-world terrors, too, as the quotidian horrors on the news seem to sink in deeper. Recently, two deeply alienated, violence-soaked, hate-poisoned teenage boys went on a frenzied rampage at their high school in Colorado, setting off dozens of bombs and personally gunning down twelve other students and a teacher before killing themselves. One of our friends described it as "going out in a blaze of gory." The news media dubbed it the "Columbine massacre" and sent the whole nation into a state of morose and humbled soul-searching. Rather than musing on various social ills and legislative solutions, though, I found myself shooing away thoughts that my children would never grow up at all. That there was simply no way they could escape all the landmines of this world and make it to adulthood. If a drunk driver or childhood cancer didn't get them, then some gun-whipping teenage psycho would.

My dear friend Susan and I were discussing our fears for our children one day in the context of her concerns about her third baby, Joel. She and her husband, David, are scheduled to bring him in for testing because they suspect he can't hear. He does not respond to loud noises, and his babbling sounds seem quiet and bland. As we talked about her anxieties for baby Joel, she said that in order to cope with their fears, she and David have tried to imagine the worst-case scenario, and then remind each other that no matter what, they can trust that God will care for them through it. But we agreed that even knowing things could be worse, and even finding a place of peaceful trust, doesn't dilute the sadness. She then told of five other families in her church who are struggling with an ill child: one with a neuro- logical disorder, one with leukemia, and so on. She asked if I had heard of the five little girls who were playing in a car, got trapped in the trunk, and all died. No, I hadn't heard. But we remarked that there is a heartbreaking child tragedy in the paper every day. "I can't even read the paper anymore," she said. "Some days," I replied, "I don't know how we can get through the day, knowing all the things that could hurt our children and rip our hearts out." Francis Bacon, the pithy seventeenth-century essayist, once observed wisely that any man who marries and has children gives "hostages to fortune." And he had never even experienced motherhood. Susan and I agreed it's a miracle that anyone lives to be 10 years old or 30 or surely 80. A miracle.

This was a conversation between two women who believe with their heart, soul, and mind that God is all-powerful, and that no mat- ter what happens, God will provide. The problem is, this kind of belief is no get-out-of-grief-free card. I heard a beautiful sermon at the funeral of one of my retired colleagues, a man who suffered for ten years from an extremely rare, degenerative blood disease. The preacher said that life is a rhythm of death and resurrection, and that we need to practice both. The grieving times in our life prepare us for death. We need to practice dying through them, as our colleague had known so well.

What can I do to cope rightly with fear? If I rehearse in my mind or in my dreams all the possible disasters and griefs, will that exorcise the fear? St. John writes that "perfect love casts out fear." I used to think that meant that if I could just get to the point where my own capacity to love was perfect then I would never have any fears. Prospects were not good for ever achieving this, so it seemed a rather useless statement. But now I understand that John is talking about Christ's love. That's what's perfect, and that casts out fear. So what's the problem now? My friend Linda, a more courageous and prayerful woman than I, says that her fears dissolve when she prays. Why doesn't it work for me?

~

How we face our terror—that's the bottom line, isn't it? The way we make sense of the world can be winsome or cynical, intellectual or poetic, foolish or irrational. But how does it answer fear? That's the crucial test. So here I am, with my age-old answer, an ancient faith. Well, it's bad enough that this business of believing in God and practicing various pieties does not immunize against pain and grief. It's bad enough that God doesn't instantly fix this fallen world, but instead takes the long, hard way around and insists on respecting us creatures with enough autonomy to seek the path or destroy each other. But when my fear is bigger than usual, and faith doesn't neutralize the fear, then . . . what?

Still, I can't see living without faith. That way lies total despair. At least this way, there's something to hang onto in the dark. And maybe as I gain experience and become more saintly, more trusting, the fears will diminish. Maybe. Meanwhile, I can only return and return to the well, keep praying and singing and living among other people walking back and forth to the well, praying and singing.

~

In his series of children's books, *The Chronicles of Narnia*, C. S. Lewis often manages to explain confusing and difficult experiences of faith even better than the best theologians. In one of these indispensable passages, a boy named Digory is sent by the great lion, Aslan, on a mission. He is to travel to a hidden garden and return to Aslan with one silver apple to plant for the protection of the newly created Narnia. Digory manages the task, but not without undergoing a terrifying temptation: the witch Jadis slyly coaxes him to take one of the apples for himself—which an inscription on the garden wall warns against—and bring it home to heal his dying mother. Digory resists the temptation, but as he returns to Aslan, he wonders miserably if he did the right thing. He faces the certainty (he believes) of his mother's death, and he doubts whether Aslan cares anything for him. But into his fear and doubt comes the memory of Aslan's face as Digory told him of his mother's illness—the great lionish eyes filled with tears. Even in the midst of creating a new world, Aslan had shed tears over one boy's private grief. "I know. Grief is great," Aslan had said. "Only you and I in this land know that yet. Let us be good to one another."

Can I ease my fears by seeking the tears of God? Near the climax of the ecstatic rhapsody that concludes the book of Isaiah, the prophet pours out his vision of the promised new heaven and new earth. It is a vision of worldwide shalom, peace and harmony among nations, justice and righteousness filling the earth, the *tikkum olom* that Jews and Christians long for across the centuries. But this cosmic vision is shot through with intimate joys, healing of the most personal, private griefs. God declares, says the prophet:

> I will rejoice over Jerusalem
>> and take delight in my people;
>> the sound of weeping and of crying
>>> will be heard in it no more.

Never again will there be in it
  an infant that lives but a few days. . . .
They will not toil in vain
  or bear children doomed to misfortune.

In the midst of fear and doubt, I find testimony that the God who heals the world attends to singular griefs. I still live with my fears for my children and myself, but here in this place I see God's tears—falling to the earth to water and transform.

~

Still now remains the mystery of my own baby and what this child will bring to us and experience him- or herself. I haven't thought much about the person inside me; I haven't dared. If there is a new person in there, I can't feel it yet. Though the heart is beating (I hope) the baby's personhood is still dormant. The child has not yet reached out to me with its presence and made a reassuring connection.

I try to live by faith and dwell in the mystery, I really do. But I secretly consider—I wish I had the guts to do it—calling my doctor and reporting some alarming symptoms so that she will order an ultrasound.

Glimpses

As it turns out, my father-in-law *has* an ultrasound machine in his surgical practice. "Want to come down and have a look?" he asks us. Ha! So much for blind trust.

So we go in that afternoon and Dad fires the thing up so we can peek at our baby.

There it is! A fuzzy white blob in a black oval of emptiness. There is only one blob, I'm pleased to see, since my bloating belly had made me wonder if we might be facing twins. But no, that belly is indeed just the result of loosened-up muscles from the first two times around. And best of all, we can see the beating heart.

It is a baby, and it is alive. Beyond that, we can't see much. Dad is well-practiced in sounding out gallbladders and breast tissue, but his technique on fetuses presents a rather fuzzy picture. So the experiment leaves me reassured, but vaguely unsatisfied. Does the baby have arms and legs? I can't tell for sure. And why isn't it moving around? It seems so still and tiny and helpless. Well, what did I expect? At ten weeks, that's exactly what it is: still (except for reflex movements we can't see) and tiny and utterly helpless. The ghost image of ultrasound does not convey the tough elasticity of those pulsing tissues or the miraculous beauty of those miniature organs. Except for that heart, flub-dubbing steadily and saying, "I'm alive!"

8) joying in the body

For a while I thought I had entered a new and permanent stage of physical being, and I would just have to get used to feeling like a draggy lump of lead for the rest of my life. But now the intra-uterine building frenzy has slowed to a more civilized pace, my organs seem to have stopped elbowing each other resentfully, and my whole body has shifted from a grindy first gear to a comfortable cruise. My belly is noticeably rounded, beautiful, curving outward modestly so that m whole body seems a celebration of classically proportioned roundness. And may I mention my amazing breasts? Whenever I'm dressing in the bathroom, and I catch a glimpse of their glorious Os in the mirror—magnificent! I glide around all day with a feeling of pride in my body. Look, everybody: my body is doing miraculous things over here, and you can all go ahead and stare!

Best of all, I can feel the baby's movements now. Gentle little bumps and whiffles deep inside, saying, "I'm here!" At last, this tiny being has a way of communicating with me. The movements still take me a little by surprise. When they come, I think, "Oh yes—hello there, you!" We are beginning to meet each other in this quiet way, sharing secrets.

Euphemisms

When I was pregnant with my daughter, my mother dug up, just for fun, an old pregnancy book from the 1950s. Published by Better Homes and Gardens and in the seventeenth printing of the fifth edition, according to the front pages, it was a large hardcover book, pink of course, purporting to give parents good advice about pregnancy and baby care. Well, well.

As one would expect, the book is full of what we would consider, in our superior state of millennial enlightenment, amusingly quaint notions. But the first line that really made Ron and me howl was the one about working women and pregnancy: "Your condition will become rather readily apparent by the fifth month. If your appearance is important in your work, you'll want to quit, or arrange to work at home after that." Of course! No particular reason was given for this advice about "appearance." The next paragraph suggests that any physically tiring work be abandoned in the seventh month, and the next admonishes the mother to stay home with the baby indefinitely "unless it is absolutely necessary for you to work." After all, that baby needs you! Ah, things were simpler then.

Stepping around that mountain of other issues about work and family for mothers *and* fathers, what about this appearance business? Why quit for the sake of appearance? Apparently, this is based on the unspoken idea that a woman with a large belly is—how shall we say?—*unseemly* in a professional environment. People going about the important business of the world do not need to be reminded of primitive bodily functions. We can hide the porcelain trappings and embarrassing bodily processes of the "restroom" behind closed doors, but that big tummy has to be hauled around in *public*. It's attached. Then again, maybe this kindly advice for working women had something to do with the ridiculous maternity fashions of the 50s, with their tentlike lines and enormous baby-doll bows and collars. Now *that's* unprofessional.

As we paged further in the book, we noticed something else that at first seemed hilarious, and then frightening: the discussion of labor and delivery went on for exactly one and a quarter pages. You feel contractions, you go to the hospital . . . and the next several paragraphs reassure you that you will feel virtually no discomfort and be unconscious most of the time. Dad should go back to the office, by the way, and just "keep in touch with the hospital." After your uterus and the doctor (with forceps, perhaps) do all the work and you awaken from your drug-induced stupor, the book has the nerve to say, "You'll feel that you have taken part in the most rewarding experience of your life." Taken part? What, as a *prop?* The next few paragraphs are about birth certificates and circumcision.

How could this be? How could a woman be expected to face this

cataclysmic passage of her life with almost no knowledge of the process, no genuine acknowledgment that it will hurt, and no suggestion
that she might want to be awake for it? It made me shiver.

I suppose the best face I can put on this is that well-meaning
people in the medical profession wished to shelter women from the
fear, pain, and difficulty of labor and delivery. Better to focus on joyful anticipation and the busy tasks of new motherhood. When
the woman arrives at the hospital, these folk apparently thought, the
professionals should get her through that hard part. And indeed,
that's what happened. My mother remembers very little about my
brothers' and my birth, because she was given nitrous oxide during
contractions and delivery. When she "woke up," there was her baby
beside her. Like many women of her generation, she has no particular
feminist anger about it. She's darned glad for the way things were, in
fact.

And by the way, the good doctors wished to spare women the
difficulty of breastfeeding, too. The Better Homes and Gardens book
does recommend breastfeeding, while detailing the procedures for
bottle-feeding as well. My mom, though, was so convinced by "the
experts" of the scientific superiority of formula-feeding over the
primitive, creepy practice of breastfeeding that she still can't understand why anyone would want to do it, especially her daughter.
When I experienced the inevitable pain and fatigue of the first few
weeks with my other babies, she kept telling me that I should quit
and "have them give you something to dry up your milk." And of
course, like all staunch bottle feeders, she was convinced that breastfeeding mothers never manage to produce "enough milk" for that
poor, scrawny, starving baby.

I realize that male-dominated obstetrical professionals who disempowered women by withholding knowledge and control have already been thoroughly thrashed, burned, and excoriated. I'd like to believe that obstetricians generally had many benevolent thoughts; they were just doing the nicest things they knew how, really. They couldn't help it if they were trained to be paternalistic. Didn't the seething anger and surging grief of their former patients take *them* by surprise when women's health activists started pushing (sorry!) hard and sometimes furiously for change? Women have rightly insisted that we should be able to experience, listen to, and enjoy our bodies. Maybe labor and delivery isn't the best occasion for emphasizing that enjoyment part, but even in pain—no, especially in pain—our bodies speak wisdom we must hear.

Body Hatred

We hear all kinds of cultural back-patting lately about how women today are better informed and more at ease with their bodies than ever, that the days of ignorance and superstition are long relegated to the disgraceful past. Well, sort of. Women *know* more about reproductive functions, birth control options, breast and other cancer risks, osteoporosis, labor and delivery, and of course STDs. But greater knowledge does not transform automatically into greater ease, appreciation, or enjoyment. In fact, I think young women especially are more divided from their bodies than ever.

I taught an introductory literature class a few semesters ago, and during the poetry section of the course, I spent a day on poems about the body. We read a wonderful poem by the African-American poet Lucille Clifton, "homage to my hips."

homage to my hips

these hips are big hips
they need space to
move around in.
they don't fit into little
petty places. these hips
are free hips
they don't like to be held back.
these hips have never been enslaved,
they go where they want to go
they do what they want to do.
these hips are mighty hips.
these hips are magic hips.
I have known them
to put a spell on a man and
spin him like a top!

When my women students wrote about this poem, they remarked on how great it was that this poet had learned to value herself for "who she really was," because "it's what's on the inside that counts." Meanwhile, the men students found the poem slightly threatening. They noted how the speaker seems to be using her body to control men. Spells and spinning? Yikes!

These responses shocked me. First of all, the men's responses told me that the relationship between the sexes is so charged with fear these days that even the good-natured, fairly nonpoliticized fellows in my class could read scary power games into a cheeky, humorous poem. More subtly troubling, though, was the women's response. While they could easily pick up on the poet's acknowledgment that her body did not conform to cultural conventions of beauty, they seemed incapable of perceiving that this poet was rejoicing in her sexuality anyway. Not, as in Maya Angelou's similar poem, "Phenomenal Woman," in the sexiness of her personality and spirit. No, Clifton's speaker celebrates the sexiness of her big hips, her big everything. My students just couldn't see this; to them it seemed the best a woman could hope for was to be pleased with her character and spirit, *apart from her body.*

By the time I had figured all this out, it was too late to ask my students to respond to my observations. But the more I thought about it, the more it made sense. Where, in our culture, is a young girl given permission to celebrate her body as it is? I hardly need to comment on the cult of impossibly perfect, computer-enhanced feminine beauty pumped into our minds through the media. This is grotesquely obvious; and frankly, the portrayal of women as the ornamental half of the gender equation is nothing new. What is new is the high profile of abortion, date rape, domestic violence, teen pregnancy, sexually transmitted diseases, and sexual harassment, even in elementary schools, all of which constantly sends girls and women the subtle message that their bodies are the location of risk, danger, pain, and at the very least, deeply destructive political controversy.

In *A Woman's Book of Life,* Joan Borysenko remarks that when she first got her period, her mother's "talk" tersely announced the arrival of fear and danger: now you can get pregnant, her mother told her, so don't let any boy take advantage of you. Borysenko laments this old-fashioned, threatening approach to an important moment in a young girl's life. But is the approach currently receiving public approval—the frank-and-factual, so-called open-minded approach—any better? Now we're supposed to say, "Since you're going to have sex anyway, here's a condom. And by the way, there are plenty of diseases you can get even if you use it."

Wendy Shalit recently provided, as a certified young woman herself (age 24 when her book came out), a powerful countervoice for young women in her book *Return to Modesty*. She argues that while our wonderfully liberated and nonsexist culture is busy "educating" about sex in grade school and preaching to young women the happy gospel that they must "be comfortable with their bodies" and that all things sexual are "no big deal," young women are more miserable than in previous generations. They have entered a savage and misogynistic culture, as they are expected to be promiscuous at a young age and to suppress any misgivings, embarrassment, or revulsions they may feel about early and casual sex. To have regrets or hesitations is to have "hang-ups." And whose interests do these supposedly freeing attitudes serve? Mostly immature or even predatory males. And, I would add, a corporate world that profits most when people's souls are shaped to respond immediately to all impulses. Shalit marshals a depressingly massive 244 pages of anecdotes, quotations, and other kinds of evidence to prove her point that so-called liberation in sexual mores leads to misery among young women and to a horrid outbreak of self-loathing as expressed in eating disorders, self-mutilation, substance abuse, and depression.

These terrible maladies are not exactly rare on my campus. But for the most part, the young women I teach come from backgrounds that give them some means of resisting the cultural messages Shalit decries. Most of them come from religious homes and have highly involved, even protective parents. The men and the women typically learn words like "holiness" and "righteousness" even before they get to kindergarten. Many of them have gone to parent-run parochial elementary and secondary schools. So, much to their advantage, as

Shalit would probably observe, they are quite well aware that they don't have to swallow the lies; they know how to say "no." They may not always say it, but they know how.

Nevertheless, the savagery and fear of our sickly sexualized culture marks them, too. Even the ones who have avoided eating disorders and substance abuse still take refuge in a kind of conceptual disembodiment. They appear to be trying to get through life paying as little conscious attention to the body as possible. I'm thinking their "lower" impulses probably grab them off guard sometimes. But in their conscious, best-face-forward selves, they're focusing on "what's inside."

Running Free

We have got to do better than this. The feminist revolution reclaimed a woman's right to knowledge about bodies and to sexual pleasure. Awareness of abuse and other crimes is better than silence. But something is still cruelly skewed if young women are so fearful and conflicted about their bodies that they hardly know what to do with those things they're walking around in. Is it possible for us to teach our daughters to love their bodies? To show both our daughters and our sons that they do not have to allow their bodies to be sites of cultural conflict or tokens of exchange in destructive power games? To show them that their bodies are beautiful and honorable, whatever their shape or muscle-to-fat ratio?

Reveling now in the beauty and power of my body, I realize how pathetically narrow is our imagination. We seem to think that joy in the body equals physical pleasure and physical pleasure equals sex. But this is a conceptual rut that traps and oppresses as stiflingly as any degree of Victorian prissiness. We have to start thinking more broadly about what the body is and what it means to enjoy it. And I don't see how we can begin anywhere else but with a theology of the body that we teach children and indeed one another from the very beginning. It's really quite simple, but I think we will have to shout it obnoxiously over and over in order to be heard at all: Your body is beautiful because it is designed by God. Therefore, honor the body. Honor God with your body. And insist that others honor it, too.

Many people assume that we religious types are squeamish about bodies and certainly about sex, that we are not "comfortable with our bodies." This is surely true of some adherents in some periods of history, but it has certainly not been my experience, either in my reading or in life. Yes, some of that Pauline New Testament stuff seems to subscribe to the Hellenistic mind-body distinction. And it's true that my Christian high school did not allow students to hold dances in the school until 1983. But in its larger thought and practice, Christianity (and certainly Judaism) is profoundly concerned with the physical, or, in the case of Christianity, the incarnational. In fact, Christians value the body so much, we mean to hang on to it in the afterlife, albeit in recreated form. No tossing it away after death like the soul's dirty laundry, as some other religions propose and as various New Age conceptions would have it. Christians declare the "resurrection of the body" as a basic, but insufficiently discussed, belief. In my own branch of the faith, one of the most powerful confessions we have is in the opening lines of the Heidelberg Catechism, a document dating from the Reformation. A doctrinal teaching tool with a pastoral heart, the Heidelberg takes the form of questions and answers. And it begins, not with some abstract schema of divine ontology, but with *you*, where *you* are, suffering along through life, panting for some place of comfort and solace: "Q: What is your only comfort in life and death? A: That I am not my own, but belong, *body* and soul, in life and in death, to my faithful savior Jesus Christ."

The idea of belonging to anyone strikes many people as repulsive. It reeks of ownership, control, slavery—and dredges up the ugliest parts of human history. But to be owned by Christ, body and soul, is paradoxically the greatest liberation of all. This conviction flows in deep currents of comfort toward those whose bodies are diminishing with age or who are facing illnesses leading downward to death. If God cares for my body as well as my soul, then I can surrender its pain and failure to the One who made it: like taking a damaged violin back to one who carefully carved and sanded its every curve and plane. In youth and health, divine ownership can become a joyful statement, a kind of shining armor for all of us facing the dragons of our culture. In Sunday school, we teach our little ones to marvel over their fingers and noses as the ingenious inventions of a good Creator; why not keep this message about the holiness of the body loud and clear when kids really need it, at that time of gangly misery, powerful surges of physical desire, and intense mutual scrutiny: puberty?

One of Shalit's most bitter points is that young women are given no good reasons to say "no" since everyone seems to expect them to be promiscuous and not care. She would like to hand back to women the power of modesty, as a broad cultural code, in motivating that "no." Her solution still assumes, though, that young women should be in charge of their own bodies. But it's better yet to declare that our bodies—women's and men's—are God's prized possessions, that God is the rightful owner, and all that we do with them comes under the joyful privilege of reflecting that royal status.

There are some signs of hope in our culture for finding joy in the body, instead of shame and disgust. I see increasingly sharp, vocal, and well-informed resistance to media images of women and men. I recently heard Jean Kilbourne, a popular speaker who uses devastatingly clever humor to expose the way advertisers sell slavery and addiction to women and insult the intelligence of the populace with big, poufy helpings of lies.

Also, I'm grateful for the rise of women's athletic programs over the last twenty years, even though I'm no athlete myself. (I do have a dim recollection of putting in a fine season on the ninth-grade girls soccer team twenty years ago.) Today, when I watch my daughter and son enjoying women's soccer or various Olympic contests, I see them learning that women's and men's bodies are beautiful, agile creations. (In the hoopla leading up to the Women's World Cup Soccer games, they saw the Nike commercial featuring Mia Hamm and Michael Jordan. They knew all about Mia. But "Who's that tall guy?" they wanted to know.) I understand that sometimes the discipline of athletic training can devolve for young women into self-destructive overtraining and undereating, but there's much to counteract that, too.

Also in the hope-for-our-civilization category are some movements advocating chastity, such as the "True Love Waits" program. In my opinion, though, chastity these days has to be much more than girls and boys practicing the passive virtue of "waiting." Chastity is an active virtue. That old allegorical poem by the English Renaissance poet Edmund Spenser, *The Faerie Queene,* figures chastity as a woman warrior named Britomart. As a young girl, she sees a vision of her true love, but does she sit around and wait for him to show up? No, she puts on her armor, practices her jousting technique, and rides off for adventures. Her main task is not to find this special fella, but to rescue Amoret (who represents real love) from the evil sorcerer Busirane, whose house is plastered with tapestries and cluttered with gilded statues, all depicting violent, bestial, grotesque myths and stories about love. Get it? She has to find her way through powerful, sickening lies to rescue something genuine and lovely. Busirane's house turns out to be an illusion sustained by evil magic, by the way. The point is, chastity is every bit the harrowing adventure, a period of moral testing and courageous action. Actually, *The Faerie Queene* is an extremely long and harrowing poem. High school teachers might try assigning it to their students as a courageous exploit in its own right.

Chastity is only part of joying in the body, though—the brush clearing so that the really colorful blooms of body-joy can find the sun. Shalit argues for modesty (not quite equivalent to chastity, I acknowledge) with essentially an erotic argument: modesty prevents misery and promotes real pleasure. Not technical, "ten tips for a mind-blowing big O" pleasure, but the deeper human pleasures of romance, mystery, satisfaction after delay, and genuine spiritual union. It's a good argument, but still focused mostly on the realm of between-the-sexes body issues. I would offer the words of the psalmist: "I run in the path of your commands, for you have set my heart free." Letting our sexuality, sensuality, and plain physicality honor the Maker ultimately sets the heart free. Free from shame, insult, regret, self-hatred. The commands of God are not, to the psalmist, repressive and judgmental, but freeing: they are the edges that define and mark the path of life.

Eat, Drink, and Be Merry

This business of chastity aside, what about the pleasure of physicality itself? This deep physical attentiveness of pregnancy is awakening me to it again. Eating, for example, is a source of extra delight these days. I have never so much appreciated the beauty of an orange. I slice one of those perfect packages into four or five fleshy disks of

intense color, swim in their fragrance, pull the disk open into a curving string of sunny little triangle sections, suck their juices before
pulling with my teeth and savoring each one. I feel a little naughty
enjoying food so much. My feelings of naughty pleasure make me realize something I haven't thought about much: women especially are
not supposed to like food. We can be footloose and moral-free in the
sex area, but eating is clearly a realm of intense and irrational moral-
ism. The multizillion-dollar diet industry is out there selling indul-
gences, as it were, acting as the priesthood that can expiate us from
our food sins. No need to pay the pros, though, to participate in this
religiosity: witness the undercurrent of guilt when someone brings
a birthday treat to work and then sheepishly apologizes that she
"baked out all the calories." I say it's time to get subversive with pleasure. I wonder what would happen if we started taking physical
pleasure in every delicious bite. Maybe we wouldn't overeat or hate
ourselves for every tasty morsel. Savoring every crumb of a fresh,
warm bagel, licking your fingers afterward. Sipping a cup of coffee
while doing nothing else, not reading the paper, not driving to work.
Just enjoying the ability to smell and taste. I wonder.

Eating is one basic pleasure of the body, but pregnancy also makes
one appreciate breathing. I usually give breathing no thought at all.
Except when I have a cold, during which time I think about it constantly with great wistfulness. Like a nasty head cold, pregnancy
draws attention to breathing simply by making it more difficult, especially in the later stages when the baby presses upward and grows
heavier. In childbirth classes, breathing becomes the focus of intense
technical training, but never a source of pleasure. There it's more like
a sport, something you try to do well in order to please your coach.
But why not enjoy it? Meditative traditions from all over the world
encourage quiet, concentrated breathing as one step on the way to a

higher state of consciousness. We Westerners are usually too busy for such "nonsense." If we're thinking about breathing, it's because we're huffing and puffing on some exercise contraption. But we're missing something.

And then there's the digestive system. I have a line drawing of a very pregnant woman in cross section, showing where the baby lays and how all the other organs sort themselves out to make room. Her stomach is a flat little disk above the big uterus and her intestines are all squished down behind and beneath the baby. Wow! So maybe pregnancy is an especially appropriate time to marvel at the ability of the digestive tract to get the job done even under very trying circumstances. The digestive distresses that some pregnant women suffer surely make digestive ease seem a most happy function of the human organism. Anyone who's been seriously ill or even just had the flu knows this, too. It may seem a little creepy to thank the Creator for the digestive system, but it has at least one distinguished precedent. Julian of Norwich, a fourteenth-century English mystic, was never one to be squeamish or ethereal about the spiritual life. She wrote:

> Food is shut in within our bodies as in a very beautiful purse.
> When necessity calls, the purse opens and then shuts again,
>   in the most fitting way.
> And it is God who does this, because I was shown that the Good-
>   ness of God permeates us ever even in our most humble needs.
> God does not despise any part of creation, nor does God disdain to
>   serve us in the simplest function that belongs to our bodies in
>   nature, because God loves us and we are made in the image
>   of God.

This kind of spiritual meditation is probably not exactly what the writer of Thessalonians meant by "give thanks in all circumstances." But pregnant women know that in some circumstances, even basic bodily functions call for thanksgiving.

Perhaps one of the best categories of body pleasure, though, is that of skilled, ordered motion: the practiced tricks of the feet in a familiar aerobics routine, the power released in the circling shoulders of a good golf-swing, that surge of strength through the arms for the last triumphant chord in the piano sonata, the cool water gliding across the back during a swim in the lake, the simple and second-nature gesture of hoisting a toddler onto the hip, and a thousand other examples. How often do we celebrate these as physical plea-sures? We do things with our bodies to keep them healthy and "have fun," which often means "to say we did it." But why not just because it feels good? Sex is a marvelous thing, sure. But the loveliness of physical pleasure spans a much larger field, and we can, if we choose, run in it free and jubilant as children.

~

If I want my little ones to learn joy in the body, I can try to model it, and try to preach it in small doses that won't gag them. I guess when I say model, I'm not being entirely figurative. With only one family bathroom in our house and all the popping in and out my little people do while we big people are dressing or showering, impromptu na-ked modeling is pretty hard to avoid. I don't want to duck behind curtains constantly or parade around, but with my daughter, espe-cially, I do want to demonstrate an attitude of happy appreciation for my grown-up woman's body. I try to refrain from any mirror-front fretting about my looks. I admit, it helps that I'm naturally skinny, even bony, so I don't worry much about committing the severe American "offense" of being "fat." And now, with this beautiful full- ness, I'm always rhapsodizing about the marvels of female physiol- ogy: "Look, Miriam—see how my tummy's getting bigger?" I'll let her know about the less delightful parts, too. I thought it would be only a matter of time before it dawned on her that babies come out of the vagina—a pretty small opening—and that this procedure might possi- bly hurt. To my surprise, my son thought of it first, and—being smart enough even at age three to imagine the size differential between a baby and that mysterious opening between my legs—he looked quite horrified, as if he feared for my life. I explained to them both that in- deed it was a painful process, but that amazingly enough everything went back to normal (pretty much) afterward. My daughter didn't worry any more about it, but my son still seemed rather dismayed until I pointed out the living proof that he and Miriam were sitting right there, and here I was, too, perfectly fine and able to tell them about it.

St. Paul insists in the book of Romans that we "present our bod- ies as living sacrifices, holy and acceptable to God." That verse used to make me squirm, because any mention of the word "sacrifice" smelled of martyrdom to me, a possible outcome of the religious life I would prefer to avoid. But pregnancy has taught me to think of this as an invitation, instead, to a joyful life caring for and honoring the body, resisting endeavors sexual or otherwise that would dishonor one's own or anyone else's body, and instead finding pleasure in all the amazing things our bodies do. In pregnancy and childbirth, I do one of the most amazing physical feats humans can do: I present my body as a living sacrifice for the sake of creating by God's power another person. I would like to think this is how all sacrifice should feel in the religious life: the hurts don't go away, but eventually they make one glad. They are markers on that path to wonder.

9) ordination

Is it better to know the sex of the baby before birth, or is it better to be surprised? Here's another small dilemma expectant parents face courtesy of medical technology. I decided this week that it's better to know ahead of time. Well, I think so.

Of course my biggest concern going into the ultrasound appointment was simply that the baby would be fine, that all the parts would be in the right place. I expected that when we saw the little person's palish outlines, I would feel a wave of relief and gratitude and reassurance. We did want to know the baby's sex, mostly for practical reasons. I wanted to sort out all my boxed-up baby clothes ahead of time. And I admitted to myself that I liked the idea of having another girl, so it would probably be better to know ahead of time if the baby was not going to wear any of those darling little dresses I had saved. But I thought I would be truly thrilled with a normal baby either way.

Then the sonographer said, "It's a boy."

Well, well. How full of pretense our little maternal pieties can be. Yes, I was relieved that all the parts were in the right place. Yes, it was wonderful to see the actual baby moving about on the screen. No normalized line drawings or fetal photos of someone else's baby this time. This was our little person moving his hand to his head and opening and closing his little mouth as if laughing hello. But it was *his* hand and *his* mouth. And my relief was eclipsed by disappointment.

This is a very unattractive confession. But it's true. I suddenly realized how much I had planned on a girl. I had imagined holding a little girl's hand, I had thought of my daughter with a little sister, I had thought of a baby smearing strained carrots on a little pink jumper. I had looked forward to bestowing upon this child what we had determined last time around was the perfect girl's name: Lydia.

But this is not to be. Period. This baby is a boy, and that changes everything.

I am grateful for the intricate finger and toe bones we saw and that circular blank of a stomach and the bumpy ladder of a spine. But as for those other little parts . . . what can I teach a boy about life?

I already have a boy, of course, whom I adore. But I know him. He's Jacob, he's my Jacob. Two boys seem altogether different. One boy is himself, a person. Two boys introduce a critical mass of boy energy into the family. Suddenly, my daughter and I are outnumbered. There's Dad and "the boys" and then there's Miriam and me. Suddenly my world seems filled with males. A male-focused world outside my doors, a male world inside my house. A husband to please, a boy to attend to, a boy inside my body. The *other* everywhere. I feel strangely lonely.

And indignant. Is all I do designed to serve this male *other?* Even the breathing and eating and sleeping that keeps this fetus buoyant within me? I have so much to tell a girl about being a woman in this world. Can I offer any wisdom to two brothers? Or will they look to their father for the hard stuff of life, and to me simply for the archetypal warm, nurturing memory of early childhood, regarding me as the cipher of Mom at whom they affectionately or dismissively roll their eyes and whom they barely even see after age ten?

I attempt to focus on more sensible reflections, such as the fact that early in my first pregnancy, I wanted a boy and was convinced I was having one. Once again, a stoic sonographer set us straight with anatomical fact. That took a few days to get over, too. Then, the moment Miriam was born, she could have been no one else, and I wanted no one else. From her and Jacob, I know very well that a child is an individual. Girl or boy is only part of it. Each is a unique person. Theoretically, I could have an obnoxious, pain-in-the-neck girl just as easily as a delightful and wonderfully charming boy. After all, Jacob is immediate proof that a boy can be sweet and funny and darling. And maybe this boy will turn out to be a musical genius and I'll be able to go to his performances and . . . no, no! Stop! Fantasizing a life for one's kid is a swamp of trouble.

Still—here's where I wonder if it's better to know ahead of time after all. If we had refrained from consulting the sonographer's oracle, then I would have gone on expecting a girl in firmly unconscious ways, while dutifully intoning that we would be happy with either. But then, in the delivery room, when someone pronounced "It's a boy!" it would be no abstract matter to brood over. *There he would be* to see and touch and hold—himself, a brand-new person. What would I care then about generalizations and half-confessed fantasies?

Well, it's done and we know and I can spend the next few months anticipating the arrival of this still-mysterious person, knowing at least one important thing about who he is. Meanwhile, my mom, who shops months ahead for every occasion, can happily browse for blue things. And I can sit down at the sewing machine and deal with this sudden and irresistible desire to sew Miriam a very frilly Easter dress.

What Is Determined?

Now that we know what the baby's sex is, I begin to wonder what else is determined already, even before this child makes his official start in life.

We live in strange times when it comes to explaining why things are the way they are. In my world literature class, we read several dramas and poems of ancient Greek origin in which the characters and their experiences are manipulated by an unruly band of deities. I like to ask students to think about how much control these characters have over their actions and destinies. At times it seems that the Olympian gods, with their petty rivalries and cupiditous moods, play with the human characters like puppets. On the other hand, the reason these old tales still hold our interest, I think, is that we see human characters like the wily Odysseus and the determined Oedipus and the impressively single-minded Clytemnestra attempting to carve out a place for human autonomy in the fissures created by divine conflicts or indifference.

My students, being generally on the religious side—many of them devoutly so—would claim ultimately that God's will shapes their own characters and their lives. But they're sophisticated enough to recognize that this is an ultimate, theological answer, and not always an experiential one. We feel ourselves to have choices, and real ones—not just illusory ones that will turn out to be what God wanted all along. We are free to make mistakes large and small, and free to clean them up or leave the mess. Sometimes we are freer than we wish to be, when we earnestly ask God to tell us what to do and receive silence as the apparent reply. "You choose," God seems to say. Sometimes that's a frighteningly existential place to be. We want a nice, curly-edged treasure map, and instead we're floating in cold, dark space.

Among the various species of experts we hear from in magazines and TV documentaries, neither Zeus and his cohorts nor God-the-one-true-God are the typical explanatory techniques deployed in accounting for our nature and destiny. Advocates of biological determinism, for instance, propose that human nature is knowable and is programmed into our little neurons according to patterns developed over thousands of years of evolutionary work. These are the evolutionary psychologists who propose theories such as the one that men are more promiscuous because Paleolithic males found it advantageous to inseminate as many females as possible, thereby ensuring the continuation of their particular brand of Homo sapiency. Meanwhile, Stone Age females needed a man around to supply food while they were busy nursing or toddler-managing, so they sought to corral a man into monogamy if possible, in order to ensure the survival of their offspring. Of course, the next thing you know, someone else is coming out with a book proposing that, no, in fact, cavewomen were actually quite promiscuous because they wanted to keep the tribal males guessing about paternity. It's all based on the thinnest threads of evidence fluffed over with wads of speculation. Articles reviewing these books always sport titles like "Stone Age Roots for Infidelity?" I cannot imagine why I should care how Stone Age humanoids arranged their society, even if it were possible to know—which, I insist, it isn't.

Another form of biological determinism is the current serious and not-so-serious fascination with the human genome project. Are our character traits mapped out in our genes? Not only might our genes determine our vulnerability to cancer or heart disease, some propose, but also our intellectual capacity and our tendency toward violence or love. Will we be able to massage our genes to make designer humans? A little more muscle mass, a little more compassion?

On the other side of the nature-nurture debate are those who attribute our adult behavior patterns to the sundry dysfunctions of our families of origin. As in: he's a serial killer because his father abused him. Or, more commonly: she can't manage to keep a marriage together because her parents' divorce made her unable to trust or commit. One recent counterargument is that it isn't the *family* of origin, it's the *peers* of origin. This may come as a great relief to parents of wayward children, parents who have agonizingly searched every dark corner of their psyches wondering what they might have done to screw up their kids. Now they can blame it on those good-for-nothing junior high buddies.

All these ways of explaining why we are the way we are have the potential to be used as excuses for our behaviors, relieving us of responsibility for repentance (the heavy-duty religious term) and genuine change. I doubt this is the intention of people who work seriously to advance our understanding of human origins, say, or human genetics or human psychology. They're simply trying to understand, or maybe advance their careers, or in the most unsavory cases maybe, make a buck. Many of the explanations have some usefulness. But sometimes even armies of grad students doing funded studies and cases of Ph.D-authored books do not add up to a big improvement on the obvious. And it seems to me everywhere evident that no one model fits all the data.

When I think of the child now preparing for life inside me, or the little children blooming and bouncing around in my house, I see all these factors at work in a confusing tangle. It's obvious, first of all, that they are unique from before birth. My daughter was as wiggly and energetic in my belly as she is outside. My son strongly preferred his mama from the start, and he's still affectionate and loyal to me. A friend whose son is a prize-winning college-age jazz drummer claims that her son was drumming rhythmically in her womb. The minute a child is born, we see that he or she is unique not only in physical features but in temperament, too. There is significant credibility to the idea that some traits are simply hard-wired.

On the other hand, little human beings are impressionable and resilient. My daughter doesn't spout skepticism at TV commercials because of her genetic code. She's learned that from me. Yikes! Sobering as it is, what I do as a parent matters. The family-of-origin theories have their validity, too. Living through their parents' divorce really does work on some daughters and sons to make them commitment-shy. Theories that downplay parental determinism are meant as a corrective to skewed psychological practices that blame all on the parents. But I don't want to lose the intense importance of parental influence,

either. On the contrary, I would like to get rid of the underlying as-
sumption that parents can follow their bliss and the kids will be all
right as long as the parents are happy. Instead, I would like to see
parents insist ferociously on the importance of doing their parenting
well, resisting a relentless work economy and a culture of selfish in-
dulgence and transience that only grudgingly makes space for it.

But it's undeniably true that parents aren't everything. Peers are
important, too, as are all kinds of experiences. A book the child reads,
a journey to an exciting city or gorgeous desert landscape, a stray
comment from a wise aunt, a concert that inspires a love for
music—who knows what might sink into a child's heart and change
her life's path? Parents also love to believe that the world is open to
our children and full of wonders for them to explore. Thank good-
ness they will meet people and go places that will provide some relief
from the distortions we inevitably hand them in the form of our own
tattered selves. In a way, we like to think that nothing is determined.
Children who grow up to surprise all predictions and overcome
enormous disadvantages, like poverty and abuse, seem to demon-
strate this theory's validity.

Then we're back to autonomy. Another piece my world lit students have to read is called "On the Dignity of Man," by the fifteenth-
century Italian scholar Giovanni Pico della Mirandola. Pico nicely
represents extreme Renaissance enthusiasm about human will and
possibility. In his essay, he imagines God saying to Adam at his
creation:

Thou, like a judge appointed for being honorable, art the
molder and maker of thyself; thou mayest sculpt thyself into
whatever shape thou dost prefer. Thou canst grow downward into the lower natures which are brutes. Thou canst

grow upward from thy soul's reason into the higher natures
which are divine.

My students like the idea that we can choose for ourselves what we
will be. That's deep in American mythology, after all. And it's deep in
our religious faith, too, that we have choices, that we are responsible
for them, and that much is at stake. It's a heady philosophical stance
for young people who every day, it seems, are making major, life-
directing decisions. Yet they're skeptical of Pico's enthusiasm. They're
old enough to know that their powers and possibilities are not abso-
lute. They're working within limitations already.

Somehow it's all mixed up together, choices and limitations,
freedom and boundaries. Whatever we're handed genetically, or so-
cioeconomically, or from our parents or peers or schools, we do have
some range of motion within these limits. Some psychological models, such as the "diathesis-stress" model and the "reciprocal gene-
environment" model, attempt to explain behavior as a combination of
inherited traits or vulnerabilities and environmental stresses and conditions. But it's one thing to speak broadly of behavior tendencies
and quite another to account for a particular person's choice in a
particular situation. We are fantastically flexible amalgamations; we
are what we are and become what we become through a calculus
whose complexity will, I suspect, always elude us.

Originals

So when the psalmist writes, "You knit me together in my mother's womb," and "All the days ordained for me were written in your
book before one of them came to be," what does that mean? What

exactly is ordained for us before our days begin? Other translations use other words for ordained, like "formed" or "fashioned" or "shaped." So what days are shaped for my new son? What will be his character? What will living with Ron and me and Miriam and Jacob imprint on him? Who will be his friends and what will he come to love in this life? What griefs will he have to suffer? Ah, there's where the idea of a life divinely preshaped loses its charm and comfort and turns chilling. Could he be destined for a diminished life, like the little boy at my church, born with microcephaly, an underdeveloped brain? Could he be destined for some terrible end, like my friend's sister, a beautifully devout young woman who at 27 was raped and murdered? Or like the teenagers murdered by their classmates at Columbine?

These darker places, shadows that any formulation of God's sovereignty over this world must cast, lead me to prefer the word "ordained" in the Psalm 139 text. Ordained doesn't mean destined, exactly; it means put in order, appointed, given purpose and meaning, made holy and set apart. So although the genetics roulette continues to come up short in this fallen world, and little babies like Dalton are born with severe impairments, God still sanctifies his life, through the faithful care of his weary parents, through a baptismal service that spoke into the heart of darkness with a sermon on Abraham's near-sacrifice of Isaac, through the teenagers at church who carry and play with Dalton just as they do with the other kids.

That our days are ordained means that God knows from an eternal perspective the whole of our lives, in their overall contours and their minute detail. My belief in this, my experience of God's intimate knowledge and care in my own life—"you discern my going out and my lying down; you are familiar with all my ways"—leads me to reject that other increasingly common explanation for our nature and purpose: reincarnation. I understand the appeal of this belief. That we come from somewhere past and enter another future seems to soothe the loneliness of our discrete little existences. The notion of past lives contributes some sense to our complexity, offering teasingly mysterious explanations for our aberrations or habits. The notion of future lives eases our fear of the "undiscovered country" beyond death, and holds out the possibility that we might indeed get to gather up the many regrets we string along behind us as we travel. The notion of karma, through which our conduct in one life determines the shape of the next one, appeals to our thirst for justice and justifies our fear of it. We want the universe to make sense, we want good to bring good and evil to bring evil. The alternative—a random, careless cosmos—is far too terrifying for most of us to accept.

I recognize its allure; but I'm too proud to believe in reincarnation. First of all, I'm already too tired to imagine working at enlightenment in another life. That *other* wicked people might pay in the next life for their deeds in this one sounds like it might satisfy eventually the justice that is never fully paid out in a single lifetime, but what about *my own* wicked deeds? No, thanks. I'll take my chances on grace in this life; justice is not nearly so appealing to me as forgiveness, healing, and renewal, right here and now.

And besides all that, I cannot believe that I am only a temporary *I,* morphed from some past life, poised to melt again into something else, and then—at least in some versions of the belief—eventually dissolve altogether into a Great Spirit of one sort or another. It's not that I am uniquely wonderful; rather, it's the wonder that I am unique. And beyond that, the wonder that my unique *I* can love another unique *I*—mother, father, friend, husband, each child, this singular new child forming inside me, already so fiercely my own. The sweet communion of human love, lover to lover or parent to child, patiently touching every detail of the beloved's life with its gentle gaze—this argues eloquently for the durability of the self, and for the magnificent personhood of the God who created a multiplicity of creatures able to honor one another's uniqueness with love. Love is not content with the temporal; it strains toward the eternal.

So I have no interest in a life beyond in which all the great individuals of history, or even all my friends and family members and I, collapse into a great vibrating mass of life energy. Instead, I want God to burn away all our failures and distortions, and from out of the sparks let each singular person emerge, recreated and unspeakably beautiful. Then we will know how intensely love can radiate among us, in the presence of love's Original.

~

Sometimes in a crowded place, like a Wal-Mart parking lot for instance, I look at the people—gray-haired older women struggling along with their carts; plump, balding men slinging their bags of purchases into the trunk; smooth-skinned teenage girls in tank tops and ankle bracelets—and I try to imagine that God knows every detail of these people's lives. Doubt is my usual impulse on such occasions. Can there really be a God who knows all that? Maybe it does make sense that all these masses of people are just recycled versions of other masses of people, our wombs the remanufacturing plants of humanity. How can God possibly manage all the details of all these individuals' lives? But it must be so, if I believe God knows *me,* knows "when I sit and when I rise." Psalm 139 meditates on this phenomenon of God's infinite knowledge, and the psalmist winds up in about the same place I usually do, giving up trying to get it:

How weighty to me are your thoughts, O God!
How vast is the sum of them!
Were I to count them—they are more than the sand.

God knows the intricacy of our created givens, and the mystery of our interactions as unique creatures with all those other people and experiences we will encounter, and indeed with God's self. To be known like this, in totality, so rare and mysterious a thing—what can it mean except that we are, even in our ordinariness, precious and ordained, held in the patient hands of God like so many dusty but finely cut jewels.

1 0) *n e s t i n g*

It's hit me now, this powerful urge to clean up, throw away, clear out. I swooped down on Miriam's room tonight, and many of her precious little treasures—hair clips, plastic beads, shells from Lake Michigan—got swept away in my ferocious whirlwind. "What the heck is this crap doing in my house? Get it out of here!" I muttered, flinging helpless items ruthlessly in the direction of the nearest wastebasket. When I get in this mood, the other people who live in my house do best to take shelter in some small inner room, maybe with a mattress over them, and stay out of my way.

The other night I ventured into our basement storage room with that woman-warrior look on my face, ready to open and sort through a dozen boxes of baby clothes. Ron generously offered to help, but minutes later it became clear that it wasn't going to work. He couldn't do anything right. "No, no. Put that box there." "Yes, just take that one out into the laundry room and set it somewhere for a minute while I clear some space here." "OK, now this we'll need after about six months, so put that over there." The look on his face pleaded, "Why are we doing this anyway?" and he had the audacity to utter the following blasphemous thought: "Can't we just pull out the boxes as we need them?" My obvious exasperation sent him retreating upstairs, where he began tidying the mountain of papers and magazines that we must regularly move out of our kitchen. There were to be *no* infidels in my basement. If he couldn't assent to the absolutely imperative nature of the project, I did not want him around.

The traditional wisdom is that nesting is primitive behavior related to our animalian ancestry, in which the female of the species prepares a place to give birth. Makes sense. But I can think of some pretty uniquely human motivations, too. For instance, if I don't clean out the house, where on earth are we going to put all the baby paraphernalia? We need at least a whole room for the crib, changing table, little dresser, bouncy seat, glider rocker, dozens of blankies, and basket of infant toys. So if we ever expect to prepare a nursery upstairs we *obviously* have to begin by cleaning out the basement storage room. Besides, if I don't clean and sort and organize now, it could be three years before I can do anything around the house without either a baby on my hip or all my mental energies focused on preventing a toddler from impaling himself on some sharp household object.

The most amusing part of this nesting urge is the element of anger. Where does that come from? Why does every little bead on the
floor and fuzz heap under the bed seem a personal affront? Why am
I on this vendetta against all things dusty and cluttery? Perhaps it's
my own revenge against that law of the natural world that my scien-
tist brother would label the second law of thermodynamics: all things
tend toward entropy. In other words, left to themselves, things fall
apart. Keeping them together requires constant energy. This is true
both of galaxies and children's closets. So I may well be lashing out
in anger at the very nature of the universe here. Well, why not? The
universe could use a little sprucing up.

Too bad this anger does not currently seem aimed at the great
messes of the world. What might happen if expectant mothers everywhere would band together and sally forth, buckets and mops raised
in their rubber-gloved hands, and aim that nesting energy at problems
like interethnic violence or environmental pollution? Unfortunately,
this instinct seems quite determinedly limited to the small scale—
kitchen drawers and car interiors. If anything, I want more than ever
to shut the big problems of the world out. I am fiercely focused on
bringing a child into a world of beauty, wonders, and love, and I can
only make that appearance take effect in my own little domain. My
nesting is just for the nest, not for the whole forest.

Maybe I am moving a little unnecessarily beyond the basic, logistical needs of preparing a bed and getting diapers and a few items of
clothing together. Clearly, this tiny person is not going to care
whether the arms of the pink chairs have been shampooed. All this is
obvious to Ron, as his furtive eye rolling reveals. But after all, we are
about to welcome royalty into our home. There's something in my
motherly soul that urges me to prepare as if for the arrival of a prince.
Wordsworth had this instinctive infant regality in mind, I think,

when he wrote in his poem "Ode: Intimations of Immortality" that "trailing clouds of glory do we come/ From God, who is our home:/ Heaven lies about us in our infancy!" Of course, these beautiful lines do make me wonder if Will was ever present at an actual delivery. Probably not. Births are exceedingly earthy affairs, leaving the floor strewn with blood-soaked linens and wads of gauze and various fleshy items that used to be tucked neatly into one's private insides. But Wordsworth was right about the fresh wonder of a newborn baby's very breaths. Out of the earthiness, a star of mystery rises. We understand so much about the body and its processes, about gestation, about delivery, about infant physiology. And yet the personhood, the soul-essence of each infant, appears as a mysterious glory.

It's hard to know how to honor this properly at the moment, or how to prepare for it. So as women have done for centuries in the face of the great and mysterious events of existence—birth, death, illness, marriage—we clean and cook. We turn to the plainest tasks and perform them with reverence and determination. Sometimes with a ferocity that annoys everyone around. It's simply a time-honored and productive way of dealing with something we recognize is much bigger than ourselves. For so long, so few women learned how to honor the magnificence of existence with the larger, louder poetry of art, architecture, music, and poetry itself. We've learned that now, too. But still the simple responses of the hands, or maybe I should say, the hands and knees, remain. In the face of the profound, we begin with the simple, and work.

No one must underestimate the importance of simple work. I will forever remember with deep gratitude the night Ron and I took our new baby Miriam home from the hospital and my friend Jennifer came over and made us omelettes. We were so bewildered with this infant, but Jennifer's simple act calmed us, and fed us, too. And I envision before me the armies of women who have labored behind the scenes in church kitchens over the years, making the food and brewing the coffee for funerals, weddings, and council meetings. In my neck of the ecclesiastical woods, standard fare at all such occasions is ham-on-bun, potato salad, Jell-O, frosting-laden cake, and coffee, with little bowls of nuts and mints on the side. Sure, women have been marginalized and denied opportunities to exercise their gifts as leaders in the church; they've been showing up at crucial moments and feeding the congregation instead. Welcome them now into full leadership, but let no one denigrate that old work. These women put more wisdom into one swipe of the mayonnaise than could be found in many an hour of council discussion.

My mother taught me to respect simple gestures in times of crisis. She has many spiritual gifts, but I think her most natural and important has been to provide acts of mercy for those in need. That sounds so noble, like winged angels descending, but mostly it amounts to a chicken dinner or a layer cake or a card sent to the hospital. I know one young woman who remembers when she was only three or four years old, and her dad had just left her mom, and they were so poor. My mom showed up one day at her house with a bag of goodies, including some pairs of panty hose. The little girl saw her mom burst into tears for joy over those hose, and to this day she is grateful to my mother.

I try to be like my mom in this way, but there really is a knack to it and I haven't quite got it. When my husband was in seminary, our friends Leanne and Steve had a baby, so I decided to bring them the meal my mother would have made: breaded pork chops, baked potatoes, and fresh green beans. I brought it over, they enjoyed it, and later I called my mom, feeling pretty proud of myself. "That's great,

Deb," she said. And then, just to make conversation: "What did you make for dessert?" Dessert? Oops. It never occurred to me to bring dessert. Mom would have had a batch of homemade cookies already in the freezer so she could just pull them out as she walked out the door.

I'm not a hugely skillful cleaner, either, despite my Dutch blood. (Those pristine Vermeer interiors? *Nothing* to your average West Michigan Dutch household.) Fortunately, there's no knack to nesting. The energy and skill wells up from within. Not all the time, though. The urge seems to alternate with periods of fatigue so weighty all I can do is plant myself on the couch, Miriam on one side and Jacob on the other, and read books they fetch for me from the bookshelf. Since Christmas we've read half of Laura Ingalls Wilder's entire opus, and it looks like we'll make it through every page before the baby comes. Meanwhile, don't expect me to get up to answer the phone.

Humbaba

Do expectant fathers engage in nesting behavior? My mother-in-law vividly recalls how, during her first pregnancy, Ron's dad ordered one of those "Heathkits" popular in the 1960s, and spent hundreds of his evening hours peering and poking at tiny circuit boards, until he finally succeeded in building his own TV set. "He wanted to be building something, too," she says.

And Ron does seem to have his own uncontrollable work impulses these days. He toiled in our yard for three solid days redirecting and replacing the edging, adding mulch, planting flowers and vegetables, adjusting the perennials. I don't think this was directly in preparation for the prince's arrival, however. He does this every spring when he emerges from the mental labors of the school year and needs to rest his mind by working his body. Similar to nesting-induced frenzies, though, his garden labors give him a sense of control over the world, a sense that he can stake out a small territory and exercise good dominion over it. I call it the "Humbaba impulse," after an episode in the *Epic of Gilgamesh*. Gilgamesh and his buddy Enkidu determine to go out and conquer Humbaba, a forest-dwelling giant who more or less symbolizes the wild power of nature. After much hemming and hawing, they finally conquer the beast, extending the borders of civilization and making a lasting name for themselves.

The Humbaba story reminds me that the primordial labor issue is definitely gender inflected. When I read *Gilgamesh* with my world lit class this spring, I thought they might be able to make better friends with the thing if I introduced them to the notion of archetypal criticism, in which readers examine a text looking for universal figures or patterns that might be presented there. So, for example, we discussed the journey-to-the-underworld pattern that appears in many ancient epics, and the figure Ishtar, your typical scary fertility goddess. Since *Gilgamesh* is a thoroughly masculine story, about the development from raw to mature manhood, I thought it might be helpful to discuss some female archetypal patterns we knew about from fairy tales and other sources. We came up with the figure of the virginal maiden, the bride, the madonna, the sexpot/whore, the wise woman (this one appears twice in *Gilgamesh*) and the crone, and we discussed some examples of where these archetypes make their appearances in the latest movies at the cineplex.

After class, though, I wondered, *Where am I in the archetypal scheme?* I'm going to be moving beyond the madonna stage pretty soon, but I really don't want to be a crone just yet, even though some feminist literature has reclaimed the crone archetype as a figure of wisdom and prophetic energy. What comes between madonna and crone? What are the archetypal resonances for, say, a mother of teen-agers?

This one puzzled me for months. The Bible didn't seem to have any one answer. There are plenty of interesting women in the Bible—Ruth and Martha and Esther and (my favorite) Deborah, and little lessons to piece together from all their stories. And of course there's the legendary "Proverbs 31 woman," who clothes everyone in her household in red, trades real estate, gives to the needy, and wheels and deals in the marketplace. I know there are books out there in family bookstores on "how to be a Proverbs 31 woman." But closely reading the biblical chapter reveals the insidious fact that this woman never seems to sleep. That right there disqualifies her as a model for me.

Finally, while sorting the family laundry and trying to corral doz-ens of unruly white socks into four piles based on their different owners, I thought of the myth of Psyche. Whatever the archetype for my stage of a woman's life might be, I thought, it surely has to include work. And love. Psyche has both.

I knew the story of Psyche from the secret mythology handbook I use to cram for teaching the ancient Greeks (Edith Hamilton's *My-thology*), and also from C. S. Lewis's masterpiece *Till We Have Faces*. But after going back to these two sources I decided to venture a little farther, and I discovered that Jungian psychologist Erich Neumann wrote an entire book called *Amor and Psyche: The Psychic Development of the Feminine*. So much for my brilliant original insight, although I bet Erich didn't think up his ideas while sorting socks. The more I ponder her story, the more I think Psyche deserves a fresh visit. She captures basic truths about an adult woman's life, offering metaphorical pictures of a woman's inner work as well as reflections of her outer life.

Psyche as Archetype

Psyche's story begins in the beauty and promise of youth, in her maidenhood. She is exquisitely beautiful—so beautiful, in fact, that Venus is jealous of her and sends her son Cupid to make her fall in love with something despicable. The plan goes awry, however, when Cupid himself falls in love with Psyche. So without Venus knowing, Cupid makes Psyche his bride, bringing her to a gorgeous palace, but never revealing his identity or letting her see him. At this point, Psyche reflects the naivete of the young bride, easing the loneliness of her maidenhood by marrying the idea of love itself. The actual husband in her bed remains a mystery to her. Is he a god? Or is he the vile serpent Venus intended her to marry? She is happy with the sweet flowers and soft beds of romance, but she does not fully understand love's ancestry; she does not yet see its potential as hard taskmaster.

Eventually, at the urging of her jealous sisters (more experienced, less naïve women?), Psyche becomes conscious of her naivete and she longs to encounter the true identity of her husband. So she breaks her promise never to try to view his face, and she lights a lamp after he's asleep. She's relieved to find that he is no vile monster, but rather handsome as a god; meanwhile her shaking hand causes a drop of oil to fall on his shoulder and he awakens. Seeing that she broke her promise to him, he flies off without a word.

Now the naivete is gone forever. She has committed a deception to get to the truth. She has rejected living only in an idea, and by doing so she has gained necessary knowledge: she has found that the dreamy newlywed relationship is very fragile and that love is both more beautiful and more terrifying than she had thought. She also finds herself, now, alone.

The solitariness of Psyche's subsequent adventures is frighteningly right if the myth can be read as a parable of adult womanhood. Young women believe that marriage will bring them companionship, but once the honeymoon glow wears off, they realize that they still need to do their inner psychic work alone. Sometimes the young marriage actually breaks up; but even when the marriage presses ahead past naivete, each partner may be surprised to find that real intimacy takes work, and there will be betrayal, disappointment, and lonely journeys on the way to it.

Psyche, distraught with the disruption of her contentment, resolves to find real love. She knows that the love she lived with was the son of Venus the beautiful and powerful, an unpredictable figure who amuses herself both by delighting and enslaving. So Psyche ends up trudging off to meet Venus herself and plans to try to win her over through subservience. Perhaps then she can find her husband again and rebuild some kind of joyful life. Venus, meanwhile, is after Psyche, too, intending revenge. They meet; Venus laughs at Psyche in scorn and proposes to train her in the service of real love. Suffering is the method Venus has in mind, and she sets Psyche a series of four tasks or labors, analogues to Hercules's famous twelve.

So Psyche finds out that winning the favor of real love, getting it on your side in order to reclaim its satisfactions and rewards, entails work and trials. At the outset, each task seems impossible, but nevertheless it must get done. I think the labors of love, so to speak, that Psyche undertakes are resonant to every mother and wife and professional, or every woman—single or divorced, mother or not—who wants to find connection and selfhood.

Psyche's first task is to sort an enormous pile of tiny seeds, all different kinds, into separate piles. There's a time limit, too: it has to be done by nightfall. Now this is a labor I understand. Sorting laundry, sorting out dresser drawers, sorting my piles of papers at work, sorting my priorities so I can sort out my schedule: literally and figuratively, many of my psychic tasks involve sorting, and there's always a time limit. Cleaning and clutter-purging counts as this kind of labor, too. In fact, if I were to rewrite the tale, the task would involve gathering the seeds from under beds and couches, then sorting them, then wiping up the floors afterward. Perhaps because the literal sorting and cleaning is a picture of inward sorting and cleaning, this kind of physical work does not always feel like a hardship; there is a deep satisfaction in it. One of my colleagues told me that after she had surgery for a skin condition on her face, she couldn't lean her head down. So she perched her glasses on the end of her nose and sorted out all her recipe boxes. She said that afterward, she felt her whole life had been refreshed and renewed. I think therapists ought to order all their women patients who suffer from anxiety or depression to spend an entire day cleaning out all their kitchen cupboards. It could spring them months ahead in their progress toward good health.

Psyche has no idea how she can possibly manage the sorting task she faces. But friendly ants show up and do the job for her. The ants have been seen as symbolic of instinct, but I think they represent persistence and determination. Ants are not brainy creatures; they're very primitive. But they're organized and they plug away till the job gets done. Sometimes, that's what it takes. I often get all tangled up in worry about the things I have to do, and the solution is to stop fretting and get moving: make Miriam's lunch, bring the clean towels upstairs, then go to bed.

Psyche's next task is to fetch the golden wool of some very big and fierce sheep. She almost despairs at this one and thinks seriously about drowning herself in the nearby river, but instead a tiny reed whispers to her and gives her a great idea. She has only to wait till evening, when the sheep come to the river to rest. On their way they brush past the prickly bushes and she can simply walk over and gather the wool that gets caught there. Neumann suggests that the sheep's wool represents masculine power, a persuasive notion since the sheep are aggressive and have big horns. But the fleece can be anything rare and precious that can only be obtained if one is willing to face danger: the completion of a goal, a reconciled relationship, some accomplishment at work. Now if this were a myth about the male psyche (which one famous Jungian believed it was), then the way to get the wool would be to go crashing in there, maybe with some flaming prickly bush branches, frighten the sheep half to death, and overpower them. But Psyche has to use a patient strategy. The time will come. The reed, I think, suggests an inner tenderness and quietness that Psyche listens to in order to find her answer.

This part of the tale validates that waiting mode so characteristic of women's lives, that mode of which pregnancy, I've already come to learn, is a vivid picture. Waiting is part of the task. Not a passive, helpless waiting, but rather a time of patient attention motivated by strategic knowledge and sustained by confidence that the prize will be hers.

Psyche's third task is to collect water in a flask from a waterfall whose source is the river Styx, border river of Hades. The trouble is, no one can reach the waterfall because of all the steep, slippery rocks around it. This time, an eagle appears, seizes Psyche's flask, fills it, and

returns it to her. Then she must walk it back to Venus. One inter-
preter believes the water represents emotion, and Psyche must find a
way to contain her emotion to bring it into the service of love. To do
this, she needs intellect and reason. Neumann is a little hazier on this
one, seeing the river as representative of the "paternal uroboros" (i.e.,
cosmic circularity) with Psyche's job being "to encompass this power
without being shattered by it." Another simpler and more helpful
way to look at it is to see the water, with its connection to the world
of the dead, as all the dark things a woman must face: grief, fear, illness, pain. These will defeat her unless she finds some way to contain
them. So perhaps my mother's cakes and sympathy cards, ham-on-
buns at funerals, and Jennifer's omelettes are all ways of putting the
waters of life and death into a flask so that they do not overwhelm
us. The eagle, I think, represents wisdom, faith, and vision (and is not
necessarily a masculine principle, as Neumann believes). These come
to assist Psyche from a divine source, mediated through centuries of
human history and tradition. They are the energies behind simple
acts in the face of powers far beyond us.

Finally, Venus sends Psyche on an errand to the realm of the
dead. She must carry a box to Proserpine and fill it with beauty to
bring back to Venus, who feels she's getting a little frayed around the
edges. Psyche receives help this time from a tower who whispers
instructions to her. Among other directions, the tower tells Psyche
that several seemingly worthy people will ask for her help, but she
must ignore them. That's part of the task. Psyche makes it to the
Queen of the Dead, obtains her beauty charm, and returns. On her
way back, however, her curiosity overwhelms her and she decides to
peek into the box. After all, these labors haven't done much for *her*
beauty, either. So she opens the box hoping to freshen up a bit. Inside
she finds: nothing. She falls into a deep sleep.

This task, I think, is actually quite directly about beauty. Women need to reconceive what it means to be beautiful as they age, as they approach the realm of the dead. Maiden freshness doesn't last for-ever, and each woman needs to work through what her deeper beauty will be. One good possibility is to serve others, to gain value by being needed. But this can be a trap, a distraction from real beauty of the soul, as many middle-aged women have found after overworking themselves into illness all in the name of "service." The tower strikes me, then, not as a symbol of masculine culture, as Neumann has it, but as a symbol of inner fortitude, self-esteem perhaps—an instinctive, solid perception of where to place the boundaries in order to protect and value her soul.

Psyche looks into the box out of vanity, thinking maybe she can revive her maiden beauty—a temptation we know is hard to resist, bombarded as we are with advertisements for youth-preserving cos-metics and diets and surgeries. But the box is really empty, and that's why Psyche falls asleep. Her lapse into trusting old forms of beauty subdues her consciousness. Thankfully, Psyche receives understand-ing and forgiveness for this slip-up. Cupid comes to her and awakens her, assures her that all will be well, and tells her to complete her er-rand. Meanwhile, he advocates for her among the gods, and they agree to make her immortal.

Oh, and one more thing. While Edith Hamilton and C. S. Lewis never mention this part, Neumann preserves a key element of the tale found clearly in the Latin source: through all of these labors, Psyche is pregnant. Of course she is. Pregnancy is that complex inner work, so beautiful a picture of love's labors, so full of the potential for ma-turing and strengthening womanhood. Finally, united with Cupid and residing on Olympus with the gods, Psyche gives birth to a daughter, whose name is Joy.

So Psyche gains, after much labor, a love far more tested, lasting, and expansive than simple romantic passion. She has had to make use of resources, both inside and outside herself, that she didn't realize she had at her disposal: persistence and determination, patience and strategy, faith and wisdom, and an inner strength and self-assuredness. That there are no specific figures in the tale clearly and simply representing the important people in a woman's life—the husband, the children, the parents and relatives, the coworkers, the friends—makes the tale, in my mind, better able to offer wisdom to women in many situations. The basic psychic elements are still there—the labor-intensive nature, literally and psychically, of a woman's life; the struggle to keep going despite discouragement, difficulty, and self-doubt; and the essential goal toward which all the work is aimed: enduring, mature love.

~

My sister-in-law Janelle made a cross-stitch and framed it for us one Christmas. It sits on the windowsill above our kitchen sink, and it says Work is love made visible. Janelle got the idea from a similar plaque that hung in the kitchen of her uncle's family during the many years that he and his three daughters and son cared for Aunt Judy. She had multiple sclerosis, and each year she could manage less and less until finally she needed round-the-clock professional care. Hard work is the hard truth about love.

I usually take little notice of the plaque in my kitchen. It's usually splattered with dish soap, which I suppose is appropriate. One of these days, on a kitchen rampage, I'll clean it off and think about how that truth is programmed into my body. Nesting is a way of making that inner, loving work visible as we prepare for our prince.

1 1) him

We toured the hospital delivery suite tonight
with about six other married couples. Since a
third of the women who give birth in the United
States these days do so without a legally attached
man in the picture, I'm guessing that our neatly
paired group was the result of discreet hospital
segregation.

The women padded around the corridors, ro-
tund and docile, while the husbands took turns
making cute remarks: "Yeah, we better stop at the
ladies room!" "Do the doctors wear catcher's

mitts to catch the baby?" One guy, especially, gunned for everyone's nervous titters, offering witticisms at the expense of his wife, who was shamed to weak smiles and silence. At the end of the tour the nurse offered the men some written information:

"Here's a handout listing forty-one things the coach can do to help during labor."

"Be out of town!" offered mister smart-ass.

Har har.

If I were his wife, I would take him up on that offer.

Why couldn't the husbands just shut up and listen? Were they jealous that for once they weren't the official center of attention? Were they scared about the uncertainties and dangers of childbirth, but couldn't deal with fear except with silly posturing and flippant remarks? Grow up, men. Deal with it.

Even my own dear man just didn't get it. He was decent enough while on the tour, but all the way to the hospital, he harangued me with some crazy financial investment scheme he'd come up with, and on the way home he chattered away about which kind of edging would most attractively accent our shrubbery. After sullenly putting up with this for fifteen minutes, I finally interrupted to announce that I had no interest at the moment in either finances or gardening.

"I just want to think about labor and delivery."

He, a bit chastened: "Are you nervous?"

"Of course I'm nervous!" I snapped.

Men don't seem to need to do any mental or emotional preparation for childbirth. They just look at the birth, I guess, like any other piece of work: fixing the lawnmower, jogging a few miles, writing a report. I suppose what keeps them nonchalant is that they do not have to face the physical pain of delivery. I remember going to childbirth classes before the birth of my daughter, feeling a weird, heightened intensity that seemed at odds with the cheerful tone of the class. Ron was wonderfully willing to play the role of "coach," but he also seemed to get a little bored halfway into the first session and kept up his part only as a matter of courtesy and care for me. I, on the other hand, even though I could easily have absorbed the actual information conveyed in each hour-long class in about four minutes, hung on every word of the teaching nurse as if she were preparing us for a stealth operation behind enemy lines.

He can't understand. That's the simple truth about the man, the husband, the father, whatever. To assimilate something he doesn't feel in his body is too difficult an imaginative exercise, so this whole business becomes an abstraction for him, like the difference between watching a sailboat from shore and actually flying along across the waves. This is not entirely his fault, and many men, the good ones, really do try. They ask "how are you doing?" and they put together the crib and they run out for Chinese food. Many men stick around, which is the most important thing by far. But why can't they get it *all* right, instead of acting like boneheads half the time? Why can't the husband do as he should: observe his volatile wife throughout pregnancy with constant vigilance, continually calibrating his responses to her ever-evolving needs? I admit this is a tall order. All right, it's impossible.

I'm exquisitely sensitive these days. I can't help it. It feels as if so much is at stake. One stray comment can send me spiraling downward into a sulk. I told Ron I didn't feel like going to a church meeting one night, and instead of the correct response, which would have been "Well, whatever feels right to you, honey," he pressured me into going. "If there were really something wrong with you physically, that would be one thing," he said. "I'm on the committee trying to make people excited about this project, and how's it going to look if

I can't even get my wife to go?" Of course, this all seemed instantly relevant to what I could expect from him in labor. What would he say to me then? "Oh, come on! Buck up, honey. Now if you were *really* in pain . . ."

I steamed about this all morning. Wouldn't it be terrific, I kept thinking, if I didn't have to put my trust in anyone's help through this? I began to reconsider this relatively recent cultural phenomenon of having the father participate in the delivery. Do we really need that? On the one hand, men should know what it costs to bring a life into the world—every bloody, flesh-splitting detail of it. On the other hand, why should women put up with the keen likelihood of the lunkhead factor exactly at those moments of our most profound vulnerability and triumphant power? Just in order to teach men a valuable lesson? Always working to redeem *their* souls. Pooh. Why not declare male participation in childbirth a worthy experiment of the twentieth century and then return to the ancient wisdom of shooing them out the door and surrounding the process with an air of mystery, a holy woman-rite, only mothers and wizened midwives allowed. (Wait—we'll keep the advanced medical technology on standby. Thank you.)

Distance and Fear

If only the father didn't have his own needs, desires, issues, pressures, griefs, and all the other inconvenient commonplaces of human personhood. I need him to put his own needs aside right now and support *me*. I need him *always* there, always ready to absorb the thousand natural shocks my flesh is heir to. He's planning to be there for me when the birth comes, but he doesn't realize that the crisis is *now*, too. I want constant proof that he's ready, stalwart as an oak, to shelter and hold me.

I should trust him. After all, I have evidence of his heroic qualities in a crisis. When we were both sophomores in college and only sort-of dating, he rescued me in shining armor on a brave white steed. Something like that, anyway. Walking out of the dorm's back door by myself, I slipped on some icy steps and fell smack on my tailbone. I blacked out and cut my ear on the way down. Ron came around looking for me, wondering why I was late to meet him, and he spotted me lying there just as I was regaining consciousness, bleeding from the ear. He trundled me into my clunky old white Ford Maverick and sped me to the hospital over dangerously icy roads. Thinking I might have a head injury, he made me talk to him the whole way to keep tabs on my mental state. Thankfully, the blood came from a simple cut in my ear, but call that exhibit A for being there when I need him.

Exhibits B and C would be his perfectly fine and attentive assistance during two previous births.

Oh, but he's human, I fret, so maybe this time will be different. Maybe he's bored with the whole birth drama the third time around, figures I've done it fine before and why should I need him this time. Maybe, at the crisis moment, he will be caught up in himself, thinking about getting back to work or getting himself some dinner. After all, I see it happening now, see him receding into the distance, a smudge of resentment on his face.

A few nights ago, when we were both feeling some stress—he over a sermon that wasn't quite taking shape and I over a poetry reading I had to do—we found ourselves talking out this distance. I accused him of being uninterested, shrugging off the pregnancy as my bothersome thing that he has to put up with. He replied that he's merely doing what experience has taught him works best with me:

leave me to myself when I'm irritable or moody. "But that's not what I want now!" I protested. "I want pampering." And how is he supposed to know that this time is different? He's supposed to read my mind, of course.

I can see how he might become a little exasperated.

Here's the conflict: I long to bring him into this experience with me, placing his hands on my tummy so he can feel the baby squirming, dissipate the abstraction with warm touch. At the same time, I want to be left alone. One moment I depend on his intense energy, lean on it, take it for granted. The next moment, I want him to back off. I need him, but I need the distance, too.

In my leave-me-alone moods, I look around this house and suddenly realize nothing here is exclusively mine, except maybe this little table in the corner of our bedroom where I write. Even the laptop computer I write with is usually downstairs in the living room, where Ron checks his e-mail whenever he can kidnap the thing. I share a bathroom with everyone else in the family, and God forbid I should ever get three minutes of privacy in there. I share a room and a bed with a husband. Even my own body I share with another person. I'm tired, tired, tired of all this enmeshment. Will everyone please just leave off with your demands and let me be?!

But there's nowhere to go for rest.

One time when we were discussing what we were anticipating and what we were fearing about another baby, I said (predictably) that what I fear most is lack of sleep.

"Yes, I know that's hard for you," he said, in a tone I thought sounded a little patronizing. "That part is not that big a deal for me."

"Well, what is the hardest part for you?" I asked.

"Having *your* emotional energies taken up with the baby," he answered. This was the worst answer he could give because I don't know what to do about it. Conversations like this make me feel like I'm the city electrical supply, flowing emotional energy into the family. Since babies need enormous emotional energy, adding one to the system is definitely going to drain power from the rest of the grid. Between the pregnancy, the birth, and nursing, I will be low on energy for Ron for about a whole year. I know this isn't an entirely accurate metaphor. But it becomes a zero-sum game in our minds, a question of finite supply and infinite demand. It becomes me vs. him instead of us for us. It's hard to snap together as *us* when this great big belly bounces us apart.

The pressure builds, we start keeping secret score of who's doing more or putting up with more, someone gets angry or hurt, then we talk it out and we each apologize and we both feel better. And then the little cycle repeats itself. Pregnancy isn't causing all this; it's just magnifying the usual issues, making every touch point more tender and sore.

So we carry on living in this space, reaching across it for each other. He has to steer away from loneliness, and I from fear that he will turn away my need with anger or indifference. It makes any kind of intimacy difficult, not just the physical engineering of it, but the emotional connection. We're floating around like two spaceships in a nebula with no long-range sensors and only running lights to guide us.

The Task of Trust

We each have our tasks to do here. He has to remember that he's a grown-up, and he's chosen with me to have another child, so he'll have to face that his needs will not come first for a while and he won't always feel like he's getting his proper dues. He's normally a rather gallant fellow about this, but sometimes the pressures make him blow up over little things and complain that he's "carrying the bag." Which he is. He works hard and does more than his usual share of thoroughly tangible things like taking out the garbage and doing dishes and making supper. I am simply not capable of everything I can usually do, and he knows that, but sometimes he loses hold of that understanding and gives me that straight-mouthed look that says, "Are you really trying?" I tell him I hate that, hate the subtle sense that he thinks I'm being lazy, making excuses. He admits that it's hard to remember in the sharp-edged moments that the intangible work (to him) of carrying the baby is part of the much larger team load.

My task is to choose trust over withdrawal or revenge. Withdrawal is my first temptation. When there's a conflict, I find myself determining not to ask for any help, not to complain, not to say a word about any discomforts I feel. If I ask for no help, I figure, he can never complain about giving it. No obligation means no risk of resentment. My other temptation is to play the trump card he can't ever beat. He can never win the game of "I'm-suffering-more-than-you-and-you-don't-even-care" when I have those pregnancy-and-delivery cards to play. And I like to play them. I like the sweet taste of self-pity, and I like using this leverage to get some attention, to get the courtiers to bow down to the queen.

The resentment and the trumping so easily become a cycle in a marriage, and not just during pregnancy. What happens in my marriage may be different in degree but not in kind from what happens in the marriages that implode. Just like everyone else, we carry stresses in from the outside and they ricochet around in the house, injuring everyone. Just like everyone else, we start keeping score. For us it's usually division-of-labor issues, but it could be about in-laws or money or freedom or child-rearing methods or any of the other usual suspects. I've seen couples keep score like this, even silently, and then the field of play gets muddy with anger and the ruts form and harden and then it's too late. Much easier to walk away, it seems, than to try to smooth out the field and find each other again. Much easier to be on one's own than to deal with the repeated humilities of entanglement.

There is no such thing as self-sufficiency, however. It's an illusion, a fantasy. We can walk through our days offering only a passing word to our fellow travelers, or we can let other travelers use and trample us—or we can find true companions and travel together. But we are entangled as a matter of course.

So I will choose trust, that delicate dance.

How can I do this? How can I get out of these dark sulks, these times of distance and hurt?

I miss my friend Jennifer. At times like these, we used to know how to blow off some steam. When we lived in Iowa, Jennifer and I played in the Des Moines Symphony. One week a month we rehearsed every night, and we had to drive an hour each way. As we sped by the pig huts and the soybean fields in the sealed environment of the car, it felt as if certain moral freedoms applied, and now and then we indulged in some rollicking husband-crunching. I remember one night we decided we ought to start a "widow book," wherein we would record all the annoying things our husbands did. Then, someday, when our husbands were gone and we were rocking and knitting and listening to the clock tick away the hours, we could open the book and remember, perhaps with the slightest tinge of satisfaction, just what we were missing.

I suppose reporting exasperating incidents to one's women friends is a time-honored way to ease tensions. It feels good, but it doesn't solve the "issues." For that, conventional wisdom recom-

mends that couples must be totally honest and open with their feelings. What a naïve view. I may be self-pitying, spoiled, and have a
low resentment threshold, but I've done this long enough to know
that sometimes love means keeping your mouth shut. Some of my
feelings, after all, are so selfish and petty that they don't deserve to
take up space in my heart, let alone be spoken aloud. Cokie and Steve
Roberts, the Washington journalists, relate in their book about marriage their own philosophy about this: "The success of a marriage can
be measured by the number of teeth marks on your tongue," they
write. Dietrich Bonhoeffer, the theologian who wrote the famous
little book on community called *Life Together,* also thought that "communication" is not always the answer. He wrote: "Thus it must be a
decisive rule of every Christian fellowship that each individual is
prohibited from saying much that occurs to him." We've come to regard "expressing our feelings" as sacrosanct, a preoccupation suppressed or thwarted only at great risk to our psychic well-being. And
it's surely true that no one should be completely silenced. But sometimes our feelings deserve to be thrown into the psychic garbage can.
Let them sit out and they'll stink up the place.

Then again, sometimes love is about speaking the healing word. I
think of the golden moments in my marriage, those times when we
are fully ourselves in the orbit of one another, and I see that these
happen when we touch each other with our praise and admiration,
not dutifully but spontaneously, when we see the best qualities in
each other and say so: "You spoke very well tonight." "The band
sounded great." "I'm proud of you." "You amaze me." Then we rise to
the level this genuine respect deserves, and our partnership makes us
both transcend this mortal coil and glow somehow, perhaps in the
promise of our God-imagined fulfillment.

Ideally, marriage changes the trajectory of the individual for the better. In describing Adam and Eve's inaugural union, the Genesis narrative says that they clung to each other as "one flesh." The Hebrew phrase refers to sex, the literal fleshly one-ing. But in its sly profundity, the word *flesh* reaches beyond the meat of our bodies toward all living things on the earth, all beings in whom invisible animates visible. One flesh in marriage is that complex and sturdy thirdness that takes life when two join. We are growing soul-roots in each other, intertwining and metamorphosing into a new living thing.

And this heartbeat in my belly! This child is an embodiment of the way he and I are entangled in a creation mystery. We have surrendered ourselves to each other, and this joining bears the fruit of a new person. Shouldn't we feel closer than ever with this two-become-one-flesh inside me?

Then why do these visions of golden moments, these things I know to be true, seem so far away right now? Why does the distance seem so much more real than the union?

Apparently we greet this miracle of one-ing as we do most miracles, with considerable resistance. There's something reflexive and satisfying about staking out one's own selfhood, grabbing for one's own needs. There's something delicious about the sulking, the guilt trips, the self-defense.

Oh boy. I should reach out to him first. But this is so hard, I can hardly do it. Well, he could reach out first, too. In fact, I think it's *his* turn. After all, *I* have very big needs right now. Here I am making a baby! Let him pull himself around and come to me.

The Tumbler

These are the times that I find Christian teaching about love thoroughly annoying. All that self-denial and sacrifice and patience and kindness comes off as simperingly sweet and even dangerous. I should be going to the scriptures for inspiration and reading the great poem of love in I Corinthians: "Love is patient, love is kind. It does not envy, it does not boast, it is not proud," blah, blah. But this seems exactly the empty gonging St. Paul dismisses in the opening verses of the chapter, as I can't even do the first phrase successfully. "Love is patient with him constantly leaving his stupid empty soda cans in the car even though I've explained a million times that this bugs me." Nope, can't do that one. "Love is kind and does not display obvious annoyance when he is stressed about work and telling me every detail of a very boring meeting." Nope, can't do that one.

I wish St. Paul had written it more like this: "Love keeps at it. Love knows it's all right to be mad at each other as long as you are both committed to working it out somehow. Love knows that a little time apart and a good nap can make apologies come out much more easily. Love is based on mutual respect and fairness and keeps coming back to that even when scorn and impatience creep in." Now that I could work with.

Paul isn't necessarily talking about marriage (he was not an unqualified fan of it, as an earlier chapter of Corinthians reveals); he's talking about human community, for which marriage is like a greenhouse or lab. Congregations, clubs, work teams, and communes have plenty of trouble functioning together, but marriage is a smaller, hotter version of human community than any of these. And trying to do marriage as an equal partnership rather than a simple hierarchy is a relatively new, still-experimental model. Unlike the marriage systems of the past in the West, and of many other cultures still, the roles in today's marriages are not solidly defined, squashing each other is not allowed, and the constant negotiations are extremely demanding and exhausting. No wonder so many set out to do it and fail. No wonder one-third of the women giving birth this year will do it without a husband. Marriage as genuine human community, I believe firmly, is the most honoring ideal for the soul's well-being; but practically speaking, this kind of marriage is a *lot* harder to keep together than a socioeconomic contract.

All right, but let me remind myself again of the reasons to keep at it. I've seen us work shoulder to shoulder and accomplish goals that came from two hearts. I've seen us air painful truths and find that forgiveness and healing are possible. I've seen him glow brighter than he thought he could, because of my belief and encouragement—and he's seen the same in me. I've laughed till my cheeks and sides hurt at his impossible tales and he's dreamed for me and seen it come true.

Maybe Linda, my missionary pastor friend, is right. When I told her how the love poem in Corinthians annoys me, she said that she reads it not so much as how *our* love ought to work as how *God's* love *already* works. When we open the door to that, sweeping behind it all the selfish power crap between us, then God can do in us what we can't do for ourselves. Call the power games off, let the roots grow, change our souls. Let me hold to these things, then, to this more excellent way.

~

Our friends Mark and Karen recently bought a stone polisher for their kids. They opened the thing up, all excited about having some nifty polished stones by suppertime, only to discover that the process involved several steps and took weeks. *Weeks!* So they had to plug the thing in somewhere in a quiet corner of the house and just let it churn, round the clock. No one ever told me this before my wedding day, but I'm beginning to understand, after eleven years, that marriage sometimes feels like climbing with another person into a stone tumbler. You keep spinning over and over, half the time up in the air and half the time clattering into each other on the way down. Sometimes, you want some relief from the tumbler; you start thinking you could be perfectly happy with how beautiful a stone you are without it. But if you're both willing to stay in there a long time and accept the same amount of tumbling, you get smoothed out and polished enough to reflect a light beyond yourselves. If you can laugh about all the ups and downs, it can even be fun.

Oh and here's a sobering thought: the little pebbles who wind up in the polisher with us are subject to the same tumbling. Oh, little baby, your parents have so many faults. But we're in this together. Wheeee!

1 2) *fullness*

We have a little cherry tree just outside our front door, and I can see through our dining-room window the hard little green balls, poking straight out from the branch like tiny, perky Christmas ornaments. Now that the weather is hot and humid, they soften and enlarge each day, changing from green to orangey-pink to the deep winey red I'm waiting for. Cherry pie is the one food I've craved longingly, lovingly, during all three pregnancies.

I'm glad to live in Michigan in this pregnant summer. All the summer fruit trees and bushes are

fulfilling the foolish promises of spring, turning their maiden blos-
soms to hard green stones and then to soft fleshiness, swelling with
juice until they seem a pinprick away from bursting. The strawberries
and sour cherries first, then the sweet cherries, then the blueberries,
then blackberries and raspberries in the sweaty heat of August, then
the sweet, crunchy apples when the nights turn cool and frosty. My
own belly mirrors the roundness and overabundance of all this delicious ripening. To be ripe is to reach the extent of possibility, to become as great and heavy and drooping as it is possible to be before
crossing over to the grotesque, and to decay.

The term "ripe" is commonly used in relation to pregnancy to
describe a cervix ready to stretch open in labor. It's a reasonable
enough term, as the cervix does have to soften and pull itself larger in
order to open. But of course, the cervix is not the fruit. And feeling
the weight of the baby-loaded uterus pressing on it as I do now in
these last weeks, I think a more appropriate term for a ready cervix
might be "exhausted" or "stressed out" or "fed up." Save "ripe" for the
real fruit of this labored growing, the baby.

Colossus

At thirty-two weeks now, I glory in this ripe fullness, but I also
feel the strain toward bursting. I'm big, awkward, and uncomfortable,
and I know very well from my two previous experiences: Just when
you think you can't get any bigger—you get bigger. Some women
seem to balloon from neck to ankle. I'm one of the protrusion types.
My pregnant belly sticks straight out, like a basketball—or these days
more like half a watermelon, oblong with a little knob at the center.
The rest of me looks about the same as always, except for those mag-

nificent breasts and a slim layer of fleshiness, a maternal sheen that turns me, as Ron puts it, into "a more substantial whoa-maahn."

But now that buckling my sandals involves an elaborate procedure—sink down to the floor, sit on my bottom, contort one leg, buckle, then the other leg, buckle, hoist myself over to hands and knees, one knee up, then stand—I start to imagine how lovely it would be to maneuver belly-free again. But it's going to get worse before it gets better. In a few weeks, I know, the achiness will start as my pelvic floor protests its unfair workload. Just getting up and walking around will seem like an act of heroism. And visits to the potty will shift from frequent to constant as my already overstressed bladder will be further compressed to the size of a squashed grape. But I suppose one has to be good and sick of being pregnant before being willing to go through labor to end it.

The waddling and hoisting involved in this stage make me a somewhat comic figure. The funny comes from the vulnerability; as I grow larger, slower, and more ungainly, I need more help. While climbing stairs (when I can't find an elevator), I lean harder and more wearily on handrails, and I lean emotionally on willing shoulders, too, slipping closer toward those birthing hours when I will have to submit almost completely to the care of others. It's right that I visit the doctor's office more frequently in these last weeks, as I become more and more the patient, more in need of alert professionals and wary, protective friends.

But I wonder if the protectiveness of the modern health-care system, luxury that it is, encourages us to emphasize the vulnerability of these late weeks and ignore the paradoxical other side: the beautiful power. Routinely supervised by bustling medical pros, filled to the eyeballs with minutely detailed information about pregnancy and birth, overwhelmed with advice, do we forget the power surging through us at every heartbeat, the power of creating life? Pulsing with this life now, I want to plant my feet in the earth, feel myself towering over it, grow to a colossus, fill and subdue. The hours of birth combine desperate vulnerability with the thunderous power of life, and I can feel both the sinking and the rising within me. But how can I celebrate that power?

I have many times in my life felt swept up into something grand and beautiful, most often when playing in an orchestra or singing in a choir. When I produce a beautiful sound with my voice or my instrument (I have to struggle for these moments), and that sound surges into the greater sound of the music happening, living, around me, rarely do I feel a greater sense of well-being, of touching the highest possibility of human nature. But this pregnant fullness in my body connects me to an even deeper and more elusive grandeur, one whose roots sink to the ground of all things. I feel as if the chord of my being is in tune, resonating the whole spectrum of sound, like the way my viola, resting on my knee, vibrates in sympathy when the trombones play. This resonance with the energy of life itself must be the reason many women long from girlhood to be pregnant, even knowing it isn't always fun. This is also why infertility hurts so much, I think; it seems to women who are unable to do this as if a whole possible dimension of being has been refused them. I think communion with creative energy can be found down other paths, but there's no doubt that holding a baby inside is an exquisitely profound human experience, profound in the exact sense of finding the bottom of things. In this, God allows some of us a small communion with God's Creator-self: we can feel, fleetingly, what God must feel over all creation—a bursting joy, an ache of longing for that which is both other and within. The life energy of this child in me is the same divine spark infinitely multiplied and quivering in all the atoms of the universe. I can barely contain it, this microcosm of all. I am grandiose, resplendent, a goddess.

The Goddess's Terrible Aspect

Actually, the fertility goddesses represented in the little statues dating from the most ancient times are not exactly how I picture my own grand figure. Those squat, round, frowning statues pictured in books sometimes move way beyond the line into grotesque disproportions: enormous bellies that dwarf their bodies, huge breasts, sometimes many more breasts than any self-respecting goddess sculptor should have dared to admit imagining. Erich Neumann, the Jungian psychologist, speaks of the ancient Great Mother archetype as having a "terrible aspect," a side of her personality literalized in many statues as an angry or stern facial expression. Ancient peoples apparently recognized not only the sacred power of creating life, the essential mystery of it, but also the utter fearfulness of this mystery. The poet Adrienne Rich, in her 1976 book *Of Woman Born,* challenges the trite idea of woman as a passive vessel. In many ancient cultures, she contends, vessels were not simply receptacles, but places of magical transformation that ensured the continuation of life. Women were responsible for pottery making, presiding over this activity as a reflection of their own bodies' transformative power. Women as stewards of life-magic were not derided, but accorded great respect. Transformative power is a fearful thing.

Sometimes I feel the terrible aspect emerging in me. I went to the college the other day to get some books from my office, and several of my male colleagues were in the conference room innocently eating their lunches. I went in to join them for a few minutes, and they asked kindly how I was doing. Soon I heard myself describing how much I hate it when people give me advice, and how no one should dare tell a soon-to-deliver mother what to do. I felt anger rising in me, and I caught the subtle scent of fear from my slightly bewildered colleagues. I enjoyed this. People often seem to regard me with great respect and even fear these days, as if they believe touching me might set off powerful zap-rays emanating in all directions.

I think pregnant women should cultivate this response. We should enhance our grand figures in this stage by abandoning cute maternity tops and jeans with knit panels stretching over the tummy, and instead we should wear elegant, drapey robes, like you would see on a Greek statue or a West African woman in one of those gorgeous, full-length tunics. Artist Judy Chicago, as part of her Birth Project in the early 1980s, also thought that typical maternity clothes failed to convey the power of the pregnant woman. In fact, she called maternity clothes "obscene" because "[t]heir whole point is to neuter the form and reality of a pregnant woman." In response, she created a series of birth garments (for display, not for wear) that emphasize the belly. I would be in favor of some wearable possibilities. Hugely pregnant women could parade around, their gorgeous garments swirling behind them, and people would stop to stare and maybe bow their heads to acknowledge the Creator's power mirrored in the woman, and the woman would bow her head in return out of thanks that God has enabled her to mirror the poignance of bearing life. Hey, maybe I could try this with my academic regalia—a bright red robe with black velvet trim. Well, maybe not. This is the balmy month of June and my robe is heavy as a theater curtain. Wearing it would probably just make me hot and crabby.

Serenity

Perhaps some grand resonance with cosmic flow is producing this other unexpected gift right now: serenity. Where before I felt more permeable to frightening and distressing things, now I simply turn them away. I don't want to read about mission efforts in the slums of Cairo, or an accidental fire that killed six in rural Michigan, or corruption in the city police department. Frankly, I don't care. I know I'm supposed to care, but I don't. I care about my family, my baby, my body, my house. My job seems miles away. I kept my brain focused through conscious effort till the end of the school year, but now I feel it melting into a puddle. I look ahead to projects due in the fall and spring, and I feel no agitation about them. They're over there, and I'm here, and I am actually doing what I can never do: letting tomorrow worry about itself. I don't even want to be bothered with family troubles. My sister-in-law's marriage is dissolving around her and I can't get myself to feel upset about it. It seems layers removed from my world, as if it's happening in a book I read years ago.

Instead I feel a peacefulness as on those days when Lake Michigan is smooth as glass, and one wonders how deep the water might go. On rough days, one doesn't think about anything but that roiling surface and the noise of the wind in one's ears. Now, though, I feel as on those glassy days, when what matters is the depth of the now. I'm floating on that depth, undisturbed. I feel my mental powers focusing in on fewer and fewer things. This slow shrinking of the mental scope will continue right into labor, when the whole world will disappear except for the pain and the physical task at hand.

I know from experience that this sensation of quiet slow motion snaps off when the baby is born. I remember lying in the hospital bed only hours after Jacob was born, actually experiencing the sensation of fog lifting. So I can curiously observe the fog this time, enjoy the floaty sensation, and know that my drive and sharp thinking will eventually return, likely with all the attendant and unwelcome anxieties. Meanwhile, I'm focusing on this new person, this holy and monumental task of bringing him into the world. No one else can bring this baby to birth. He's depending on me. Others will simply have to keep the rest of the world spinning for a while.

~

Ron is my first line of defense against that clamoring world with all its irrelevant business and fuss. Sunday afternoon and I'm looking a little dreamy and droopy:

"Go upstairs and take a nap, Hon," he says.

"Oh, I can clean up the lunch dishes first."

"You let me worry about that. You go work on the baby."

So I heave and hoist myself up the stairs, pulling the already wiggly handrail a little looser, and pad into our bedroom. Our big bed seems like a liferaft (it *is* a waterbed), and I want to sink my body into it and let it suspend me in this *here*, this *now.*

As I change into a loose shirt, I pause to admire my huge belly in the mirror, especially the strong blue veins crisscrossing under my skin like great tree branches, arching around the secret, pulsing garden of my womb. Inside, the placenta is an enormous jelly of blood and tissue connected by the tough, ropey cord to the fruit wiggling in its snug nest. One poet, George Ella Lyon, speaks to her newborn infant of the placenta as "that red pad of which you were the lily/ with the cord lying bleached across it/ like a root pulled from the water/ like a heartroot torn free." For now, this heartroot buries itself in me, in my body, in the depths of myself. We are close to full ripeness now. Soon we will reach the extent of possibility, and the baby must be plucked free.

1 3) danger

I've been feeling too good to think I'm advancing in any way toward giving birth to this squirmy bundle in my belly. With my second baby, by this time, those pelvic floor muscles—the ones I never even knew I had until I started having babies—felt achy and sore even when I lay down. My insides felt like a tent after a hard rain, with a twenty-gallon concave pocket of water sagging its roof. Now add a bowling ball grinding around in the water pocket and the picture is complete. This time, amazingly, I seem buoyant enough, so the doctor surprises me by reporting that the baby is indeed descending in preparation for birth. The cervix is "nicely effaced"—80 percent—and even beginning to open a little.

Suddenly I'm excited! I've been resigned to a long wait yet, putting off last-minute preparations for a real baby—like buying teeny diapers—for at least another week. But the reality of this grips me now. Just in case the doctor's words didn't make it real enough, after the appointment I feel dozens of quite strong, irregular, crampy contractions radiating from my lower back down my legs. Ow! Oh, but they feel strangely good, like an electric surge evidencing the power coiled in my body. The jolts of power are comforting reminders that my body is not depending on my consent to do what must be done. It will happen. One indisputable truth about pregnancy is that once the baby is in there, it must come out somehow.

The end is near, the end is real. The only way out is through. Now comes the fear, the quiet, tensing fear, a constant, high-pitched hum that no one can hear but me. I will have to trust Ron and the hospital staff to help me get through the birth. When I am feeling confident about the competence and eager well-meaning of others, this falling into their hands gives me peace. But what if someone's carelessness or indifference leaves me stranded?

Trust seems very hard right now. My mother calls, and of course every word out of her mouth seems like unwelcome advice or a challenge.

"Gee, Mom," I say, "I don't really feel like going out for lunch."

"Well, you've got to keep going out and doing things, you know. You can't just sit around."

"Yeah, well, I feel like the baby is going to come in the next few days."

"Oh, sure. It's nice to think that."

I decide I don't want to see her at all since everything she says drives me nuts. She doesn't hear the hum.

It's not just my poor mom. No one can say the right thing. How can I gently remind everyone in the world that I don't really care for their advice right now? Over the Fourth of July weekend we went out to the lake to Ron's folks' house for a family gathering. A huge glob of 90-degree heat and humidity squatted right on top of Michigan, causing my feet to swell up like marshmallows and my whole body to throb with low-grade misery. Everyone had a suggestion for how I could feel better: "Sit under the fan!" "Go in the lake!" "Don't you have a sleeveless top?" "Well, what you have to do is sit with your feet up." "Say, we could turn on the air conditioner in the camper and you could go in there!" "It really wasn't so bad last night once that little breeze came through at five A.M." You know, people, it's better just to say, "Gee, I'm sorry you feel so awful. Let me know if I can help."

Annoying, these other people, because they don't hear the hum.

The only way out is through. The only way out is through. I repeat this to myself in order to steel my mental strength. No one can experience the pain for me, no one can manufacture the mental preparation or concentration I will need, no one else can do for me what I must do. I am afraid.

Valley of the Shadow

It's difficult to appreciate today that until this century, giving birth was always shadowed with the fair likelihood of death. Freedom from this fear is still a luxury reserved only for people in developed countries where health care is readily available. The centuries stretch out behind us, and on that teeming river of human life many quiet bodies float along, mothers laid to rest with their silent infants.

A breech presentation, a too-small pelvis, a premature labor, hemorrhaging after birth, and of course, puerperal infection—any one of these things, alarming but completely manageable for us these days, was and in some places still is enough to bring darkness and sorrow to whole lifetimes of husbands and children left behind when the infant, or mother, or both, succumb to death.

I'm deeply grateful for modern health care. For all its complexity and excess, for all the often justified complaints that "the system" strips human life and illness of its spiritual dimension, I still see modern health care as an aspect of God's mercy and redemptive action in the world. I can face worries and fears about labor and delivery, about the health of the baby, with abundant confidence that all will be well, no matter what harrowing moments we might pass through on the way.

But this great blessing, this emancipation from extreme fear, can conceal from us what people without modern medicine have understood better: how closely death clings to life, life to death. Our foremothers had to be ready to pass through the valley of death (not just the shadow of it) with every birth, and if they came out into the sunshine on the other side, what great rejoicing there was! All the more so because the outcome was never certain.

Obviously, not every soul held life more precious because of death's nearer companionship. There have been plenty of unwanted pregnancies and indifferent parents, plenty of violence, abuse, and neglect in the tight circle of family. In some ways, our culture values human life more than any culture in history because we so highly prize the individual and because we have achieved a *mythology,* at least, of a classless society, if not the reality. We have developed a far

greater repertoire of physical, mental, and emotional rescue mecha-
nisms to promote some kind of well-being for all people.

On the other hand, I sometimes wonder if our turn-of-the-
millennium culture understands either life or death at all. These days,
with my metabolism wildly increased in order to create a new life, I'm
even more astonished than usual at the noxious bilge of violence and
degradation belched out of our TVs and movie screens. How can we
piously intone about sanctity of life or human rights and still let this
stuff seep into our souls? Flip the channels on any night and see on
every second station someone pointing a weapon at someone else
and blowing him away. Movies are even worse: mindless strings of
explosions, wreckages, and shattered bodies. Normally I can tolerate
action movies and maybe even a police show on TV. But not these
days. They seem completely preposterous. It's bad enough that many
people on this globe have to live with the reality of war, slavery, epi-
demics, violence. What does it say about our souls when we fake this
stuff in order to entertain ourselves? Why should we inure ourselves
to destruction, harden our shells, and make it even more difficult to
remind ourselves: life is precious, death is real and final?

~

Life is precious; death is very near. I feel this now, as my world fun-
nels downward toward this point where the two come together with
unbearable weight and density. The childbirth books I have on
my shelf say very little about childbirth as a nearpoint to eternity. But
this hasn't always been so. Literature from the historical period
I study for my work—the sixteenth and seventeenth century in
England—regularly visits that fearful place. We have records of
"mother's advice books" in which mothers urge their children to live
godly and noble lives even after their mums have passed on. Some of

these were written by women in their older years during a serious illness; others were written by pregnant women to their unborn children. Women of the period had a keen understanding that the childbed could double as the deathbed. The Book of Common Prayer of 1559, which contained all the officially approved Protestant services and prayers, includes a service called "the Churching of Women." In this practice, a very ancient one in fact, women were supposed to come to church about a month after giving birth for a formal thanksgiving that they had survived. The priest was directed to pray:

> O almighty God, which hast delivered this woman thy servant from the great pain and peril of childbirth: Grant, we beseech thee (most merciful Father) that she through thy help, may both faithfully live and walk in her vocation, according to thy will in this life present, and also may be partaker of everlasting glory in the life to come.

Popular prayer books of the period included prayers for women "that travell [labor] with Child" as well as thanksgiving prayers for safe deliveries. Childbirth literature of this period, Catholic or Protestant, in England and the Continent, was drenched with a serious consideration of death and eternity.

Popular childbirth literature these days seems shallow by comparison. Much recent discussion of labor and delivery focuses not on survival—for mother and infant, this is assumed—but instead raises expectations in the reader that birth must be an exhilarating and fulfilling experience for the mother. With death at bay, apparently, we are free to worry about accomplishment and fulfillment. So now we feel as if anything less than the perfect birth is either a failure on the woman's part or a result of the hostile and insensitive actions of those oppressive medical/technical interventionists.

Of course we want to rescue the birth experience from terror and ignorance. It makes theological sense to me that the curse of Eve is not to be preserved as a punishment for women—as some theologians, doctors, and other unsympathetic men used to contend when using anesthesia during birth was first proposed. Nor should childbirth pain be condescendingly valorized as the martyrdom of women for the sake of mankind, as Adrienne Rich complained. No, pain and fear during birth is another feature of the fallen creation that ought to be redeemed. The bringing of a new person into this world *should* be a deeply joyful and celebrative event, for all involved.

Rendering the mother unconscious and passive during birth, the answer to fear and danger offered to women in the West during the first half of this century, was a less-than-satisfactory attempt at this. In her book *Of Woman Born*, Adrienne Rich rightly condemns the recent Western practices of "alienated labor" in which women were "put under" or otherwise treated as passive victims during childbirth. She then describes with approval the various branches of the natural childbirth movement. Rich herself gave birth to three boys in the 1950s under the total anesthesia method advocated by her obstetrician. She writes with regret that her own birth experiences disconnected her from her body's processes, and she looks forward to the day when women can give birth in local centers where the staff understand the psychic dimensions of birth and where the birthing mother can choose exactly the circumstances under which she delivers.

In many ways, Rich's vision has come to fruition. Contemporary Western practices are a much better balance between the power of technology and the conscious direction of the mother in response to her body's own incredible processes. Rich was wisely skeptical of the natural childbirth movement's early claims to "ecstatic" experiences during birth, claims we don't hear so much these days. But Rich seemed to believe that if only the woman can be in *control* of the birth experience, then all would be well.

Having myself experienced two births with minimal pain relief, nicely supportive professionals, and a committed and attentive husband, I can report that Rich's vision, written in those early, more ferocious days of feminist body-reclaiming, may have been a little optimistic on the control issue. The fact is, despite all the information, childbirth education, enlightened views of women's bodies, technological devices, and medical expertise, no one can ever know exactly what to expect in a particular birth. From the mother's point of view, this means that one must simply relinquish the illusion of complete control. You do not know when labor will begin, how it will progress, what positions you will find most comforting during contractions, how you will handle the pain, what you might say, how long it will take to push, or if all of the normal outlines of the process will be interrupted to surgically rescue a baby in distress. We can make guesses, many of them educated and reliable, but there is simply no way to know for sure. And even when the delivery is proceeding within normal and expected parameters, I can emphatically attest that one does not *feel* in control. Active labor and delivery puts one in a kind of altered mental state. The perception of time falls away and even the room and the people in it seem to exist only on the fringes of consciousness. The body's cataclysms overcome, and the mind is only intermittently able to put in a suggestion or quasi-articulate response.

And as for the outcome of labor and delivery—i.e., the baby— even when the baby seems strong and healthy from all signs available prebirth, one simply does not know for sure until that first examination. And even then, sometimes, troubling surprises appear later on.

So the emphasis on making childbirth a pleasant and fulfilling experience in which the birthing mother is in control may promise too much while masking the inherently darker dimensions that make the birth process a profoundly instructive human experience. Dealing with this lack of control at the beginning point of life is a critical lesson, an important exercise for mother and father, and a daily one for medical staff. As my doctor says in response to those who express sympathy for her crazy schedule: "Well . . . *life* is messy!" New babies insist on thwarting our competence and the degree of control it brings. We must welcome babies on their own terms and put aside at least some of our adult dominance. My neighbor recently found out that even the most controlled birth process possible, a scheduled cesarean, can proceed and feel and heal differently than one expects. Birth is messy and unpredictable, because life is so.

And then: the pain. While I wound up using minimal pain relief during my first two deliveries, I'm no natural-childbirth hardliner. I'm not fooled by the deceptive niceness of the word "natural." Completely natural childbirths are the ones that used to kill women and infants with some frequency. After all, what is natural can be beautiful and wholesome, but it can also be "red in tooth and claw" as Tennyson pointed out. The natural world is crippled and distorted, just like the human heart. So I say, bring on the pain relief as a mercy against the darkness, a way of redeeming it.

On the other hand, pain is another instructive dimension of birth, and I don't want to refuse the wisdom it offers. Imagine what would happen if we discovered a totally risk-free way to remove all pain and discomfort from pregnancy, birth, and recovery. Wouldn't that be wonderful? No—knowing the human heart a little bit, I predict we would value human life less. That is to say, we would lose all sight of what it costs, and babies and the birth process would become even more commodified than they already are. We so easily settle with the simple, matter-of-fact surface of things. When doctors write up the charts on a birthing mother, they refer to her as a "gravida," a Latinism whose root meaning is "heavy" or "weighty." Our English word "grave" as in "serious" derives from this root. "Grave" as in "burial place" actually derives from a different root word, but the convergence into one English word is apt and meaningful. Birth is a serious, weighty, death-shadowed thing. The pain reminds us of this depth.

Dr. Paul Brand, a surgeon who practiced medicine for decades all over the world and a special expert on leprosy, published a book in 1993 with Philip Yancey called *Pain: The Gift Nobody Wants.* Brand's experience with leprosy patients, whose keenest danger is that they suffer no pain sensations, convinced him that pain is a gift, a wise body-system that we must befriend rather than stamp out at every appearance. He worries that medical practices that seek to silence pain as a matter of course actually endanger our bodies' ability to heal themselves:

> I write as a physician, not a moralist, but any physician working in modern civilization cannot help noticing our cultural deafness to the wisdom of the body. The path to health, for an individual or a society, must begin by taking pain into account. Instead, we silence pain when we should be straining our ears to hear it. . . .

Dr. Brand certainly advocates pain relief, but also an understanding of what pain offers us. His book has little to say about childbirth pain—a shocking absence. But it's not difficult to apply his principle that pain is a teacher: childbirth pain reminds us, stubborn and dense as we are, that to bring a child into this world is a serious thing and cannot be done lightly or purely for selfish pleasure or fulfillment. There is pleasure and fulfillment in it, but there is also a cost. The pain is there to speak, in the body, of that cost.

At least for the birthing mother. She's the one who gets to learn the lessons of pain, if she will. But what about the father? My friend David, a family practice physician, tells me that he can often sense a palpable change in his women patients after they give birth. Many of his patients are very young, even in their early teens, and most of them are single. Often, David says, he watches these women enter labor deathly scared, but they come out of delivery stronger, seemingly more mature. They have endured pain and survived. They have brought another person into the world, and the process has begun to imprint a new responsibility upon them. As for the fathers, when they are present, they sometimes need coaxing to face what's happening. "I find myself trying to encourage the father to pay attention and participate," says David. "I say things like, 'We're going to turn off the TV now and concentrate on Janice. OK?'"

How pleasant for the man that he can choose whether or not to look childbirth pain in the eye. The woman is pretty committed. Even with the increasingly popular epidural during delivery, the processes of early labor, recovery, and healing still hurt. So I can drone on about the tough life lessons of labor and delivery, but there's no getting around the fact that these are lessons only birthing mothers learn in their bodies. This is not fair. But what can we do about it? Well, at least fathers can pay attention. When men knew their women could die in childbirth, it was probably easier to take the process seriously.

Perhaps now, having men in the birthing room is the necessary re-placement for them of the death-fear. The man can be impressed by what the mother of his child must endure to bring the baby to birth. Despite my impatient doubts about men in the delivery room, I think it is better that a father watch, even if only in silent bewilderment. After all, whatever pain relief she might receive, the way a woman's body must split open to get that baby out is pretty shocking. If it didn't happen every day, no one would believe it possible.

It would be best if all of us, women and men, could at least try listening to what childbirth pain tells us: By having a baby we are responsible for bringing another person into a world of pain. Pain is the fire before the castle gate, the kind of fire that, in fairy tales, the knight must be courageous and pure-hearted to pass through.

The Woman and the Dragon

Amid all the busyness and antiseptic cheerfulness of a medically protected birth, I do not want to lose the deeper, even mythic dimen-sion of it. Myth can sometimes dismiss the particularity, but the par-ticularity can sometimes submerge the mythic, too. To search out the mythic and unite it with the physical reality of birth is exactly what Judy Chicago sought to do in her series of images called The Birth Project. She had become interested, during the 70s, in "marginal" ar-tistic media, such as needlework and quilting, and also in images of birthing. She researched art history and discovered the shocking fact that artists had almost universally neglected to depict the moment of birth. Wars, decapitations, crucifixions, martyrdoms—sure. And there were, of course, fertility goddesses, madonnas, and nursing mothers.

But no births. So Chicago, not a mother herself, decided to research birth by asking mothers to tell their stories and by actually witnessing births with sketchpad in hand. She created dozens of designs and commissioned volunteers, highly skilled but mostly nonprofessional craftswomen, to create her designs in lavish, complex needlework. The resulting pieces are stunningly moving depictions of the real thing: bodies split open as the baby emerges, heads thrown back in transcendent agony, women's legs spread wide with swirls of creation flowing out from between them, fountains of milk flowing out from breasts and spreading liquid life across the earth. I can see why Chicago had difficulty securing engagements to display the show: it is almost too powerful to bear. In her book about the project, Chicago quotes poet Muriel Rukeyser: "What would happen if one woman told the truth about her life? The world would split open."

One of the most hard-edged mythic treatments of birth I can think of is the scene of the woman and the dragon in the biblical book of Revelation. Revelation is a terrifying text indeed, one before which I was raised to practice severe humility, and about which I was taught to refrain from speculation. But I am still fascinated with Revelation's cauldron of strange, sometimes brutally impenetrable images, and I'm grateful for its surpassingly beautiful healing vision of God's ultimate destiny for humankind.

On the way to those final chapters, though, the episode of the woman and the dragon speaks to the danger of childbirth with a harrowing comfort. Commentators, of course, allegorize the episode. I like philosopher Jacques Ellul's interpretation: the woman is Eve, Zion, Mary, and all of creation at once. The child is the incarnate Christ. And the birth of the child infuriates the dragon because it realizes—makes real—his defeat. Christ as God-united-to-creation closes the space in which the dragon could create evil. All this is

profound and archetypal. But the writer of Revelation reveals fundamental realities with these particular metaphors because of resonances we can recognize. A woman in labor is extremely vulnerable,
but also connected to powers far beyond herself, powers of the heavens. And the world into which she brings her child is full of dragons,
poised to devour.

The writer describes the scene as "a great and wondrous sign." A
pregnant woman is "clothed with the sun, with the moon under her
feet and a crown of twelve stars on her head"—a mythic picture indeed of every woman in the last weeks of pregnancy. The sixteenth-
century German artist Albrecht Dürer made a woodcut of this scene
in which the woman stands in the foreground, quite serene, looking
firm as a pillar on a medieval cathedral, barely glancing at her dragon
nemesis. Some contemporary artist ought to capture more accurately
the way the text actually portrays the drama of the scene: the woman
cries out in pain, the text says, and as she strives to bring her child to
birth, an "enormous red dragon with seven heads and ten horns and
seven crowns on his heads" stands over her, ready to devour her infant.
In the text, she seems to feel his hot breath singeing the ends of her
hair.

How many things in this world swirl up into the horrid multiplicity of that dragon! How many things stand ready to devour an infant!
A careless, abusive father. A mother crippled by ignorance or self-
loathing. Racism. Addictions. A marriage on the path to disaster. Mi-
sogyny so systemic no one even perceives it. Illness, accident,
heartbreak. Poverty, hunger, death. I read about the dreadful conditions in which women still give birth in this world, the filthy and
shamed birth-huts of rural India, the quiet and persistent practice of
infanticide for female infants in China, the utterly oppressive sorrow

and degradation of so many birthing mothers, and it crushes my heart. The dragon, the dragon devours and thrives.

The passage witnesses to the dragons, but also to a surprising, tender mercy sent directly from God. The mother gives birth, and the child is "snatched up to God and to his throne" in order to protect it from the dragon. And the poor mother? She flees into the desert, "to a place prepared for her by God, where she might be taken care of for 1260 days." It's hardly an ideal situation—the precious mother-infant dyad is separated by the desperate circumstances—but while the world staggers in upheaval around them, they are given mercy and protection.

This is not the end, though. The dragon battles angels and loses, and in his fury he goes after the woman again, pursuing her and spewing a torrent of water to "sweep her away." But the woman is given "wings of a great eagle" in order to reach her place of safety and rest, and the earth itself helps the woman "by opening its mouth and swallowing the river that the dragon had spewed." The woman escapes. The dragon is still angry, and determines to "make war" against the rest of the woman's offspring (those who obey God, the text explains). But the woman is left, in this scene, safely out of reach of the dragon. She receives gentle care for a good long time.

Though this scene points to the great clashes of good and evil in this world—battles between the Church and its angels and the great powers of domination, violence, and lies—it still gives us a glimpse, from God's point of view, of a more intimate reality. The mother and infant, glorious but in danger from the threats of this world. God and the earth itself at God's command, tenderly protecting and caring for the mother and "snatching" the infant to safety. The terrifying nature of this saga, the imminent and powerful threat, the chase scene, as it were—all these remind of the danger of birth, our desperation for God's mercy.

Breathing

The dragons of this world lurk only in the distance for me, but fears drag on me with a near presence. This unease that slips into dread is of a whole different quality from any other stressful anticipation I've felt. I've sweated and quaked before musical performances; I've turned mute and serious before facing a class of new students; I've ached in the gut before facing someone who's angered me or whom I've angered. But this is different. I think I'm more afraid this time than the last two times because I *know* what it feels like. Sometimes it's worse to know.

No one can walk this path for me. I can only hope for someone to walk this path with me. Since childhood I've seen people face desperate times by offering each other words—words of Scripture, words of familiar hymns, words held out in sober sympathy, like medicines and ointments to relieve and soothe. So I go instinctively to the Bible to find a way to pray, and I go to that place where prayers of Jews and Christians in all time seem mysteriously condensed: the Psalms. For the last two births, I went straight to the serious stuff from Psalm 22: "O Lord, be not far off; O my Strength, come quickly to help me." I memorized some of the verses about the psalmist's suffering to give my mind something to focus on during the pain. (I found out later that I'm not the first to take this passage, normally associated for Christians with the suffering of Christ, and apply it to childbirth. Devotional books of the English Renaissance encouraged women to make the very same move.) Then I found verses of rejoicing for after the birth, too, from Psalm 40: "I waited patiently for the Lord; he turned to me and heard my cry." And, later, "Many, O Lord my God, are the wonders you have performed. The things you planned for us no one can recount to you. Were I to speak and tell of them, they would be too many to declare." I've got these words all prepared, I thought, so God won't let them go to waste—right?

This time, searching again for something to grip on the descent, I came across Psalm 20, which has elements of both plea and praise:

> May the Lord answer you when you are in distress;
> may the name of the God of Jacob protect you. . . .
> We will shout for joy when you are victorious
> and will lift up our banners in the name of our God.

I change the words in my mind, though, to make the psalm a first-person prayer: "O Lord, answer me when I am in distress."

When there is nothing else to hang on to, I hang on to words. The words of the Psalms have living presence, having been in the mouths of so many thousands in so many centuries, having taken into themselves the substance of the ages; they are as dense and present as bread. Repeating these words is far more important preparation for me than doing breathing exercises. This is a spiritual breathing exercise; perhaps that's what the inspiration of Scripture means in practice—these are the words that, taken into ourselves, keep us alive. When I have lost my presence of mind, perhaps they will help me invoke the presence of God.

Wrenching Redemption

I gave birth to my first child, my daughter, on Good Friday. I was pleased about this coincidence; it seemed fitting. Good Friday is the day in the Christian year when Christians meditate on suffering and seek to find meaning in it. Other world religions and philosophical systems have more or less compelling answers to suffering—it is an illusion, it is the result of inordinate human desire, it is the way in which one people atones for the rest of the world's peoples, it is the result of human foolishness that we must work to evolve beyond. But Christianity presents an answer to pain in the form of God himself suffering it with us and turning it to grace. Far more eloquent an answer to human suffering than any philosophy or theological system is the silent image of the crucified Christ. In this moment, God says to all of humanity in pain: I have not forgotten you. See? I suffer it with you. I suffer it with you and wrench it toward redemption.

Pain becomes redemptive, death leads to life. The suffering God is a divine gesture of solidarity but also a creative, transformative act. The only way out is through. The only way to free us, ultimately, from death and pain, is to suffer through it. Anything less would trivialize both suffering and human responsibility. Life has the cost of pain now. But there is also the promise: pain can have the result of life. This is the promise Jesus established in the Good Friday-to-Easter event: that the pain of all human history will give birth to a New Creation, in which, as Isaiah prophesied, "sorrow and sighing will flee away."

When I gave birth on Good Friday, I tried consciously to experience the parallels between this pattern, the redemptive suffering of Christ, and the birth of a single child. It didn't quite make sense, though, because it seemed that I should be thinking about Mary's birth-giving rather than Jesus' suffering. What did Jesus know about giving birth, anyway? Mary is the one who did that! Actually, medieval Europeans sometimes espoused the idea that Mary didn't feel any pain during Jesus' birth. The theory was that she was sinless and therefore did not need to participate in the curse of Eve. This makes no sense to me. However innocent she may have been, *of course* Mary felt pain in childbirth. That's the *point* of the incarnation: welcome to the world of pain. Mary's pain was a kind of herald, a foretaste, of Jesus' later suffering, perhaps. And Good Friday was, in a sense, the concentrated labor of God, the transition to the New Creation.

At any rate, it was difficult to think about all this while in labor. It turns out that the mind doesn't operate quite on that level while the body is focused on pain management. I had to think it all over afterward instead.

Simone Weil, in her essay "The Love of God and Affliction," reflects on pain and its possible meanings by distinguishing between suffering and affliction. Suffering is pain that can be redeemed toward growth. Affliction, however, is an "attenuated equivalent of death," particularly death of the soul. Affliction moves beyond suffering to incorporate social degradation, shame, and the extinguishing of personality. Christ's suffering, she also asserts, reached to the depths of affliction so that even in the darkest of human miseries, there might be hope. For many women in this world—the ones who are made pregnant against their will, or who have never had the education or love required even to form a will—birth pain gathers into itself and concentrates all the burdens and sufferings of their lives. It becomes a distillation of their affliction.

For mothers like me, however, coming to this birth crisis with the luxury of expert care and meditative reflection, birth pain represents simple suffering—pain that is deliberately prepared for and accepted because it has evident meaning and purpose. I still dread it deeply, to my core. But what do I do with the privilege, as it turns out to be, of this kind of suffering? Weil also says that "pain that is only physical leaves no trace in the soul." It is possible, though difficult, I imagine, to refuse the trace in the soul childbirth can bring. I welcome the trace. But I wonder. Can the meaningful, eased pain I will experience be something beyond a temporary glimpse of the world's dragons? Can the experience of rich, privileged women like me lay down a path away from affliction, leading us to act as the wings of the eagle or swallow the torrents for other women, becoming the mercy of God to them? Can our births, touching the pain but full of the promise, catch the world in a net of hope and witness to the renewal of a creation now "groaning with eager longing"?

14) birth

The world is different, for a new person has arrived in it. He is here, he is real, he has a name
and a birth date. Each of us is different, too. I,
the mother, given over completely from dark
clouds to light and joy. Ron, a buoyant father
now of two sons. Miriam and Jacob, feeling their
bigger-than-ever status as sister and brother.
This tiny infant will go on changing each of us,
God willing, for the better. Philip Aaron, born
July 10, 1999.

My heart says: *Many, O Lord my God, are the*

wonders you have done. The things you planned for us, no one can re-count to you. Were I to speak and tell of them, they would be too many to declare.

~

Each birth story is unique. Dreadful, rash, charming, exhilarating, each story needs to be told and retold, meditated on and explored for its meaning, savored in its singularity. Helen Sterk, one of my colleagues and a professor of communications studies, recently discovered how rarely birth stories have entered our cultural discourse. One would think that a drama as daily as birth might appear commonly in literature or at least in oral traditions. But not so. Birth stories have remained in the silent places, the tatters of women's lives not told. The relatively few birth stories that do appear in literature are typically mediated by historians, male writers, or expert observers. Sterk, astonished when her search for unmediated birth stories turned up so little, compiled an archive of 131 interviews during which birthing mothers representing several generations told their stories any way they wished. The resulting aggregate of women's narratives—the stories of some 300 births are now recorded for history—convinced the five scholars who studied the interviews that women *must* tell these stories. Transformation of the world, even in small ways, begins with transformation of the mind and heart. Rather than remaining tangled in and even silenced by the discourses about their bodies and their experiences that experts and other "mediators" impose, women must narrate their own lives, sort through their hearts and memories and weave into the human story each new strand.

A new story is now embedded in my heart, embedded with two stories already there.

Miriam

Miriam's story is sweetened with the charm of small-town life. She was born in 1993 in Pella, Iowa, a town of 10,000 people forty miles southeast of Des Moines. The Pella hospital was small but well-equipped and well-staffed. On the day Miriam was born, I spent a long and fairly ho-hum morning and early afternoon laboring in one of the two labor rooms. My doctor, Dr. John, suggested midafternoon that we could break my water to get things moving, and Ron and I readily agreed. After that, a few more hours of mild but very close-together contractions and then, all of a sudden, POW! Hard labor.

The story gets more interesting about nine-thirty P.M. when another woman came in, also a patient of Dr. John's. There were only three rooms in the delivery suite—two labor rooms and a delivery room—which were, except on exceedingly rare occasions such as this one, quite adequate. They put the other woman in the other labor room and I could hear her yelling her guts out. By this time killer contractions were hitting me in waves. Dr. John gently and soberly assured me, "Those are the kind that do the best work"—a comment for which I will always be grateful. Then, shortly after Yelling Woman arrived, I found out what the famous "urge to push" feels like. Ron went running out into the hall calling out, "We need a doctor in here right now!" Dr. John came back in to "check me" with the usual invasive digital procedure that makes you cringe the first time they do it and then after about ten times you don't care and then during hard labor you're deeply grateful because it provides information such as, "You're ready to go! Start pushing," which is what Dr. John said then.

But then he trotted out of the room. Ron heard him on the phone, first talking to his father, another doctor in the Pella medical practice, and then to his brother-in-law, a medical resident who was visiting for the Easter holiday. He was asking them to come down because the other woman was already being wheeled into the delivery room—Dr. John had two moms ready to deliver simultaneously. Within a few minutes (everyone lives minutes away in Pella) the whole doctor family was there, suited up in surgical duds and ready for action.

The next thing I knew, there was a big commotion in my room as nurses wheeled in all kinds of equipment. They were setting up my labor room as a delivery room. Dr. John stayed with me ("because you were admitted first," he later explained) and then the baby race began. "Push, Push!" the nurses must have been chanting in chorus across the two nearby rooms. My beautiful daughter seemed to appear suddenly, all at once—I remember looking down at her and seeing *all* of her, and thinking how beautiful she was. She arrived at 10:05 P.M. and the other baby at 10:06. Whew!

The next day, my choir director from church called at eight o'clock in the morning to say congratulations. News travels with mysterious speed in Pella. Apparently, everyone knew already at the Good Friday service the night before that I was in labor. One of our pastors, Jill, came to visit later that morning and reported that the choir had sung a verse of the hymn "Come Labor On" in my honor at the pre-service rehearsal the night before (it's actually a hymn about mission work). After the service, several people from church had come over to the hospital to peer into the nursery and see if a little Rienstra had arrived yet. They were there about ten P.M., and wondered why the whole maternity hall looked so deserted. It was because every nurse on the floor was busy helping with the two simultaneous deliveries.

We brought Miriam home on Easter Sunday. Before we left the hospital, Dr. John invited Ron and me to join him in the lounge area.

We sat down together—Ron and I still staring in constant amazement at our baby—and Dr. John gave us a little instructional talk
about taking care of baby and ourselves. He finished, this good man,
by speaking out of a faith he knew we shared with him: he reminded
us that our daughter had a soul, and our most important job was to
"train her up in the way she should go."

Jacob

Jacob was born two years and four months later in Pella. By this
time the hospital had begun construction on a brand new labor-and-
delivery wing, complete with the fashionable do-it-all rooms with the
pretty wallpaper and the heavy mauve curtains behind which were
lurking huge, scary medical machines. None of this would be finished
in time for my baby's birth, of course.

This time I went into labor while standing around in the waiting
room waiting for my regular weekly appointment. Dr. John was in
Romania doing volunteer medical work (could I complain about his
leaving me to help suffering Romanians?), so I had my appointment
with Dr. Galen. I had had quite a few stray contractions during the
day, but by the time I saw Dr. Galen, I was having regular contractions
right on the exam table. "You're going to have this baby tonight," he
said cheerfully. "How about if we meet over at the hospital in an
hour?"

I expected hours of hard labor, just like last time, and I planned to
proceed as before: stand with my arms around Ron's neck, pulling
downward on him with each contraction, breathing in faithful obedience to the birthing class rules. But this time, labor seemed to move a
lot faster. Before I knew it, the contractions were hitting me hard. I

whipped the fetal monitor off and threw it to the floor, clambered onto the bed, and assumed the only position I could endure: on my hands and knees. During the contractions I moaned and breathed erratically, and between them I crumpled my head and shoulders onto the pillow to rest.

By this time, the nurse had figured out that we were galloping through the labor stages here, and she offered me some IV pain medication. I accepted the offer, but before she could give the meds, she had to perform this nice leisurely procedure that includes "checking your progress." At this point I remember a hubbub: "She's ready to go! Cancel the order! No meds!" And the quick trip around the corner to the delivery room, and the urge to push.

Then there were the intense minutes of quiet concentration and businesslike communications among the medical people, punctuated by bursts of "Push! Push!" every few minutes. "I want to see that baby!" I groaned. "That's good," said Dr. Galen. "Think about seeing the baby."

Fifteen minutes later, Jacob was born, my dark-haired boy. Jacob had a little trouble breathing at first, so after I held him for those first few moments, the nurse put him in a little oxygen tent next to my bed. I remember it as a good and quiet and intimate time, me gazing over at him, weak from the fast-and-hard delivery and sleepy from lack of oxygen myself, trembling like crazy from the waist down, and him gazing back at me with watery dark eyes, his tiny dimpled fists like flower buds.

The doctor and nurses all hovered around and monitored him, concerned but not frantic. If he had not improved quickly, they would have sent him by helicopter to Des Moines. But as the minutes passed, his breathing and blood oxygenation got better, his "crackly" lung steadily cleared. So we waited. At one point, the conversation having turned relaxed, Dr. Galen asked me what my dissertation was about. I had finished it just three months before, but I thought and thought, searched my poor weary brain. I couldn't remember. Finally I said, "I think it had to do with the Psalms." Ron had to explain the rest.

After an hour or so, Jacob was pronounced safe to stay and we were all settled into a regular room. Ron went home about eleven P.M. Our friends Jennifer and Peter had been staying with Miriam since we left for the hospital at five. When Ron came home at eleven, Jennifer said, "Home already? It's like you just went to the mall!"

P h i l i p

I remember everything. Even more than with my first two deliveries, I was completely alert every moment, keenly aware that *this* is happening *now.*

The end came with a crazy, surreal acceleration, but the beginning took place over about two days. Two days of teasing contractions here and there. A little bleeding and crampiness Thursday night after our family outing to the zoo. A few contractions in the middle of the night, the strange sensation in the gut that says, "Here it comes," then the vice clamp passing through the back and upward through the belly, tightening, tightening, then slowly relaxing, and then it's over. I remember how they feel and wonder all over again if I can endure it.

Then the next day, more blood in the morning, but no contractions. Nothing much all day. That night, about once every hour, in that quiet semiconscious twilight, a contraction comes and fear sets in again. Can I do this? I will surely need pain medication to get through it. Forget my determinations not to have any—that's all just posturing. I can't go through this again.

But then morning comes, and I feel impatient. Let's just do it! I can't stand this waiting anymore. Everything aches, I can barely walk without pain. Ron suggests we take the family on a slow nature walk, and I agree, needing to do something. We walk, everything aches, but only a few stray contractions.

Then, at home, they start coming, here and there. Is this it? It must be happening, but it's not time to take action yet. They need to be regular and they're not. I can't think about or do anything. Ron tries to keep the children busy watching a soccer game on TV, but they find their way upstairs and annoy me with their questions and needs. An hour later, the contractions start coming every few min-utes, but not too strong. I call my parents to pick up the children. They come right away (thank you!) and when they're gone, and the house is quiet, it's as if my body takes the signal. Every few minutes. I brace myself, breathe through them. So far, I think, I'm OK. I'm do-ing it, I remind myself. There's no more fear anymore because there's little time to think ahead or behind.

Finally, after an hour, even though I don't think the contractions are too bad yet (I remember worse from before), I decide we had bet-ter get to the hospital. Call the doctor again. I feel every bump on the ride there. We arrive at the emergency entrance of a towering big-city hospital this time. A kind, older gentleman volunteer opens the door for me, but I can't move. "Are you having a pain?" he asks gently. I nod and wait for it to pass, thinking how quaint of him to call it a "pain." I feel hyper-alert as I ease into a wheelchair and they bring me to Labor and Delivery. My consciousness seems to pierce out through my eyes: This is the day, this is me arriving at the hospital, this is happening now now now.

In the evaluation room, we wait. I stand and breathe through each contraction, focusing my eyes on a poster in the room. Contractions come and come, a little harder. Finally a nurse appears to check how far I've dilated. She breaks my water by accident. She's embarrassed and apologetic, but I'm glad. And more good news: already at six! I'm relieved: much of the work already done. I look the nurse in the eye and say firmly, "Get the doctor here NOW. This won't take long." She agrees. It's 5:45.

They need a few minutes to prepare a labor-and-delivery room for me. But there is no time. Now I feel the real ones, the HARD ones. I remember these! Oh, I feel them coming and they overpower! There's no way to sit or stand, just hold on and breathe, breathe, they pass. But then another comes, HARD HARD HARD—oh, how many more?

The nurses wheel me on the bed to the other room. Oh, here comes another one, nothing to do but moan and try to breathe. The doctor is on her way, she'll be here any second I feel pushy does she feel pushy tell her not to push yet doctor is in the hospital here she is can I push yet no wait one more they're getting suction ready pant pant pant now can I push yes go ahead Aiiiieeeeeeeeeeeee good, that's good another one push puuuuuuuuuuuuuuush!

I yell through each push, yell with total abandon. No time for any pain meds so I yell and it helps. It's loud, and I hear myself, but don't care. I feel the baby's head crown push and push why won't it come out why can't I just get it out? Doctor and resident down there working, giving instructions, fussing around. Baby's head just stays in one place. Almost there, almost there, almost there it hurts, it hurts, over soon over soon one more controlled push you don't need a contraction I feel it I feel the baby's head out—relief relief relief!

The rest hurts, but is easy. I hear the baby cry. Finally, the whole baby is out, in a towel, in my arms in a matter of seconds. Beautiful, beautiful. Wet and white, dark hair and bright eyes, a person, our person. Thank God, thank God! It's over!

Little one, thank you for coming quickly. Thank you for coming early. Thank you for being you, and here, and healthy and strong. The nurses admire him, he's perfect.

I'm wide awake, not dizzy, not in a haze. Everyone speaks in normal tones again, but with happiness in our voices. Then the awkward time while the doctor and resident examine the "war zone" and do the repairs—not bad, but it takes a while, and I tremble, especially my legs. I try to hold them still but it's almost impossible. There's much to watch as the nurse cleans off the baby, everyone coos over him—him, this new person in our midst.

So what was the time of birth? Six twenty-two. Ron and I laugh—it can't be! So fast, insanely fast. Blessedly, mercifully fast. Another birth over, I did it. Thank God. *We will shout for joy when you are victorious, and will lift up our banners in the name of our God.*

The doctor and resident clean up the equipment and gather up the towels strewn everywhere, say their good-byes and hearty congratulations. The nurses finish their work and go, leaving the three of us with one nurse to give the baby a bath right there with us and help us get transferred to a room on the nursery floor. It's still early, eight-thirty or so, still light outside on this midsummer evening. Ron and I joke—So what would you like to do tonight? Any projects around the house that still need to be done?

There is work to do yet. Baby and I must both recover. We must get to know one another, learn the give-and-take of feeding, get through many awkward days and nights before we are both adjusted to our new separateness. But right now, such joy and relief!

~

"Birth is as solemn a parting as death," wrote G. K. Chesterton. I'm not one of those mothers who feels a deep, cosmic connection to her child in the womb. A bond, surely. But the separation, while solemn, is to me paradoxically necessary. I must see the child, touch him with my hands, hold him against my cheek before I can know him and begin learning to love him as himself. Inside, he is mystery. Outside, he is still a tiny stranger. But now at least the process can begin.

15) *first days*

Awakening from some dreaming depth, in which
I was someone and somewhere else, I hear a knock
on my hospital room door. Oh yes. The hospital,
the middle of the night. I know where I am now.
"Your baby is awake and hungry," the nurse says
softly. "Would you like to feed him?" In the dark,
I raise up my stiff, heavy body on one elbow,
reach for the height-adjusting buttons on the
side-rail of the bed, and shove the pillows
awkwardly into place behind me, trying not to
wrench any of my sore muscles or put any real

weight on my bruised bottom. The nurse hands me a little cocoon of blankets with a tiny face peeping out. She shows me Philip's ID tags, but I know he's mine; I already know that face. His eyes are dark and shining, wide awake, his tiny mouth pursed open and waiting. We unwrap his upper body and two wiry little arms pop out of the blanket, like featherless bird's wings unfolding. I know how to hold him against me and place my comparatively enormous dark nipple into the pink circle of his mouth. He has a good idea what to do, too. Once we get started, the nurse leaves us alone, and I lie there, watching his jaw work and adjusting his position, keeping him going with a jiggle or a stroke on his cheek. Half vigilantly attentive, half in reverie; half awake, half dreaming; utterly joyful yet frightened; euphoric yet profoundly tired. Now begins a swirl of twilight states that will bump me across the hours for the next many weeks.

I remember, after each of my babies' births, a moment of deep, quiet joy after the birth-storm had passed and I was resting in a darkened room, holding my new infant. Now I lie in the night stillness together with this new one, and it seems we two are the calm center of all things; and even if I'm half asleep I seem most truly conscious, most connected to the real and right. But it can't last. A little more sleep and then daylight will come and baths and feedings and doctors' examinations and visits and those infernal blood pressure and temperature checks.

The resident comes round early the morning after the birth, businesslike and serious in her running shoes and blue scrubs. She asks the appropriate questions about pain and amount of bleeding. I ask her whether a fast labor can make the baby sleepy more quickly. She responds with a smile: "Yes, you really exploded that baby out!" I'm a little offended. Exploded? I am not a *bomb*. But I'm a little proud, too. I did deliver without anesthesia, thank you very much—"like a marine," as Ron put it.

A little later my father-in-law knocks on the door. He's in the hospital early to do his own rounds for his surgical patients. He enters smiling, buoyant and assured on his home turf, looking like he's ready to dash in and out. But the baby, sleeping in the bassinet next to me, stops Dad short. In the crescent formed by the edges of the knit cap and the blanket-cocoon, a tiny nose fits between two lines of soft, dark lashes, and thin, pink lips delicate as the edge of a china teacup. Dad reaches in his fingertip to pull the blanket-edge back just enough to admire these miniature family contours. "Thank you," he says to me. "Thank you for another beautiful grandchild."

Later in the morning, Ron arrives looking tired but happy. Then my parents join us with Miriam and Jacob. Mom and Dad are excited and kind and eager to report about what happened when the phone call came announcing the birth. They describe how Miriam and Jacob jumped up and down for joy and boasted that they had kept the baby's *real* name a secret for *months*. Then Miriam and Jacob noisily stake their claim on their dismayingly small brother. Philip opens his eyes for them as they perch on the big recliner and lay the baby-bundle awkwardly over their legs for pictures. Eventually, everyone goes home, nurses appear for more blood pressure checks, some discussion among the nurses of whether or not the baby has wet a diaper yet, forms to fill out, supper brought in on a tray, nightfall and more strange dreams. By the second morning, that centerpoint of stillness has long faded and I'm ready to go home.

Elusive Equilibrium

The euphoria of the first few hours after birth has worn off, and now at home I feel the tasks and needs of the day (and night) pull me reluctantly along, sluggish and skewed. Pick up the baby, ease myself off the couch, tuck the baby in his bassinet, get a glass of water—performing one small, simple task after another is all I can manage. The British pediatrician and author Penelope Leach describes the first few days after birth with concise sympathy:

> Everything is felt too much: stitches and pleasure, responsibility and pride, selfishness and selflessness. You are still desperately tired. Your hormone balance is disturbed, your milk is not fully in, your cervix not yet closed, your body striving for equilibrium.

As for the baby, says Leach, "All is bewilderment." And the husband walks an "emotional tightrope."

That after-birth euphoria does not return—it is a brief, altogether unique human experience—but it does transmute into moments of love so exquisite and undiluted they are hardly bearable. The desire to gaze and gaze at the baby's every detail—who can resist this pleasure? For months we waited to see and hold this enigmatic creature, but now his eyelashes, his ears, his fingernails, his finely traced hairline are like smooth, intricate letters spelling out mysteries if we can read them. Genetic coding's infinite permutations, life's tenacity, the holiness of creation—these mysteries hush our distracted hearts to wonder.

We gaze on his miniature perfection as he sleeps in our arms in utter stillness, but even more astonishing—he awakens! This miracle of form is alive! He sneezes and yawns and cries rather loudly, considering his size, and wiggles his scrawny arms and legs when we unwrap him. His body seems at first unsuited for action in the world. We have to pry his skinny legs away from his oblong stomach, then stuff those newborn diapers around his pointy bottom and tape the lumpy folds together. But when I hold him against me, his warm, fuzzy head nestles into my neck and his legs curl under his bottom, remembering their formation inside me. Bundled on the slope of my chest, he seems to fit into me even more perfectly than before.

Best of all, Ron can surround him now, too. Philip and I are reuniting, but for Ron and Philip this is all new. Two people who have been corresponding at a distance finally meet. When Miriam was born, Ron was the stereotypical new father, proud and weepy and ardently adoring. As we sat with her at the hospital checkout desk waiting for our release papers, the older woman who was tapping our information into the computer eyed Ron as he held Miriam on his knees, cradling her form on his forearms, his hands cupped under her head. As we signed the papers, the woman smiled knowingly and said to me, "He's smitten with her, isn't he?" Now, I see Ron the experienced father expertly tucking Philip against him, and I'm the one who's smitten.

~

These exquisite joys come. But especially as the one-week mark approaches, the beauties bob unpredictably on waves of profound tiredness, soreness, feelings of inadequacy and uncertainty, frustration, even near-despair. This is the other side of things felt too much. No one can explain to expectant parents ahead of time how hard these weeks are. Experienced parents can't remember them very clearly, probably because the weeks go by in a sleep-deprived haze. Ask parents about the first six weeks of their first baby, and you will see the puzzled awe in their eyes and hear it in their voices. "I remember," they'll say vaguely, "but I don't know how we did it."

And people don't like to talk about it. We're *supposed* to adore our infants instantly and relish every moment of their babyhood because, by God, it is a miracle that they come to birth at all, and they "grow up so quickly." We're supposed to be grateful every moment for their health and joyful about how lucky we are. People coo and fuss over infants and beam at the lucky parents, sometimes asking with a sympathetically furrowed brow, "Is he a good baby?" or "How is he doing at night?" But most friendly inquirers don't really want you to speak the truth: "Last night I thought I had reached the end of my rope when he woke up the fourth time" or "Sometimes when he cries and cries I wonder why I had a baby in the first place." And who wants to talk about it aloud, anyway? Falling to pieces is a private thing. Easier for everyone if the parents smile weakly and try to fulfill, in public anyway, the happy, adoring cultural ideal.

But the truth is that even when one does adore the baby and feel profoundly grateful for the child's very existence, let alone good health, these weeks are still hard. In fact, caring for a newborn infant tests the bounds of human endurance. At least *this* human's.

I hardly dare admit this, and as I do, I hear voices in my head accusing me of ingratitude or wimpiness or self-pity. But *come on:* isn't it all right to admit that this is hard?

My mother-in-law tells me about an article she read a few years ago written by a man who spent his early adulthood as a monk. Later he left the order, married, and had children. He wrote that while the disciplines of the monastery did indeed nurture the spiritual life, caring for infants turned out to be the "quick path to sainthood." I know exactly what he means. Loving service, relentlessly repeated all day and night for a little person who, though a miracle of design and beauty, does have scrawny little chicken legs and can't even smile in response to your patient and heroic ministrations—this is the kind of regimen that will pound the selfish stuffings right out of you.

Flowers and cards, gifts and visits taper off, and soon days and nights are filled merely with the most fundamental matters of all: eating, excreting, breathing, sleeping. Matters of simple survival. However, none of these seems to happen in the right amount or at the right time. All is bewilderment for everybody, every minute as unpredictable as the last. Will baby sleep five minutes or two hours? Is baby hungry or is something else wrong? Will tonight be another hellish one, sharp little wails awakening us with a jolt every time we manage to fall into a deep sleep? Or will this be the night baby will surprise us and sleep a long stretch? Everything is skewed; everyone is swimming in a dozen crossing currents.

Fluids

If I were in prime physical condition, caring for my infant while still trying to keep the basics going for myself would be difficult enough. As it is, my body is still dripping and quivering from the upheaval of delivery. I remember, after my daughter was born, looking down at myself the next day to find this deflated balloon of a belly. I found it fascinating. I had never seen my stomach look quite like that before—thick, loose skin with that dark, jaggy line running down from my stretched-out navel, the whole tummy so blobby and light! I like my newly weightless belly this time, too, but that sore bottom—oh oh. And for heaven's sake, all these fluids! I'm a warm, sloppy fountain.

I've never thought about bodily fluids so much in my life. It all starts, I suppose, with that pregnancy test. Suddenly, urine is a matter of intense curiosity and, probably for the first time since potty training (unless you're a health professional), a topic of conversation. A woman with a positive pregnancy test in hand had better get over any squeamishness or embarrassment immediately. The minute the pregnancy is confirmed, the medical professionals begin tapping her fluids—more blood, this time from a vein, and yet more urine. At the OB-GYN practice where I went, the routine for all prenatal visits goes as follows: show up, tell the receptionist your name, receptionist writes your name on a cup, hands it to you, you go pee into it, they test your pee. Every time.

This is all just warm-up, though—a test, maybe, to see how cooperative you are in leaking fluids on cue. When birth comes, then the fluids really start to flow. Blood and amniotic fluid gush out with the baby, splatting all over hospital linens and even floors if the nurses aren't quick on the draw with pans and cloths. ("I can't believe all the blood!" Ron blurted out when he surveyed the wreckage on the floor after Miriam's birth.) But women have other ducts and orifices that can produce fluid, too, and after birth they all start a sympathetic production. There are the tears—of joy, fatigue, and just for the heck of it. There's the peeing, designed to release the remarkable volumes of fluids built up to cushion the baby during pregnancy. Actually, this fluidic activity has its rewards, in my opinion. After months of constantly catering to the needs of a low-capacity bladder, you can finally visit the bathroom at civilized intervals, and the trips are *worth it,* volume-wise. Wiping is a problem, but *thank you* to whoever came up with the fabulous idea of squirting off "the area" with warm water from a "perinatal bottle."

There's more! There's the sweating at night because all that peeing apparently doesn't do the flush-out job completely. There's the continued bleeding, daintily termed "lochia," that has a sweet-pungent odor but goes on for weeks, reminding you that not having your period for nine months is not a perk that comes free of charge. And then, of course, there's that most magical fluid of all: breastmilk. Amazing stuff indeed, but it doesn't come in quite the right amounts until weeks later. Usually, the body enthusiastically produces more than the baby can handle, resulting in leaking through pads and shirts, dripping whenever the breasts aren't pressed into their "scaffolding" (my term for those nursing bras), and even—so I've heard, as this never happened to me—spraying several feet across the room when the full breasts are unleashed on the world.

Baby's fluids flow, too, and become the subject of keen interest among parents and medical professionals. How many wet diapers per day? How many stools? Now *there's* a truly unique bodily fluid. At first I thought God made baby poop look like bright yellow mustard with seeds in it just to be funny. Now I suspect this design has a practical purpose that contributes to the survival of the species: in the middle of the night when you're groggy and you've left your glasses by your bedside, you can still tell for sure that baby's diaper needs changing. The stuff almost glows in the dark.

So baby and I cling to each other rather damply and fragrantly through these crazy days. Both our bodies need to heal from our separation. Each little step of healing is a milestone, looked for anxiously and greeted with relief: his circumcision must heal, then his belly button, then my breasts must get used to this hard, hard work, then my bleeding must stop. Such simple, earthy, bodily things fill my thoughts. That a woman's body can heal after the trauma of giving birth is one of the human body's greatest achievements; perhaps the healing process is a genius of bonding, too. My weakness and pain leave me connected to baby's vulnerability, and maybe in this damp, dazed, and blobby state I am also a softer cushion for absorbing those shocks of otherworldly bliss.

Mothers and Other "Helpers"

Although most of the visits have stopped, we're lucky at the moment to have two armies of casserole-makers working for us, those from our "regular" church and those from the church where Ron is guest-preaching this summer. With these two churches and assorted friends whipping up the goods, we have meals coming almost every day for four weeks. This reminds me that one of the most practical things ordinary churchgoers do in this world is provide food in a crisis. Some churches really have it together, appointing a "meal captain" who gets the tip-off about deaths, births, and illnesses in the church and then quickly designates a point person for each incident, who in turn calls people and sets up a meal schedule. Most churches just wing it, and the people who are good at this sort of thing get the job done somehow. It's the perfect arrangement for us: friendly faces knock on our door at suppertime, hand us casserole dishes and rolls and usually way too much dessert, coo briefly over the baby, and then go away.

The going away part is crucial. The fact is, I have nothing very sensible to say to anyone right now. My thoughts are fixated on blood, breasts, and baby poop, and my feelings are like terribly stiff drinks that would have visitors sputtering, bulgy-eyed, if they were to quaff them with me. Virtually anything, from a sincerely loving remark to a smarmy television commercial, can set off a crying jag. Moreover, I have small, circular wet spots on my shirt. So all in all it's better if people make their visits very short, as in about three minutes. There will be time to get reacquainted later, assuming I will eventually remember my name.

Unfortunately, just at the time when a woman feels most pulled apart, literally and in every figurative sense, custom dictates—and I do mean dictates—that new parents receive extended visits from family members, especially the mother's mother. This seems like a marvelous idea. Even with a sterling quality husband—willing to help, completely capable, and able to take time off from his job—another willing helper can keep plenty busy doing laundry, cleaning, cooking, and keeping any older children busy. And in fact, for many people, this plan works out beautifully, even inaugurating a tender new stage of admiration and love between the new mom and her own mom. But it isn't always as simple and reasonable as it sounds; it wasn't for me when Miriam was born. Instead, my parents traveled eight hours, arrived on our doorstep to help for a few days, and within minutes we were arguing and crying and stabbing each other with words.

How do I explain this? The details don't matter anymore; it had to do with who was sleeping where, and I can't bear to rehearse it all again. All I know—and it took me years of thinking about it to figure this out—is that the birth of the first child sends shock waves into the old configurations of family relationships. Weddings can do this, too—daughters and sons turn their loyalties from parents to the new partner. But often that transition has been going on for years already, so the wedding is just the icing on the three-tiered cake, as it were. Nothing, however, can adequately prepare parents or children for the appearance of the next generation. My daughter was not the first grandchild for my parents, but I am the youngest child and only daughter in my family, and as a result I often fell into the role of the little princess. So shifting our normally harmonious parent-child relationship into the next stage was inevitably going to involve some lurching and pitching. My parents saw me with this new infant and realized I would never again be their little girl. I held my new infant and finally wanted my own parents to stop parenting me so I could learn to be the parent myself. If we had seen it all coming it might have been different, but it hit us all by surprise.

The shifting of roles, so that the parent becomes the grandparent, the child the parent, absolutely must happen. But at the moment of the shift, maybe it's not such a great idea to have everyone together in a few rooms for several days and nights, particularly when mercurial hormonal adjustments and infant night-wakings are factored in. I've heard that in some circles, people hire a "baby nurse" to come and do all the extra chores. This probably works out fine, but it might have been considered a shameless extravagance around these parts. Besides, I didn't feel ready to have anyone around except Ron. What I wanted most while facing this shifting-point to a new parental role was some privacy. It seems peculiar that I should consider my parents—the ones who diapered me, for heaven's sake—an invasion of privacy at this moment. But I think I felt as if they knew me *too* well. They remember me as a *teenager,* frighteningly enough, so they can spot from a mile away my most juvenile qualities, my tendencies toward grandiose pomposity and selfish whining and wide-eyed manipulation. Not that they would *say* anything necessarily, but having them around seemed like inviting dangerous regression into former stages of ourselves, exactly the stages I knew I had to leave behind. And flayed open as I was in the days after the birth, I didn't think I could tidy all those complex emotions away for the sake of presenting a mature front.

On the other hand, being a modern and extensively informed new mother, I of course felt that my parents couldn't possibly understand me at all. They raised their first baby in the unenlightened 50s, you know.

So I tried to pretend that I was grateful for my parents' help, but the truth is, I didn't even want it. No, that's not quite true, either. I did want my mom to pamper me like a five-year-old child—bake me goodies and do all the cleaning and let me take long naps. But I knew it could never be that simple again, ever.

It took me a while to figure this out, too, but my parents arrived at our doorstep with needs of their own. Grandmothers can't help but try to be mothers again. The years since their mothering days drop away, and they want to live it again, taste that sweet concentrate of experience. It's similar for grandfathers, who recall their younger, more vigorous selves, scooping up little pajamaed forms and pacing the upstairs hall with a cloth over one stout shoulder. The problem with living out this nostalgia is that the new baby's actual parents are in the way. So the grandparents, having forgotten their raw uncertainties and gathered to their memories the confidence of years, and the new parents, armed with volumes of parenting guides and nervously eager to prove themselves competent, meet among the living-room furniture in a clash of the titans. It's not really about breast vs. bottle, cloth vs. disposable, burping positions, bath soap, or layers of blankets. It's about claiming place and giving way. When this happened to us, neither Ron and I nor my parents understood consciously the grave matters at stake—power, mutability, mortality. So we argued fiercely about small matters to cover our large griefs. We flailed our way through it and did it badly.

This all led to one of those frightening moments in life when experience drags us to the top of a mountain, despite our dug-in heels and cringing faces, and forces us to look about and get some perspective. I knew my parents well enough to understand the grief behind their words, and at exactly the same moment, I felt keenly the sheer distance between their histories and ways of thinking and my own. And then I looked down at the beautiful infant daughter in my arms and tried to shoo away the obvious, horrible, and persistent thought: someday she and I, too, would feel both the adamant ties and the heartbreaking distance between us.

There's a tidy satisfaction in all this retrospective analysis. And I do believe that this is all true. But the time of transition itself just hurt, like a bewildering case of cramps. The grief would hit me in waves. I felt grief over a relationship with my parents that would never be the same. But that was one component of a larger field of loss. Whoever I had been before motherhood was gone; whoever I was becoming had not yet taken shape. I could see that it would involve a great deal more selflessness than I was used to. I remember lying on the rug in Miriam's room at five in the morning, this perfectly wide awake infant squirming happily beside me while I quietly sobbed out an unpleasant new feeling: the irreversible, inescapable realization that I was the grown-up now. This baby's needs came first, would always come first. She didn't care how I felt. Tough shit what I wanted, tough shit that I was tired. I was at once grown up enough to love her fiercely and not nearly grown up enough to bear that fierce love.

Fortunately, all this upheaval seems far worse the first time around. This time I'm used to being a mother and my parents are far more relaxed, too. Also, there's the simple geographical mercy of living within an hour's drive of all the grandparents this time, allowing us to sidestep completely the question of lengthy overnight stays. My mom and Ron's mom take turns coming over for a few hours, doing a little laundry, sweeping the kitchen floor, tucking in the baby. Then they go home. It's nice. No one is scrabbling quite so hard to get what they need. My dad comes over, too, and holds the baby, beaming and jibbering feverishly, and I can feel his deep pleasure healing over the disappointments and conflicts of the past.

Maybe becoming a mother or father would be easier for everyone if we all admitted that a new baby is not merely a crisis of hands—you need more hands to do all the baby-holding and cooking and washing required—but of the heart and spirit. My practical mother has little patience for emotional wallowing—I admire her for this because it gives her great endurance. And she would probably dismiss all this blathering about emotional transitions as "getting carried away" and then thrust her hands back in a sinkful of sudsy water. Oh well. My parents walk their own stony paths to wisdom. Me, I have to paddle a rough river of words.

Unfamiliar Hours

As the days pass, I become reluctantly familiar with each hour in the middle of the night, hours that for most of my life have swept right by as I lay there happily asleep. The way a crescent moon can hang cold in a lightening sky at four in the morning was something I knew, before having children, only from reading about it in books.

Now Philip at least sleeps between feedings at night—usually— but we can never be sure when he'll wake for the next one. I get through the unpatterned wakings by establishing a routine of my own: when baby cries, I check the time, wait a few minutes, then crawl out of bed, visit the bathroom, fill the water bottle and put on the glasses I've left on the bathroom counter, quietly enter baby's room, turn on closet light and leave closet door open a crack. Bring baby to changing table, check baby's diaper with a flashlight, change if necessary. Sink with baby into the rocking chair and drag the large pillow from the floor onto my lap. Nurse baby, checking my watch to even out the time on each breast. After nursing, burp baby on shoulder, then move baby to crib, wrapping him in the same little blankie the exact same way. Place him on his side against the little support wedge, alternate sides each time (if I remember). Turn off closet light, close baby's door, hitch up bra in the bathroom, replace water bottle and glasses (if I remember), shuffle back to bed.

The routine is supposed to help him establish regular patterns and learn that the world is a familiar, comforting place. But I think I'm the one who needs it the most. I can't think straight in the daytime these days, let alone in the night, so I tether up a routine as a kind of rope to lead me through this daze. When I sink my body into bed—lying flat on my back because lying on my side squishes my big, sore breasts—and I think rather desperately, "What will I do if he wakes again before morning?" I know what to answer. I'll wait a few minutes, crawl out of bed, visit the bathroom . . .

But how to pass those thirty or so minutes while he eats? Prayer would be the perfect answer, now wouldn't it? So I try to pray: "Dear Lord, please remember Michelle and help her to get pregnant soon. And Jennifer, too. And remember Betsy and Karen and Joy and help them to bring their babies to birth, healthy and strong. And . . ." (Mind wanders for a while. Eventually I realize mind has wandered.) "Um . . . Dear Lord, . . . uh . . . where was I?"

I've found I can handle this time of semiconsciousness better if I merely repeat in my mind something I've memorized. So let's see.

What's been rattling around in my memory long enough that I can manage to find it in the middle of the night? Hymns. Many progressively minded Christians complain these days that hymns are boring and we've sung them too long and we need new music in worship. Some of that is true, but I'm convinced that what we sing in church isn't for the thrill of the moment. It's a matter of doing the drills in order to be prepared for the real battles, the ones that happen outside the sanctuary. So there's a reason to sing the same songs all your life: then they'll be there when you need them.

The hymns that rise out of the fog in my mind during these nights are the ones that speak with a melancholy beauty about intimacy with God, or a longing for it: "Spirit of God, Descend upon My Heart," "Jesus, Lover of My Soul," "What a Friend We Have in Jesus." The second verse of "Jesus, Lover" takes on a quirky new resonance as an accompaniment to midnight nursing:

> *Plenteous grace with thee is found,*
> *Grace to cover all my sin.*
> *Let the healing streams abound;*
> *Make me, keep me pure within.*
> *Thou of life the fountain art;*
> *Freely let me take of thee!*
> *Well thou up within my heart,*
> *Rise to all eternity.*

All that flowing and welling seems fitting as I sit here, flowing into my baby. As I am a fountain of life for this infant, and he freely takes of me, so Jesus is a fountain of life to me. I don't know what that means, though. Right now I think I need a pillow more than a fountain. I do know, in these deeply weary hours, an inarticulate desire for comfort, for *someone* who *is* comfort. It is a hunger my baby knows in his way, and I in mine.

Now that we're living these first days with a newborn again, I remember that, mercifully, the difficulties are all very much in the moment. Even if the night is difficult, I'll hardly remember it the next morning, although I'll feel the thick residue of fatigue. And next month it will all blur together. I find myself taking comfort merely in the fact that time inevitably passes. I nurse the baby, carefully timing ten or fifteen minutes on one side, then switching, and I think about how the minutes do pass, and the hours, and the nights and the days. Things do get better. I know this from experience. Meanwhile, these are the days of small things. Small diapers, small fingers and toes, small prayers of gratitude when baby wakes up safe another time, small moments of pleasure when the family has a quiet meal while that baby finally naps, small triumphs when the baby feeds well or sneezes adorably, and days going by in very small units of time.

16) breastfeeding

Settled firmly into the contours of our old living-
room couch early on a sunny afternoon, I feel
Philip's soft puffs of breath against my neck as he
rises and falls on my chest, on the great ocean
swells of my own breathing. He drifted into a
snooze after finishing off the contents of one
breast, so I lifted him to my shoulder, one of
my hands folding his curled feet like leaves around
his bud of a bottom and the other hand blanketing
his flat, narrow back. My hand is so large on his
back that my fingertips curve around to trace his

pencilly ribs. Pat pat pat pat pat pat pat. So gentle, so quiet.

Then come the voices in my head. "Nurse on both sides at every feeding." "Awaken the baby with a tickle or a diaper change if he falls asleep between breasts." "Don't let the baby fall asleep after nursing or he won't learn to take a full feeding." "Snacking and snoozing leads to trouble." "You should put him down in his bassinet—babies need to learn to sleep independently right away."

Get out of my head, you stupid voices! Oh you nag me, and I'm so dazed and weak right now, I can't summon the anger to resist you. Maybe you're right. I don't know what I'm doing. I probably *am* a bad mother. Maybe I had better just do what all you experts say.

I thought it would be different this time, that with my third baby I would feel confident and competent. I read all my baby books again—couldn't help it. I chewed on them addictively, almost as hungrily as during the first two pregnancies. Had I forgotten all the details in the four years since Jacob was a baby? No, I still knew many phrases from my old books from memory. So just for a fresh hit I went out and bought a new book recommended by several friends. It was dogmatic and patronizing, written by two men, but I figured I could cull one or two good ideas from it and ignore the annoying tone. As my due date approached, I was informed, knowledgeable, experienced, prepared. But now I hold this brand-new, totally different, consternating, and often noisy little person whose perfect well-being is more important to me than anything—*anything*. And I'm so tired. What did you say I should do?

Ah, but I manage to turn down the expert-chatter volume today, just this time. My own voice comes from somewhere and says, "For heaven's sake, that poor baby was inside you just a few days ago! He wants to be close to you, and you want to feel his warmth. Just enjoy it." So we do.

C o m m i t m e n t

When I take Philip to the doctor for his two-week checkup, the scale reports that he has not only gained back his birth weight after losing seven or eight ounces in the hospital, but he has gained an additional thirteen ounces as well. I'm delighted and proud. He's all right, he's doing well, and—I give myself the credit—it's because of this magical elixir that comes from my body. So *there* all you doubters (including myself): I *am* a good mother.

And it hasn't been easy. Breastfeeding takes commitment. At first, the hours spent sitting with baby seem sweet and natural. The baby has emerged from my body into the outer world, but my fleshy self still seems his most natural nest. With my pregnancy-expanded hips and legs spread out amply on the sofa, I cradle this little piglet across my waterbed-bulge of a stomach. His head feels like a heavy marble fitting into the bend of my great, rough-skinned arm. He takes into his mouth my spongy flesh, and it seems fitting that we should spend hours joined together like this.

After a few weeks, though, a little separation starts to sound pretty nice. My energy reserves are getting mighty low and all I want is some small relief. Simple instinct only lasts so long, and then comes a suspicion that maybe what's going on here is a kind of entrapment. Some women love to be needed and thrive on the constant companionship of the little suckling, but I'm starting to feel a hint of panic, like the edges of myself are starting to blur. I need some time alone to reconstitute—just a day off or a few hours off or, oh luxury, a night off—that's all I ask.

But it's no use. I could leave baby in his daddy's good hands for a while, but my body is still producing his food, my breasts still need to be emptied. In these early weeks, the windows of free movement for me are slim and unreliable. Baby eats for twenty minutes (at least), then we get a window of forty-five minutes "wakey time," as we call it. Half of this time involves baby fussing or crying and me or Ron bouncing up and down with him, doing "the baby dance." Then, if we're lucky, baby naps for forty-five minutes, then . . . I'm on again! Take a seat and whip out the nipples! I could never do this hour after hour if my breasts weren't committed for me. I consider trying to sneak away, but the old milk ducts keep right on secreting relentlessly. "Sorry, sister," they seem to say. "We don't make the rules. We just do our job!" Philip needs me for food and I need him for relief. We are connected by mutual need, filling and emptying and filling and emptying in a still-awkward dance of dependence.

I spend a great deal of my meager mental energy on breastfeeding administration. I have to hold in my crumpled mind what time the baby last nursed and on which side to begin nursing this time and which of the three positions I used last time. I'm trying to rotate positions on the right side to ease the soreness, but so far this strategy has succeeded in making the entire circle of nipple desperately sore. My bottom still hurts, too, so that I have to walk slowly and ease down onto chairs. I'm tired of hooking and unhooking these dumb bras. And Philip may be growing, but he's still a high-maintenance nurser. I could never lie in bed and sleep while he nurses, as some women claim they do (although I don't entirely believe them). This baby likes to nod right off the minute he has a breast in his mouth; he does need plenty of coaxing to take a full meal.

At least I can honestly say that I don't mind some of the more comical coping tasks of these early days. I don't mind, for example, breastfeeding in public. My friend Leanne says she always felt embarrassed about breastfeeding her daughter in public because she (the baby) *slurped* so loudly. My babies have all been pretty quiet nursers, thankfully. And I've perfected some slick maneuvers with the drapey shirts and the hooks on the scaffolding bras. Besides, even if someone were to catch a glimpse, no one would mistake nursing prep or cleanup for a titillating display. There's nothing sexy about a lactating breast, in my opinion. Breasts in milk-mode achieve epic proportions, it's true—and we bigger-is-better Americans adore breast size far beyond reason. But there's nothing coy or flirtatious about those darkened, enlarged areolae. They cover sheer acreage; they suggest powerful weaponry; they stare in cool defiance at those brave enough to look. Good thing babies don't focus well or they might be too frightened to eat.

And I don't mind the smells, either. This is lucky, because breast milk tends to get smeared all over my front, one way or another. Fresh breast milk, wet on baby's chin or on my breast, has only a delicate odor. The sour version is less appealing, but familiar and wholesome anyway. Ron's Aunt Carol, a breastfeeding enthusiast from way back, held Philip the other day and sighed, "Oh, that wonderful sour smell! I miss it!" This smell migrates quickly from me and baby to everything else. Sour milk fumes emanate from my bra, my nightshirt, and my sheets every morning. The shirts I wear during the day smell like milk, too—especially the leak-zones and the left shoulder, where baby spits up the fresh stuff. Then I throw my clothes in the hamper, and soon all the laundry smells like sour milk. Baby's blankets and clothes smell like spit-up milk, and people who come over and hold the baby tend to leave vaguely perfumed.

The smells and the dampness aren't so bad, and I think I could even handle the constant, round-the-clock duty for a while, if it weren't for: the pain. Occasionally, even the most dedicated breast-feeding enthusiasts will concede that breastfeeding hurts. Yes indeed. Some women claim they feel a physical euphoria after breastfeeding, and some sociologists and feminist writers like to examine breast-feeding as a dimension of female sexuality. All I can say is that some women's physiology apparently allows for breastfeeding nirvana. My experience leads me to consider other aspects of mother-infant phys-iology, such as the fact that healthy, full-term infants' most highly developed muscle system is—that's right—in their jaws. Moreover, their little gums are hard as stone. After all, suckling is a matter of life and death for infants, and they're not taking chances; they've got the equipment in place to make those breasts put out. So what happens when a powerful jaw clamps down on a breast that has up till now led a pretty sheltered life? It hurts. I found out with Miriam that, while the pain issue arises frequently in discussions of childbirth, pain in nursing is more successfully clouded with propaganda. First I was told that the pain peaks at the twentieth feeding (which occurs, believe it or not, on day two or three). After two weeks of painful nursing, I was told that it typically takes six weeks to get "estab-lished." When six weeks passed and I was down from torture cham-ber levels to mere mild soreness, people started confessing that it was only after four months that "things get so much easier."

With Jacob, I found out that even experienced breasts need weeks to "toughen up" again. In fact, I had worse pain with him, al-though after six weeks it did get much better. This time, with baby Philip, one of my breasts, after two weeks of round-the-clock duty, is fairly comfortable. However, the other is slightly sore all the time and treats me to three seconds of excruciating pain whenever the baby latches on, as if his jaw were a misfiring staple gun. Because this breast also has the grim audacity to be the more readily productive of the two, Philip fusses at it, latching and unlatching several times before he gets himself into a comfortable rhythm. You would think I could manage to have a matched set of breasts—but oh, the infinite variety of nature!

The big hospital in town does have a lactation consultant. I've called her, and she's made some good suggestions about getting baby to open his mouth wide and so on. She's invited me to bring baby in so she can watch him nurse. Thank you, but figuring out how to arrive at her office with all three kids in tow at the exact time when baby is hungry—the logistics are beyond me. Anyway, technique may improve things some, but I suspect I'm dealing with one ornery breast.

During the day I can tolerate the soreness—I grimace like a gargoyle to get through the latching-on drill—but at night I can barely survive it. He wakes at 1:20 and 3:45 and 6:05, and his snuffly wails shoot like electrical current through my whole body and right out through my breasts. I groan in my bed, thinking, *Here comes that pain again.* Before dawn this morning, after feeding him every two to two-and-a-half hours all day and all night, he latched on to that sore side and I just cried—cried because it hurt, cried because I was so tired, cried because it seemed I would never ever know another way of life. Me and this needy, squirmy, staple-gun-jawed infant—forever. The tears streamed down my face and neck as he pounded innocently on my breast. I thought I couldn't do it anymore; I had reached the end of my rope. After he finished, he didn't want to go back to sleep. Ron took him downstairs for a little early morning bonding time. I went back to sleep, and God gave me just a little more rope.

The Measure of Motherhood

I know the magic is true. There are moments of great pleasure, even in these early months, despite the pain and the relentless non-schedule and sleepy-boy's need for an alert meal manager. Unfortunately, navigating the physical and logistical troubles of this "simple, natural" infant nourishment plan is not the only challenge for modern moms. There's also that problem of the voices in our heads. Nothing causes more guilt for new mothers than breastfeeding, whatever you do about it. I breastfed Miriam for nine weeks, until she decided she liked those little floppy bottle-nipples she got once a day better than working away at that big fleshy mountain, and she started refusing to nurse. I endured several days of guilt as big and painful as my engorged breasts, bought a case of formula, and vowed to "do better" next time. With Jacob I nursed for three months, dutifully hauling a breast pump with me to evening orchestra rehearsals and pumping during breaks. (I found out that men do *not* like to think about breast pumps. I once had to ask the orchestra manager for extra time at break, and when I told him the reason he nodded at me with a pained expression as if he wanted to cover his ears with his hands, close his eyes, and go "la la la la la la la la" to block out my words.) Overall, Jacob nursed well, he weaned quite happily, and I still felt guilty. I wanted to do better.

Why the feelings of failure? Because breastfeeding is "the measure of the mother" these days. We all know breast is best. Everyone says so: the American Medical Association, my doctor, most other moms I know. Even the formula companies dutifully remind us on every can and every free sample of formula we drag behind us in our little goodie bags on the way out of the hospital: "Breast is best. But if you ever need a formula . . ." And being a good girl, a good mom, I do what's best for the baby. Of course.

I'm willing to put up with a lot in order to do what's best for the baby. But it bothers me that I also want the doctor's approving smile, that I'm reduced to a child waiting with shining eyes for that pat on the head. Sociologist Linda Blum, author of a book on breastfeeding called *At the Breast*, explains with deadpan professionalism that my little-girl feelings are the result of a historically located, class-connected cultural ideology. Oh. Right. Well, it makes sense. Breast-feeding is the most obvious measure of how a woman stacks up against the ideal that requires mothers to be intensive, exclusive care-givers, doing whatever it takes to maximize the precious child's po-tential. Turns out, according to Blum's research, that the orthodoxy of "breast is best" in the United States is a recent phenomenon, and that middle-class white women are the only ones willing and able to swallow this orthodoxy whole. Working-class white women have gotten the message, too, but their tougher home situations—it's less likely, for instance, that they have a reliable "manly provider" around—mean that they are much more likely to tell their breastfeed-ing stories as tales of failure. They tried, but couldn't keep it up; they're angry at the hospital for not helping more; they're angry that they have to work because their husband is unemployed, and so on. African-American working-class women, on the other hand, are more likely to go for the bottle and not worry about it. Blum suggests that for these women, going against the orthodoxy has the cultural benefit of signaling the woman's ability to decide for herself, to make inde-pendent choices.

Meanwhile, those of us who are middle-class white women are nursing away, doing the "right thing" but still feeling guilty as the dickens because no matter what we do we can't possibly get it right.

If you don't nurse for a year, you've "quit early." If you join the La Leche League and nurse religiously, you're "a little *too* into it." God help you if you choose not to nurse at all, whatever your reason. And of course, since the message from the experts on high is short and simple—because we women are not too bright, I guess—everything about breastfeeding that *isn't* simple comes as a big surprise. If it hurts, if you feel discouraged, if you find that using a breast pump at work is more than you can stand, then it's all your fault. You're not good at it. Your body has failed—or maybe it's your *priorities,* sister. Obviously, you're willing to make *compromises* when it comes to what's best for baby.

Blum pointedly observes that breastfeeding "successfully" requires a major support network, but none of the public service information explains about that. No, it's all about fuzzy-edged, softly lit photos in which mother and infant share a heartwarmingly intimate moment together in the nursery. Real mothers, however, have to make the crabby, hungry older kids wait for dinner because baby wakes up and needs to be fed at just the moment dinner needs to be made. Real mothers have to put the baby down in the middle of a feeding—and listen to him wail—while they run to the kitchen and grab the toddler off the counter and clean up the glass she knocked over and broke. Real mothers have husbands who say they "need their sleep to be sharp for work" and refuse to take a wakeful baby at night. Real mothers only get six weeks paid leave and find out that breast pumps—the high-tech "solution" to combining breastfeeding with going back to work—cost money. Real mothers have cracked nipples and run out of clean breast pads and shed real tears.

I'm not disagreeing with the orthodoxy. I believe breast is best, and I hope I believe it for rational reasons and not just because I'm the victim of unconscious middle-class ideologies—although, clearly, I am. But I resent how the formula companies and medical associations and even doctors and hospitals hide the hard parts behind a simple message and soft silhouette, and imply that it's all about the mother's choices and character. Mothers are doomed to feelings of failure when they are told on the one hand that their "success" with breast-feeding equals their "success" as mothers, and then, on the other hand, when they have to deal with husbands, medical professionals, and employers who either don't care or don't get it.

Or extended families. I took the baby to a family birthday party at my brother's beach house. I fed the baby and then left him with his very pleased grandpa for a little while so I could go down to the beach. After a half hour or so, baby started fussing, and soon I had an envoy of alarmed relatives coming to fetch me. "You know," my dad confided, "I don't think he's getting enough. You're going to have to supplement eventually." Apparently, people forget that five-week-old babies fuss because they fuss, not necessarily because something's wrong. My mom, too, cannot bring herself to believe that a baby can survive merely on whatever pathetic substance oozes out of my breasts. After I mention getting up in the night with the baby, she replies, "You know, *our* babies always woke at two and six. Why don't you just give him some pablum?" I know she's just worried about me being tired. But I wish she would accept that I am capable of making wise choices about how to care for my baby. Come on, Mom, I'm following the current cultural orthodoxy—just like you did!

Nursing mothers need the other people in their lives to give them sleep and time off from work and help with the older kids and occasional moments of privacy and more than anything else, encouragement. It takes a village to breastfeed a baby. The sooner we all figure that out, the better.

Meanwhile, I'm trying to give myself permission to feel ambivalence. The deep connection of breastfeeding, like any good human connection, both blesses and binds. I could not bear to give up this intimate magic, but I'm trying to remember that I don't have to feel sweet and fuzzy and noble and self-sacrificial about it—not all the time.

Dreams and Archetypes

Somewhere beneath the ideological complexity, the emotional ambivalence, and the minute-by-minute mental and physical management is the basic urge. Holding the baby to the breast and feeling him tug this life-giving fluid into himself—this urge is buried in some ancient human collective memory and it wells up now in my body, pulling me, dragging me even, through the difficulties. Something ancient and universal shades and colors, too, the moments of bliss, when I lift Philip away from the breast, his tummy full, my breast blessedly slack, his scrunched little face all contentment, eyes closed, mouth still smacking lazily, my body encircling his in a combination of power and tenderness too intoxicating to resist.

This is the deep magic, the weird and simple phenomenon that commits me to this practice more than any ideology could. My body sheltered this growing creature for months, and then when he came out of me, my already swollen breasts underwent a final, bizarre transformation and began producing his food. The separation of birth is eased by the togetherness of breastfeeding. He drinks what comes from my body, and he grows.

Before Philip was born I had many dreams about breastfeeding. Sometimes I dreamed of nursing a normal baby, finding it pleasurable—assuring myself in my dream, I suppose, that I would know what to do. Sometimes my dreams revealed fears. I dreamed once that the baby was born weirdly large—it had a huge face, big blue eyes, and blond hair. I had been away from the baby for about two days after its birth for some reason I couldn't help, and when I came back I wanted to nurse the baby. But since I hadn't nursed him from the start, I had no milk. My dreams were asking, *Could I do it again? Would I be a good mother?* I suppose I had to sort through these worries, too.

That I would dream about breastfeeding so vividly suggests that doing it creates a memorable imprint on the psyche. As is true for birth-giving, breastfeeding is a profound archetype and metaphor. Many ancient cultures meditate in their art and sculpture on the figure of the madonna, the woman with an infant either at or near the breast. It is an indelible image, ancient in its dignity and beauty. In the Western tradition from the thirteenth to the seventeenth century or so, painters treated the Virgin Mary with her holy infant as a standard subject. In the earlier part of this period, it was fashionable to paint Mary with a breast exposed, even with Jesus' mouth attached. "Look! Christ was human in every way!" was the theological message. Speaking of human, the baby Jesus is usually depicted naked and with *all* his proper parts. "Yup, he had one of those!" these paintings assure curious viewers. In later paintings, the baby Jesus still wears either nothing or what looks like a wispy handkerchief (Didn't Jesus need diapers?), while Mary is often fully covered in folds of rich fabrics. The emphasis shifted, apparently, from Jesus' humanity to Mary's royalty as Queen of Heaven. And the symbolism became more complex: Mary's lap as the altar, the wispy diaper as the shroud, suggesting the Son's future sacrifice and the sacrament that commemorates it. My favorite painting of this genre is one called "Madonna of the Book," by fifteenth-century Italian painter Sandro Botticelli.

Mary sits at a reading desk, tracing her finger over lines of Scripture, while Jesus, clearly a wiggly toddler, stands up on her knee. Even Mary, it seems, had a hard time getting a moment's peace.

We don't often see contemporary, real-life images of the nursing mother. It seems we are a little embarrassed, partly because the breast has been so intensely sexualized in our culture—in a way that, we forget, is foreign to the past and to other cultures. We are also embarrassed, I think, because breastfeeding is part of the whole pregnancy-childbirth cycle that we have attempted to relegate to the medical realm. The image of the nursing mother pushes uncomfortably against that fencing. We do see mild madonnas in formula brochures and on hospital maternity floors, but the nursing mother is usually depicted in fuzzy outline with soft lighting caressing her gently glowing face—a kooky juxtaposition with the science of baby formula. Such images are domesticated, tame. The mother and child float in a safely circumscribed world of soft yellow blankets, bumper pads, and comfy rockers. There's little sense of the power and dignity of nourishing a new human out of one's own body.

Those European Renaissance paintings of Mary, varied as they are, present in the Virgin's clear features and queenly brocades and in their ancillary details—a cross in the background, a local landscape— some sense of the deep implications, for the mother-child pair and for the world around them, of what they are doing. Mary is situated in the world—one can see it out the window behind her, for example. And what she does shapes human history and shakes the universe. Perhaps it would encourage and empower modern mamas if we could return to this kind of located realism, in which we would see modern women going about their tasks in the world matter-of-factly connected to their busily nestled babies. Imagine a photo of a softball coach with a baby snoozing on her shoulder while she instructs her team from the bench. Or a judge with her robe open, nursing while she goes over a brief.

We could stand to reemphasize the cosmic implications of this uniquely feminine work, too. While the development of safe, reliable infant formula in many ways frees women and saves babies, symbolically speaking it removes women from their sole position as indispensable nourishers of life. From ancient times, breastfeeding has been one vital practice that connects real live women to divine powers. In an age when many are hoping to regain a sense of the divine feminine, this is still an area of potential reconnection.

All the contemporary major religions have some way of representing a feminine aspect of the divine. Kali, for example, from the Hindu traditions, or the Great Mother figures of Taoism, Buddhism, and Native American religions, or the concept of God's mercy and compassion from Islam. The figure of the Virgin from Christianity contrasts with all these conceptions of divine femininity in that Mary, however exalted, remains human. Technically, she is not part of the godhead—a distinction that some might complain makes Christianity the great discriminator: the feminine principle can't break through the celestial glass ceiling. But Mary's humanity is useful in its meanings both for women and men: she exemplifies the great paradoxes of God's relationship with human beings. God chooses Mary and Mary obeys. But this leads to an astonishing emptying of Godself (the Greek work is *kenosis*), the humbling of the God-lover before the soul-beloved. Mary becomes the mother of God, the nourisher and shelterer of the Most High; she nurses the First Principle at her breast. In this way, God honors the creatures of his making in a reversal profound enough for many centuries' meditation.

Those who object to the exaltation of Mary sometimes complain that Mary presents everyday women with an impossible ideal—virgin and madonna. How are we supposed to emulate *that*? Others suggest that Mary as a figure of surrender and obedience perpetuates the association of these fundamental postures only with women. Perhaps to resolve these difficulties we need to celebrate a Jewish concept of the divine feminine: the Shekinah. From the mystical practices of Judaism comes this idea—or more precisely, experience—of God as a deeply feminine presence. The term Shekinah is related to the Hebrew word for "dwelling." In the Hebrew Scriptures, the Shekinah is the glory of God dwelling among his people, the radiance of theophany. The medieval Kabbalists who meditated on the Shekinah came to think of it as the feminine aspect of God, that part of God closest to the created world, figured often in their writings as mother, sister, daughter, bride, princess. It is both the dazzling beauty of God and God's loving nearness, even amid suffering and exile. It is the part of God that God turns toward us when we look up in hope. The perfect human analogue of this is the nursing mother. As she embraces and feeds her child, she bends her face down toward the child in a loving gaze, reflecting—can we perceive it?—the glorious face of God.

Breastfeeding's Classic Hits

I sometimes get to jar my students into considering how the practical and mystical combine in the image of the nursing mother and infant. I don't exactly go out of my way to bring up breastfeeding in literature class, but why ignore it when we find it? St. Augustine's famous autobiography, for instance, from which I assign excerpts in my world lit class, dives into the topic of breastfeeding within the first five or six pages. Augustine addresses the story of his life to its original Author, and he begins in a most surprising place for a man of the ancient world: at his mother's breast, where he finds the earliest tableau of grace in the mural of his life:

> Thus for my sustenance and my delight I had woman's milk: yet it was not my mother or my nurses who stored their breasts for me: it was Yourself, using them to give me the food of my infancy, according to Your ordinance and the riches set by You at every level of creation. It was by Your gift that I desired what You gave and no more, by Your gift that those who suckled me willed to give me what You had given them: for it was by the love implanted in them by You that they gave so willingly that milk which by Your gift flowed in the breasts. It was good for them that I received good from them, though I received it not *from* them but only through them: since all good things are from You, O God, and *from God is all my health.*

Augustine here searches out every detail of God's delicate care for him. His longing to praise God's love and fathom its mysteries also takes him back to the shrouded origin of his own personhood: "Tell me, God, tell your suppliant, in mercy to your poor wretch, tell me whether there was some period of my life, now dead and gone, which preceded my infancy?" He does not understand nor remember, he writes, but like a curious child who wants to poke around in all the corners of an intriguing topic, he wonders aloud before God about infants in the womb and at the breast. One of Augustine's biographers, Garry Wills, speculates that Augustine's astonishingly frank and detailed descriptions of nursing and infant behavior came directly from observing his son's infancy—the son who was born to him and his mistress while he was still a very young man. But like all of his *Confessions* (or *Testimony,* the translation of the title Wills prefers) every passage of Augustine's particular life is placed in the context of an all-encompassing theological reality: God's gracious ordering of the ordinary mysteries of our lives.

Breastfeeding comes up in world lit class again when we visit the Christian mystics of medieval Europe. The uninitiated often think that "mystics" must be mystical, by which they mean vague and cloudy. Some of them are. But others, particularly women mystics, are almost too earthy for comfort. Mechthild of Magdeburg, for instance, who lived in the twelfth century in what is now Germany, describes one of her visions of the Virgin and actually finds theological import in leaking breasts:

> Then it was seen how nobly our Lady stood by the Throne on the left of the heavenly Father, in all her maidenly beauty, and how her human body was formed and tempered in the noble likeness of her soul; how her comely breasts were so full of sweet milk that drops of it flowed down to the glory of the Father, for the love of man, that man might be welcomed above all creatures.

Leaking breasts glorifying God? Not the first thought that comes to mind when the breast pads get soggy. But as with many mystics, once you get over the weirdness, it starts to make sense. Superabundant grace, superabundant breasts. As a symbol, it works.

As if that weren't enough about breasts in one semester, next in line comes Julian of Norwich, the fourteenth-century English mystic. Julian manages to thoroughly startle my conventionally trained

Protestant students by creating a rather freely drawn but convincing picture of Jesus as Mother:

> The mother can give her child suck of her milk, but our precious Mother Jesus can feed us with himself, and does, most courteously and most tenderly, with the blessed sacrament. . . . The mother can lay her child tenderly to her breast, but our tender Mother Jesus can lead us easily into his blessed breast through his sweet open side, and show us there a part of the godhead and of the joys of heaven, with inner certainty of endless bliss.

This is just too much for some of my students. But the less squeamish and more theologically adventurous can see that Julian wants to picture for us the gentle, attentive, "courteous" love of God. And the best picture she knows for that is the mother, especially the nursing mother. The love of Jesus, most painfully condensed in his sacrifice on the cross, is commemorated in the sacrament of communion; and in the sacrament, communicants believe that by a spiritual mystery they eat and drink the body and blood of Christ—take him into themselves for spiritual nourishment. Not so hard to see why Julian connects Jesus' love and a mother's love: both are, in their rock-bottom physical reality, a literal pouring out of the self. That reference to the wound in the side that Jesus suffered on the cross takes Julian's connection to another level—do we mothers not feel our love for our children like a wound in the gut and a gateway to bliss at once? No one knows much about Julian, whether she had ever been a mother or even if her name really was Julian. But she understood some of the deeper mysteries—of God and I think of motherhood, too.

When you consider how many hours, out of the total aggregate hours of human lives, have been spent in the act of breastfeeding, either as infant or as mother, it's a wonder that art and literature aren't well stocked with realistic depictions of breastfeeding and meditations on its symbolic resonances. Instead, references to breastfeeding either thin out to cliché or feature obvious inaccuracies. The famous, melodramatic climax of John Steinbeck's novel *Grapes of Wrath,* for instance, always struck me as suspect. Three days after Rose of Sharon gives birth to a stillborn infant, she's going to offer some old man her breast? Where's the mention of her painful engorgement to that point? And didn't Steinbeck know that an adult mouth is not at all shaped properly for suckling? It's not like using a straw, you know! Even women writers don't always get it right. Maxine Hong Kingston's otherwise gorgeous and chilling story "No Name Woman" describes a woman giving birth and then immediately nursing the infant till its stomach is full. Doesn't she know that just after birth breasts only produce colostrum, and only in tiny, concentrated amounts? Who knew this was an area requiring research?

Holiness in the Embrace

Dante at least uses breastfeeding appropriately as a symbol. In the *Divine Comedy,* he compares Dante-the-pilgrim to a nursing infant in order to describe his eager desire to drink up the light of Paradise. In John Ciardi's translation, the term "aureole" appears many times in the *Paradiso* to refer to the aura of light that surrounds the holy saints of heaven, especially Dante's beloved Beatrice. The technical term for the area around the nipple—areola—comes from a different root, but here's another apt merging of sound and meaning in the English language. The bright circle of the halo, the dark circle of the breast—the similarity of sounds reminds me that this act of self-giving and other-nourishment has a holiness about it.

So does this mean my breast is a holy thing? Am I a source of grace to Philip, a conduit of God? I suppose so. It's hard to get through all the clutter to reach that thought. And if, in the symbolism of grace at work here, I am in the position of God, well then it's a good thing I believe in a God who knows the weakness of the flesh. Because I don't feel godlike at all. Instead, I feel humbled and even, pretty often, helpless. Power and dignity are present in the idea of breastfeeding, the image of it, but the reality at first is mostly about mutual weakness. Philip and I, infants together in the caring embrace of a motherly God beyond and around us both.

I recall this hushed holiness from my first two babies in the form of deeply imprinted images. I see myself in the corner of Miriam's darkened room, rocking with her, patting her back, singing softly. But even more clearly, I remember rocking in that same glider-rocker in the downstairs bedroom with Jacob, nursing him and looking out the low window onto the neighbors' gardens in the late-summer Iowa twilight. As the shadow of the house slowly pushed the golden sunlight upward, darkening the leafy greens of the garden, fireflies bobbed over the tomato plants and it seemed, in those moments, that angels must be dancing above the lacy asparagus tops.

There have been beautiful moments with Philip, too, especially just before bedtime, when he's clean and in his jammies, and he nurses with his eyes closed until his whole body relaxes, curled warm against mine. Soon I will be able to enjoy this more, I tell myself. Right now, he and I still need to learn trust. We who care for him must simply wait and see, trying to nudge him into patterns of sleeping and waking and eating that are comprehensible to dim creatures like us. And he must learn to trust that I am there when he needs me, and that the world can be a fine and pleasant and interesting place. So I endure these hard weeks, ever hopeful that tonight will go better, tomorrow he'll be a day older, and together we'll be that much closer to a more settled existence.

17) later weeks

For the first time today, Philip looked straight at me while nursing, as if to say: *I like this—I like you.* We often have times of real communication now, wide-awake looking into one another's eyes, mutual adoration. His early, fleeting smiles have blossomed into smiles of such delight his little cheeks can't seem to spread wide enough. He's lost that wisdom-of-the-ages newborn-baby look, the one that makes a boy baby look like a miniature, smooth-skinned old man. Now he looks more innocent, as if he's forgotten the sorry truth about the world and he's ready to enjoy himself. When we bring our faces close to his and bask in the mutual love rays, it seems we can at last know *him*.

Miriam and Jacob have begun their school routine, Ron is busy again at the college. I go in twice a week to teach one class. Baby doesn't care much about our more structured fall schedule, though, so we still seem to navigate a scattering of fragments: days and nights divided into brief, erratic cycles of feeding and sleeping, Philip alternating between smiling, snoozing, waking, and crying his lungs out, and me with my mind a fluttering of thought-pieces, my moods rising and plummeting several times a day.

Fragments

This was all harder the first time around, when the shock of the baby as literal burden continually rattled me. I felt as if I would never again have both hands free. Everything I did required skewed elbows and a sturdy back, because babies like to be held. They cry less when held, which is good for one's sanity. So I was always carrying a baby on my left forearm or slung over my shoulder. Would I ever be able to hold the toast with one hand while I spread butter with the other? Would I ever be able to hoist the laundry basket up the stairs with both handles rather than dragging it, bumpety-bump, behind me? And what about going to the bathroom? Would I ever be able to do that without hitching my pants back up inch by inch, front-back, front-back, with one hand?

This time, I already know the answer: No. It's true that eventually the baby grows and lands on his feet and walks around, and you do have two hands free, at least for a few minutes at a time. Of course, then children enter a period of several years (sometimes decades), during which they are as civilized and controllable as goats. But even when baby is sleeping and damage control is not the issue, it feels as if you never put him down. People talk about how children change your life, by which they usually mean the day-to-day arrangements of what you do. But the real change is inside. A child changes the shape of your soul. No longer am I only myself; always, always this baby is on my mind, in my heart. Miriam and Jacob altered the contours of my soul before they were born and have settled there for good. Over the years, they have enlarged it, I think, stretching it even more quickly than their small bodies have grown.

This deep alteration is different from marriage, though that changes the psyche, too, or at least it ought to. I'm connected to Ron, hooked together side by side like two kids in a three-legged race (and sometimes about that graceful). But the babies, I *carry* in every way. So I'm not shocked by Philip as a new bundle on *me*—I said good-bye long ago to my independent, streamlined, hands-free self. Philip simply makes me more bulky, psychically speaking.

Maneuvering around the corners of life—changes, decisions, growth—is much more complicated when it's not just me: it's all of us now. Parents can never use the little carry-baskets in the great, crowded grocery store of life. Instead, they have to push a big cart up and down the aisles, skidding along with all the kids clinging and clamoring. And sometimes behaving like goats.

∾

Baby barely slept today—twenty-minute naps and then awake again and wanting to eat. Every time he dozed off looking good and ready for a long nap, it was time to go drop off Jacob or pick up Miriam, so I couldn't tuck him away comfortably in his bed. And of course, in transferring him from car to school or school to car or car to home, he woke up. And that was the end of naptime.

Even when I do tuck him away at home for a nap, he keeps popping up again. I close his door and lie down myself, thinking I can finally get a little rest. Just as I sink into sleep—sniffle, snort, snertle . . . waaah! This has happened dozens of times. He can't seem to stay asleep for long during the day. How can he get by on these micronaps? It's killing me.

≈

My feeling about diapers is that, unlike many problems parents face, this one I know how to solve. People without children often imagine that diapering baby bottoms is the worst part of being a parent. They think of the smells, the mess, and worst of all, becoming part of a club whose members talk constantly, specifically, and with inappropriate fascination about their baby's waste products. This is all true. But something about changing diapers puts everything in perspective. Hey, this is the nitty-gritty, down-and-dirty, honest-to-God truth about life on this earth. The uninitiated are welcome to carry on in their fantasy world where poop is a taboo topic, but the fact is, poop is part of life. Actually, anyone with a medical professional in the family already knows this. Ron's brothers and sisters love to tease their dad about all the times he took calls at the dinner table and asked patients over the phone, without lowering his voice one bit, "Any blood in the stool?"

≈

When Miriam was a baby we invested in one of these sling things, these droopy pouches of fabric that wrap around you, neck to hip. Miriam *loved* the sling. We would fold her legs up pretzel-wise (babies are surprisingly flexible) and sit her up in the sling, facing outward, like a drooling, smiling Buddha. The sling allows the parent, theoretically, to hold the baby a lot and still have both hands free. With the Buddha position, though, you have to steady the tippy baby with one hand every few seconds, and if you need to bend over, you had better swing one arm around baby to prevent an unfortunate ejection.

The greatest benefit of the sling is that it allows the father to carry the child. Ron spent hours fussing around the house, doing this and that, with Miriam happily perched up front. He turned it into a manly achievement thing: Look how much I can accomplish while in charge of the baby! He says now that literally bearing the weight of the baby against his body imprinted her on his heart. It helped him to realize that he could never again do any task without considering her needs, too. Unfortunately, Jacob didn't like the sling much and Philip doesn't seem to either. Oh well. Ron is already father-trained.

~

Days are still pretty erratic. But three evenings in a row now, we've roughed out a routine. I can't manage to feed baby at a convenient hour—either before our big-people meal is ready or after we've eaten it—so I end up sitting at the table with a pillow and a nursing baby in my lap. I hold baby with one arm and put my fork in the other hand, then switch sides with both. After supper, Philip wiggles in his bouncy seat while we do dishes. Miriam and Jacob entertain him, waving rattles in his face and singing too loudly. Then, Ron or I haul baby around on one arm while scooping up stray socks, putting books away, and pulling pajama tops over the kids' heads with the other hand.

After Miriam and Jacob are in bed, it's bath time for Philip in his little plastic tub recliner—or maybe just a quick touch-up lying on a folded towel on the bathroom counter. Once he's snapped snugly into his footie pajamas, I lay him on the floor in the living room and we keep each other company in a circle of lamplight in the otherwise darkened house. I'm trying to stretch the time before his last feeding, thinking (no doubt erroneously) that the later he goes to bed, the later he'll start the day in the morning. I'm too tired to do anything else, so I just lie there with him. After a bath his fine brown hair sticks straight up—his first hairdo—and in the dim light the soft ends glow gold like a halo. When he gets fussy and restless, I take him up and nurse him in his dark room. He falls asleep, I lay him in his crib and cover him with one of my two favorite blankets (he doesn't care which blanket, but I do), close the door silently, pad down the hall, hitch up the scaffolding, and crawl into bed. Three evenings in a row: it's a start.

≈

For some reason, babies seem to require a specialized vocabulary. Blame it on an outburst of creativity or maybe on lack of sleep—new parents can't seem to call things by their usual names. For instance, when dealing with the day-to-day pooping activities of our babies, Ron and I have used the word "sklorch," as in: "I think baby has a sklorchy-pants." After much pondering, we've decided this is the word that best describes what babies do in their diapers: they sklorch. And not only, unfortunately, in their diapers. In the early weeks, baby poo happens very quickly and in large volumes, which means that even diapers with the most advanced containment technology are helpless against the onslaught. At least once a day—sometimes after much tummy burbling and sometimes amid ominous silence—that telltale mustard color seeps through the cute little outfit, and of course baby sits there looking altogether pleased with himself. We signal the red alert like the engineering crews of the *Star Trek* starships when the engine malfunctions and threatens to explode the ship into space dust: "We have a warp core breach!"

~

So what was the point of my education again? Wasn't it designed to produce a disciplined, hardy mind, capable of vast swaths of concentration and elaborate structures of sustained thought? Ha! What a laugh! That kind of mental luxury is dandy for those not engaged in the real sweat of civilization: motherhood. Anyone can think straight who can spend whole days in the library. That's for sissies. Try having a sustained, sophisticated thought after physical trauma, weeks of broken sleep, and forty straight minutes of bouncing up and down and side to side with a fussy, fretful baby.

~

The patience, still the patience for this nursing. Seven times a day, at least thirty minutes each time. The patience I need radiates outward from the minutes of nursing, to the days till he's older, to the years when the children are in school, to the years when they no longer need me and my days are fully my own again. I tell myself to enjoy these moments, and sometimes I do. But it's hard. I'm so tired.

~

Probably one of the biggest accomplishments of civilization—I heard historian Elizabeth Fox-Genovese say this in a lecture once—is getting the father to share in the raising of the child. However complex or conflicted a woman may feel about her parental responsibility, it's unusual for her *not* to feel it. Apparently, it's not as automatic for men. But once a man becomes a father, he must not be allowed to go on thinking of himself as a hands-free individual. Slings for everyone, I guess. I have a feeling this won't be enough.

~

Spending many minutes per day putting food in one end of the baby and then wiping up the mess when it comes out the other has a way of exposing all manner of pretense in the nondiapering world. My friend Jennifer confirmed my own feeling that being a parent makes one suddenly impatient with frivolous posturing and posing. I've always inquired about famous authors, like Virginia Woolf, for example, "Yes, but did she ever clean a toilet?" My friend Jennifer, the professional violinist, tells me that caring for a baby changed her perspective on certain pieces of music. She says that she used to think a certain virtuoso violin sonata by the composer Eugene Ysaye was a fine piece. But after her daughter, Joanna, was born, she became completely annoyed with it. "It's so trite and shallow," she says. "Obviously, this man *never* changed a diaper."

Naked Babies

The days and nights cycle on, and somehow Philip's baptism slipped in and got caught in the circle of days and happened. At least I'm pretty sure it did. Man, it was nothing like Miriam's or Jacob's. I remember being much wider awake for theirs. It seems like the mother ought to be present in mind and spirit, as well as body, for her child's baptism. But I guess they happen either way. Maybe a sleepy mother better illustrates the theology behind infant baptism: God reaches out first to us in grace. It's not something we have the power to do or earn.

We were young, idealistic parents when Miriam was born, so of course we decided that the usual way of baptizing in our church—sprinkling the baby's forehead with drops of water—was not good enough for *our* baby. The symbolism of sprinkling, we decided, was positively anemic. We were going to do something *dramatic*. So with the permission of our senior pastor, a very patient man, we decided to baptize Miriam naked. Yes, even without a diaper. We brought her to the font wrapped in a blanket, dispensed with modesty, and dunked her right in. Ron's mother came in as a guest pastor and did the actual splashing. I made a little white robe to wrap Miriam in afterward, keeping in mind the verse from Galatians: "All of you who were baptized into Christ have clothed yourselves with Christ." I think we shocked quite a few of the older ladies who sat in the back pews, but they recovered. Two years later we did it again with Jacob.

All of this was extremely important to us. This time, frankly, we have less energy to care how it's done. We've since moved to Michigan and now go to a much bigger church. Instead of carefully planning a service, complete with specially requested music, we told the musicians: "Whatever." Instead of a coffee afterward with baked goods and relatives, we all went home and collapsed. We still did the naked baby routine, though. We considered going with the cute white outfit and the risk-free sprinkle. "Yes, but we've set a precedent," we sighed. "We'd better do all the kids the same way."

So we got permission from our pastor—another patient and understanding man—and Ron's mom risked getting tinkled on again.

And it went fine. We managed to show up on time and no unauthorized tinkling occurred. No one in our family was quite sure where to stand, the musicians messed up a little, and we didn't get even one good picture. But none of that really matters. God spoke Philip's name. That's what matters.

We got a kind note a few days later from a retired pastor in our congregation. He wrote:

> Dear Ron and Deb,
> Last Sunday morning was a mountaintop experience. A most precious moment for you as parents. The holy sacrament . . . and your little son's honest garb before his Savior's face. Brought tears of joy.

Honest garb. Thank you for that phrase. That's what we've wanted to remind ourselves and our babies all along: God loves us even in our naked helplessness; grace comes to us in our honest garb and sets us free.

~

Once in a while it hits me again that I have given birth to three babies. Yes, by grace and with lots of help. But *I* did it, thank you very much. When people speak of doctors as the ones who deliver babies, they're getting it wrong. Sharon Olds gets it right in her poem "The Language of the Brag." In the first half of the poem, the speaker recalls a long-held desire to do something with her body to match the feats recorded in poetry about male heroes—some strenuously physical feat that wins an appreciative audience, something courageous and impressive, something "epic." In the second half of the poem, Olds vividly describes pregnancy and the act of giving birth, holding up this feat as her answer to all the male achievements invoked in the first part of the poem. She even names Allen Ginsberg and Walt

Whitman, American poets she counts as her predecessors, and claims to have outdone them. The poem ends triumphantly, declaring:

> I have done this thing,
> I and the other women this exceptional
> act with the exceptional heroic body,
> this giving birth, this glistening verb....

The poem stands as her boast, on behalf of herself and other women, for a splendid act of strength and courage that no man has ever achieved.

Today I am feeling fierce and proud: I have delivered three babies to the world, and I, too, claim this boast.

~

I was indignant enough about TV when I was pregnant. Now I can't bear it one bit. Don't those people with their TV guns and their stupid TV story lines realize that every human being was a baby once? That every human body formed miraculously in some woman's womb, that someone had to feed the baby and shelter it, that thousands upon thousands of hours and incalculable care are required to coax a person to adulthood? I don't see how anyone who has cared for an infant can find pretend destruction of human flesh exciting or entertaining.

~

Am I getting a little cavalier, a little ungrateful? Before Philip was born, I carried right in front of my mind every nightmarish thing that could go wrong for him, and I was obsessively aware that a healthy baby is a miraculous gift. A common one, but not to be underappreciated even for a moment. If I could just be grateful enough, constantly enough, then nothing bad would happen—right?

Now that Philip is here and so obviously lively and thriving, I don't worry about lurking fatal diseases anymore. Instead, my anxieties spin round and round a much smaller circle. Will he sleep for an hour this time? Is he getting a full tummy? If I take him for a walk, will he snooze in the stroller and mess up my plan to have him nap when we get back?

~

People who are into meditation or yoga or intensive prayer or poetry are always talking about being "present to the moment." No doubt being present to the moment leads these people to golden vistas of profound experience and wisdom. Right now, though, I can't figure out how to get all of me present and accounted for at all, let alone paying attention. Some part of me is drowning, submerged, not breathing. Sometimes this takes me to the edge of desperation. But what can I do? The only way out is through—again.

The trouble is, those lost parts of me have previous commitments that just sit there on the calendar waiting for my arrival. I look ahead to the things I have committed to—a lecture, an article, my students' papers—and I want to cry. I have not had more than twenty minutes of uninterrupted concentration in a row for months. How will I do these things? How will I do them well?

Ron is gone a lot these days, working more to make up for my reduced teaching load and income. When he's away I feel an awful loneliness. The great spiritual writer Henri Nouwen says that one basic task of the spiritual life is to turn loneliness to solitude. But how can I turn loneliness to solitude when there *is* no solitude, ever?

Loneliness doesn't always happen all alone in a quiet house. Some-times, as many mothers know, the worst loneliness is the kind you feel in a house full of noise and activity. Even if I could get a few calm minutes alone, I cannot keep company with myself when parts of me are missing. God is present, I guess. But we are not having pleasant, chatty conversations these days, that's for sure.

~

There's something weirdly personal and immediate about any corpse I see on the news or in a magazine photo. The silent, still body always reminds me of—this is bizarre—a sleeping baby. I suppose a sleeping baby, with its barely visible breaths and absolutely relaxed features, has something in common with a body whose life is finished: a still-ness beyond history, perhaps, that mocks the world's frantic roilings. Or maybe being responsible for a single creature's life has awakened my heart to the fragility and vulnerability of all people and even all living things. I see my own baby in any small, needy creature—birds, puppies, anything with big, pleading eyes. I want to gather in every helpless thing I see. If only tenderness could be truer and stronger, always, than destruction.

~

I walk through the days automatically, in a fog. I wonder if my class can tell that I'm barely managing. Some days I ask my students how they're doing, and they groan dramatically about how tired they are. "Ya buncha wussies!" is what I want to say. But instead I give them a sympathetic smile.

I know I'm not as sharp as usual, but it's been so long I can't even gauge how diminished I am. At least once a day, exhausted and discouraged, I don't think I can go on, I cry. If I can get a nap, carefully timed between Philip-feedings, I can usually gain the stamina to go a little further. I long ago used up my energy reserves. Now I'm deep into credit.

I'm beginning to understand the phrase "out of your mind." I seem to occupy only part of my mind. This parenting renovation project has closed off the larger rooms and I'm living on card tables and boxes in a few cramped mental spaces.

Volume, Volume, Volume

Well, I think we can be quite sure now that we have another urping baby on our hands. I am not talking about spit-up. Spit-up is dainty and dribbles down the chin, maybe spots a little on the adorable white collar. No, we're talking big, voluminous glops of half-digested milk that soak right through the burp cloth on your shoulder—or miss it altogether and slop down your back.

Fortunately, sort of, we've been through this before. Jacob was a terrible urper. During his first few weeks, he seemed so sweet and even-tempered that Jennifer—who is Jewish by blood and Unitarian by upbringing—declared that he must be the Messiah. But when he started urping all over everyone, we knew for sure that he was just a normal guy. Jacob's urping began when he was a few weeks old and went on till he was about eleven months. It never bothered him one bit. He would lie there babbling happily, then, with no warning at all, a fountain of goo would come out of his mouth—then he would go right back to babbling and wiggling. Our doctor told us it was just a developmental abnormality of the stomach valve, and he would grow out of it. Medicating him for it would not be worth the risks. So we put up with it. At first we laughed. Then, especially when he would nail us on the sleeve or (yuk!) the back of the neck, we'd get exasperated: "Oh, *Jacob!*" Life got really gross when he was old enough to eat brightly colored baby food *and* crawl around on the carpet. We practiced our carpet-stain removal techniques many times daily. And of course there were unbelievably large and odoriferous piles of laundry.

So here we go again. In fact I think Philip might be worse. Laying him on the floor without a big blanket under him is a shockingly reckless act. And we must never, never hold him without protection. When I see other parents holding their babies, just holding them without any burp cloths whatsoever, I get jittery. I want to dash over and jab something under that baby's mouth before the little time bomb explodes.

In church the other day, I was holding Philip up against my shoulder during the service. Two teenage boys were sitting behind me, and Philip was smiling at them and charming them. I could hear them murmuring with pleasure at this cute baby. Suddenly I could feel Philip lay a big glop on his cloth. "Oh gross!" the two boys hissed to each other, giggling and horrified.

⁓

I do worry about SIDS. That's the main specter of horror for new parents, I suppose. Especially in the first few weeks I sent up a bubble of thanks every time he awakened from sleep: he's still breathing! Lately, however, even that worry is subsiding because it seems clear that Philip is extremely gifted at waking up. He does it more times per day than he really needs to, by my calculations.

The Jesus Thing

I'm not a spiritually precocious Christian, by which I mean that Jesus, as a *person,* still mystifies me. The theology all makes sense to me—the Son is the second person of the Trinity, became incarnate, atones for sins, orders the universe, ushers in the New Creation. I love the theology. I want my universe to hang together in a perfectly ordered, flexible net of thought. So I'm completely in love with the *idea* of Christ. But what does it mean, really, to *know* Jesus?

Some people are naturals at this. Some of my eighteen-year-old women students, for instance, speak about Jesus as if he were the perfect boyfriend, holding their hand all day and whispering encour-agement. That sounds too sweet and naïve, but it actually seems to keep them strong long after many of their young women peers have gone cynical and sad. The older, saintly people I know seem to have it worked out in a different way. They're more circumspect, but when they write or speak about Jesus, it's clear they've gone down some long roads in the company of this other Person.

For some reason, though, I'm still intimidated by Jesus. After all, in many of the Gospel stories, Jesus gets pretty harsh with comfort-able, brainy, religious types. When we lived in Princeton while Ron was in seminary, I would often cut through the yard of the Episcopal church on my way to the library. There was a life-size sculpture there of Jesus bent over almost horizontal under the weight of the cross. With one hand he steadies the cross and with the other he reaches out, his lips parted as if to say: "This is all *your* fault." Or maybe that's just how I perceived it. Sometimes I think that if the doorbell were to ring, and I were to open the front door to find Jesus standing there, he would be standing with his hands on his hips, frowning. "You're not very radical," he would state flatly. "And I'm kind of peeved at you for being middle class."

At least this is how I often imagine things, until I remind myself about Jesus as good shepherd and healer, friend to many kinds of people, the one who fills the big gap between what I am and what I'm supposed to be.

These days, though, the theology-savvy part of my brain has gone dormant, and I seem to have misplaced whatever neurotic Calvinist guilt I usually carry around. And in the middle of the night, rocking with Philip in the dark, I have no clear thoughts left at all. Just a kind of messy blob of me. And that's when I feel *him,* quietly *there,* like a friend who knows you so well there's no need to say anything.

So many others have testified through the ages that in the midst of sorrow or failure, loneliness or simply weakness, that's when Jesus throws off our conceptual cloaks and becomes a person, mysteriously present, closer and more gentle than the most comforting human embrace. *Jesus loves me, this I know.* Even Karl Barth, after writing huge volumes of ponderous German theology, summarized his life's work by admitting that's the heart of it all.

~

Who is this person, Philip? His eyes are fully open to the world now, his arms springing out to reach for what it will offer him, his little legs bicycling madly against earthly ills. But who will he be? We compare him so often to his siblings: he looks exactly like Jacob, he wiggles constantly like Miriam. But how will he shape these comparisons into himself?

~

I figured out today how many hours I have logged so far breastfeeding baby. It came to about 300. Then I took a little inventory of the peculiar circumstances under which I've provided meals. Several times Philip has awakened just before I had to go pick up Jacob from preschool—not enough time to feed the baby and still get there on time. So I whipped him into the car, drove to school, and fed him in the car while I waited for the bell to ring. I've nursed him right in my seat at church—we're allowed to get a little earth-mothery at my church. Once I fed him while bouncing around in a moving golf cart. Ron's whole family was together for a summer reunion, and his dad wanted to give us a tour of a beautiful new golf course. Well, just as we got there, guess what? Hungry baby. So I climbed aboard, lifted my shirt, attached baby, and we lurched off. Philip was a little perturbed by the situation, but he did OK. Later that same day, we visited an art gallery in Saugatuck, Michigan, where sculptor Marcia Perry was exhibiting her annual "goddess show." Her studio was filled with gorgeously undulating, highly polished wood sculptures of the female figure. There I sat in their solid presence, nursing my baby. I must have looked like performance art.

≈

Philip is twelve weeks old. He is still getting me up twice a night. The four o'clock feeding doesn't bother me so much. It comes, I guess, at some naturally lighter point in my sleep cycle, or whatever's left of it. But that midnight feeding kills me. It makes my head hurt. Ron has offered again and again to give the baby a bottle, but I always say no. I might as well feed him myself. My breasts would wake me up anyway by getting too full. They'd adjust after a few nights, but who can think that far ahead?

≈

Do I love him? He is not someone, quite yet, to love. And I'm not quite capable of fully conscious, mature love, either. Real love, as Martin Buber said, is an I-Thou affair. Philip and I aren't standing up that straight yet. We're more on the level of me-him. Yet even when I can barely lift my body off the sofa, when I'm completely frustrated with him, I find that I love him out of habit or instinct or something plainly physical and almost unfeeling. I'm driven to love him with my body. I perform the tasks of caring for him because he needs it and therefore I must. Well, I think this still counts as love. All of loves' days can't be filled with heroic acts of human fullness. Love goes through stages of plain, numb actions.

The numb places begin to throb, though, when I'm away from him. Even a few hours apart from him is barely tolerable. I long for relief from his demands, but then when I'm away, it hurts. And not just because my breasts are filling up. Despite that, there's a physical emptiness in the middle of my chest. Nothing relieves it except holding him there again.

~

The Bible says that God attends to all the small cares of our lives. "The very hairs of your head are numbered," Jesus told his disciples, by way of assuring them that God knows all their fears and needs. We teach our children to bring their tiny concerns to God, their bumped knees and colds and hard days at school. As a grown-up, though, I try to keep my requests on the grander scale, be duly grateful, and avoid bothering such an important deity with frivolous details.

But lately as I pad to Philip's room at four in the morning, that old warhorse of a hymn seems less sentimental and more profound:

What a friend we have in Jesus
All our sins and griefs to bear
What a privilege to carry
Everything to God in prayer.

Tiny cares are all I've got right now, and I find myself aiming my thoughts at Jesus as if he's the appointed customer rep for the small stuff. Maybe Jesus is where you go when you can't get yourself dressed up enough for an appearance in the throne room. Rocking in the dark, Philip nestled against me, hoping only for a quick return to sleep and a long stretch till the next time, I offer a vague "please please please." Somehow I know that Jesus doesn't think it's silly and doesn't mind.

~

I've reached my goal now of nursing for four months. Philip is eating solid food well, taking a bottle very happily. He's well and thriving. I'm free to wean him. But something in me is resisting.

About a month ago, I tried to begin weaning by skipping one daytime feeding. How I longed for what weaning could mean: a solid night's sleep, pain-free breasts, my nice bras instead of the scaffolding, no bra at night, more comfortable sex, all the caffeine I care to consume, a little more energy. But then I thought, "I've gone this long without those things. Why not another month?" So I changed my mind.

Now I've gone beyond my goal, and something still pulls at me. Not guilt exactly, although there is some of that. But grief, I think. For so long I have known exactly how to love him: with my body. I could be close to him in a way no one else could, literally connected with him, warm and soft, eyes closed, quiet. Some part of me wonders, how will I love him now?

~

For the first several weeks, I could pray in the middle of the night with some alertness, about other people even. Then my prayers turned to asking God to please help the baby learn to sleep. Then to fairly inarticulate begging. Now I am beyond even that. My mind can't even reach out to God. I am like the baby put to bed to cry itself to sleep, letting out the last pathetic whimper before sleep overtakes. I have no fight left in me, no protest. Defeated by a twelve-pound infant.

~

Number three was our extravagance. There will be no more babies for us. Maybe I'm reluctant to wean him because I'm grieving the end of this stage in my life. I tell myself over and over that I will have to wean him eventually anyway. I can't love him like this forever! And he would mind a lot more if we did this later, probably. He knows very well that I still love him.

I have given my body to my babies, and now I'm claiming it back. There are reasons to rejoice, freedoms I've longed for. But right now, despite everything, I'm sad that this crazy, demanding, wondrous time is over. And deeply thankful for all of it.

As I nursed him this morning, over and over in my sleepy mind I managed a simple mantra: *Thank you thank you thank you.* Thank you for this perfect baby, for this closeness, for this quiet moment, thank you thank you thank you.

18) sleep

November 21

I had thought yesterday would have been the last time. But during the night my breasts ached, and when baby woke at five-thirty, the solution for both of us was obvious. It felt so good!

This was the last time, I knew. I'm glad we shared it, he and I, in the predawn dark, all the others in the house dreaming and breathing in quiet rooms.

After eating, though, he wanted to be awake.

My head ached. I needed, *needed* to sink away again, out of consciousness, out of the November morning dark that isn't morning at all, but
the edge of night that washes farther and farther up the shore of day.
It's too early for me, baby. Please, too early for me.

November 29

A week later and my breasts still ache as if I have been hit in the
chest by a truck. The ducts inside must be contracting or something;
they feel like they're clamped in a vise. I can barely hold the baby
against me. His wiggles and kicks send shooting pains through me.
Another thrilling dimension to the breastfeeding experience not cata-
loged in the reference books: drying-up pain.

My body is doing what it's designed to do, adjusting to the baby's
growth and development. Part of me is gleeful with relief and eager
to return to more streamlined proportions, but this dreadful tenderness tells another truth-in-the-body: I'm still grieving. Growth, ex-
pansions, burgeonings—these follow the impulses of life; shrinking
and diminishment suggest a dim outline of loss and death.

Then this completely unexpected cruelty: insomnia. Baby slept
fairly well last night, but I couldn't sleep at all. What is going on? The
strange thoughts, the tears that come in those dim, frustrating hours.
It's puzzling.

Is there some secret issue I'm not dealing with, some psychiatric or
spiritual garbage heap I haven't cleaned up? I don't *think* so. Sure I have
troubles and stresses, but I know what they are. I've named them; I'm
not in their power. In fact, my life is perfectly fine, wonderful even. So
why do I feel sick and sad? How long before I can enjoy my baby and
my days, instead of stumbling through them, half-witted and dull?

December 7

After months of broken sleep topped off with two weeks of insomnia, it is time for more drastic measures. My outlook these past two weeks has swung wildly between extremes: wonderfully happy, then despairing. With this sleep deficit I'm carrying, one night of poor sleep and I'm at my wits' end, over the edge, helpless.

The early morning is the worst. Now that Philip doesn't need me to get himself fed, I don't have to get up with him in the morning, but I try to take my turn anyway. I'm not a morning person, though. Never was. Morning people muse serenely about how tranquil and lovely are the early morning hours while they sit on the back porch drinking hot coffee or put in a whole morning's work before ten A.M. I hate it when morning people talk like this. Bunch of smug insufferables, that's what they are.

When I have to be up before seven-thirty, it's clear my whole system is in rebellion. I'm cranky, self-pitying, lethargic, and resentful. "How dare Ron leave these dishes in the sink! What does he think I am, his maid? Men have it so easy. And so do rich people. And I'm sick of my job. How come I can't have servants? How many hours till nap time, anyway?" These are the kinds of personable thoughts I have before seven A.M. I'm not a fit person, let alone a fit mother.

Lately it's been feeling like six A.M. for most of the day.

Finally, Ron says, enough! Despite my protests, he cancels appointments, calls a babysitter, arranges for a 24-hour emergency retreat for me at his parents' house at the lake.

If I were a character in a Victorian novel, I would be sent off for a month at a seaside resort, probably in France. Oh, that sounds like the perfect prescription. But when offered a real-life, reduced-size version of this, I resist. It feels selfish to leave the family for so long. Ron reminds me: "You can't care for the kids well if you're in bad shape!" True, but that only reinforces my feelings of failure. What is *wrong* with me? If I had been a better mom, I wouldn't have gotten this bad. That's what I tell myself.

Then Ron changes tactics: "You're giving me time to have the kids all to myself." All right, that one works. If I can see this as a gift to him and to the children, then it's OK for me to need this. Boy, am I caught up in the whole feminine enmeshment thing—servitude as identity. Everyone else's needs first. What's the matter with me? I know better.

December 8

Now that I'm out here at the lake I realize how much I've needed this. Walking on the wintry beach this afternoon, the waves roaring, the wind scouring the cold, hard sand, I feel it all come rushing back to me: the beauty of the wild world, and myself, an autonomous consciousness, looking out, reaching through this landscape to God. Prayer comes naturally, flowing in waves of gratitude and relief. I'm surprised at the gratitude. I would have expected a passel of pent-up petitions, but out here the clamor of needs hushes before the vast horizon. I'm glad for my isolation here, for my dust-speck size before my Maker, and the gladness sweeps outward from my heart as if the wind were whirling it through me.

Now back in the warm cottage I hardly know what to do with the luxury of a whole evening and a day of time. I can do whatever I please? Without having to squeeze it into little postage-stamp patches of time? Unbelievable.

My mother-in-law, a great believer in regular retreats, tells me that she began taking 24-hour retreats too late in life. She waited until her children were all in school and she was working on a graduate degree in divinity. But she remembers the earlier years, struggling from time to time with days when frustration and exasperation drove her to declare herself unfit for motherhood. She never thought it was all right to take a little time off; she had no models who did such a thing. After having tried it, though, she recommends that mothers (and fathers, too) take 24 hours off once every season.

In affirmation of that excellent plan, I think I'll hit the hot tub.

December 21

Two more weeks gone and I don't seem to be getting much better. I'm used to it now. I panic less when one o'clock, two o'clock go by and I'm still not asleep. I resign myself to less of a day the next day, one way or another. Either I'll sleep late and cut the day short that way, or I'll get up and feel lousy again, for another too-long day. Every day seems like a wide river to cross.

Other than early in the morning, I still manage to enjoy my baby. He's darling, sweet, funny, adorable. When he smiles, nothing else matters, at least for that moment. He's scootching all over the living-room floor now, doing the breaststroke with his arms and kicking his plump, creased legs. Sometimes his back half moves faster than his front half and his little legs rev up in the air, leaving him balanced for a second on his round tummy. Of course, all this scootching around means that his other remarkable ability—urping—leaves soggy blotches all over the carpeting. We've given up on stain removal. We'll have to

replace the carpeting. Eventually, anyway—who can think of redeco-
rating now?

One of Philip's most delightful developments is sleeping through
the night. Yes, from eight P.M. to seven in the morning. Sometimes at
five we need to give him a quick snack, or lately, just a quick pacifier,
and he's back for more sleep. Finally. Finally.

So everyone in the family is doing beautifully, except me. Still I
struggle to regain some kind of equilibrium after this childbirth year.
I'm convinced now that the insomnia is partly behavioral—a result of
messing up a regular sleep routine with months of sleeping in pieces
any-old-where around the clock. How many times have I gone back
to bed at seven-thirty in the morning for a couple hours, or at eleven-
thirty, or at any other odd time of day when someone else is around
to take over? I am also convinced that something chemical is going on
here. I can feel it in my brain, some weird chemical coursing through
it, keeping it from sliding over that brink of unconsciousness, prying
my eyes open from behind.

$\mathcal{D}$*e c e m b e r* 2 7

Now I want information. I tried doing a search on the Internet
for "(women or childbearing or nursing) and insomnia" and other
key-word combos that seemed promising. There's plenty about insomnia, but nothing I could find that directly addresses hormonal
shifts caused by weaning. I have two new books on sleep, though—
one about adults and one about children.

I wish I'd had this baby sleep book sooner. In the chapter on
months four to twelve, the author, Dr. Marc Weissbluth, calmly

reports on the results of sleep studies done on infants: "After four months of age, an infant's sleep becomes more adultlike." Aha! If only I'd known. Elsewhere in the book, Weissbluth explains that periods of consolidated nighttime sleep begin to organize around six weeks, and that babies don't respond to sleep "training" until four months. This is all based on laboratory-verified biological patterns of brain maturation, as well as experience in a sleep disorders center at a large children's hospital.

Now I'm angry. I'm angry that I read that *other* stupid book that insists babies ought to be "taught" how to sleep from the moment they get home from the hospital with a program of scheduled naps and crying in their cribs. This concept seemed too rigid for me, and I never followed it. But now I see the more sinister side of this book: if baby's sleep patterns are a matter of behavioral conditioning, then of course it's up to the mother to mold the baby into a perfect little sleeper. And of course it's *her* fault, *her* failure, if the baby doesn't cooperate. Sure, that's what women need: another thing to get blamed for. Now I find out that this notion is not only patronizing, but bad science, too.

Weissbluth, on the other hand, offers plenty of suggestions for parental behavior while encouraging parents to work with babies' natural sleep development. But his attitude seems less control-freakish, more caring. Weissbluth actually accompanies his suggestions with the word "please": "Please remember that this is an outline of a reasonable, healthy sleep pattern, not a set of rigid rules." So parents, we can all relax now and stop searching our souls and blaming ourselves when baby doesn't sleep through the night at six weeks.

But now what about this miserable insomnia? I'm trying to piece together a theory, but all I've got are snippets. For example, prolactin, the hormone that surges after birth and governs lactation, apparently has some role even under normal conditions in bringing on and sustaining sleep. Also, women commonly experience insomnia during menopause. Hypothesis: Could it be that when prolactin drops during the weaning process, the other hormones that take over can, under certain circumstances, kick into overdrive? And similar acts of hormonal aggression may occur during menopause? If so, which hormones transform into chemical zealots, and why are they torturing *me?* I have been needling every doctor I know for answers, but they all respond like cheerfully quizzical scientists: "Hmmmm, that's an interesting question. I don't know."

Sleep Hygiene

Even though I can't find any decent research on women's hormonal upheavals and their effect on sleep, I am learning plenty about dealing with insomnia. Sleep doctors must be the only medical professionals who agree on everything. I bet they have very cheerful professional meetings, probably in relaxed places like the Bahamas. Every expert source I've found, for example, insists that the first step in dealing with insomnia is to rid oneself of all the chemical enemies of sleep: caffeine, alcohol, heavy meals before bed. Then they establish rules of "sleep hygiene": don't do anything in bed except sleep ("marital relations" are OK), wind down before bed, don't think about stressful things before bed, and so on. They all advocate keeping a sleep log. Then there's a technique called "sleep reduction therapy," wherein you eliminate naps and reduce the time spent in bed by going to bed very late and getting up at a set time. The idea is to increase the sleep drive so that you conk out right away every night. This is supposed to break the behavioral pattern of tossing and turning in bed. And no staying in bed during middle-of-the-night wakings. No no. You have to get up and do something boring and sleep-inducing for a while, then go back to bed. Repeat as necessary.

Apparently, sleep is way more complicated than I ever thought. It's both strongly behavioral and complexly chemical. And I've got problems on both fronts.

Raveled Sleeves of Care

"In vain you rise early and stay up late, . . . for the Lord grants sleep to those he loves," writes the psalmist. When this started, my mother-in-law said the insomnia might be a call to prayer. "Mom thinks *everything* is a call to prayer," Ron assured me. It doesn't feel much like the stirrings of some divine summons. There's no serenity about this, no gentle urgency. Just a manic, frustrating silliness.

When I first became a mother, sleep became a gift. Miriam gave me a night's sleep when she slept, Ron gave me a nap when she didn't. Now I see that even the ability to sleep is a gift. It's not something we do out of confidence, skill, and determination. We set up the conditions for it, and if we're lucky, it comes. To sink out of consciousness into the mind's private mysteries—this is God's provender for life on the level of breathing, swallowing, digesting, the beating of the heart. We take it for granted until its normally complex interplays get knotted up and trip us.

The sleep-realm is not a passive place, not an empty mirror image of consciousness. Sleep scientists have discovered, despite expectations to the contrary, that the brain is as active during REM sleep as during prime periods of wakefulness. In fact, the brain is quite busy during all sleep stages, regulating autonomous systems, adjusting temperature, releasing healing hormones to repair the wear and tear of the day on the muscles and tissues. And the mind, or even the soul, practices its own mysterious rites during sleep, healing and sorting and releasing in ways that slip through the rational fingers of conscious analysis.

I've been thinking about Shakespeare lately, because in about a week I'll begin preparing for the Shakespeare course I'm teaching for the first time next month. Shakespeare understood about the healing powers of sleep, just as he understood the dynamics of other altered mental states like madness, jealousy, ambition, and ecstasy. In *Macbeth*, a play obsessed with sleep, the ambitious Macbeth is cursed with insomnia already in act 2 of the play, right after his first act of regicide. He reports to Lady Macbeth that he has heard voices warning him that he has "murdered sleep," and he desperately laments the loss:

> *Sleep that knits up the raveled sleave of care,*
> *the death of each day's life, sore labor's bath,*
> *Balm of hurt minds, great nature's second course,*
> *Chief nourisher in life's feast.*

He would probably have gone on standing there with blood on his hands metaphorizing about sleep if Lady Macbeth hadn't interrupted. "What do you mean?" she demands impatiently. But Macbeth knows what's at stake: without sleep, his mind, already strained by the clamoring of his conscience, will soon disintegrate completely.

How am I going to heal my strained mind without sleep? I don't drink, I don't smoke, I don't do drugs. I'm a freakin' Puritan already.

So now I'm a mentally unstable Puritan? Sleep is my natural self-medication. Without it, as Othello says on the brink of his own breakdown, "chaos is come again."

Maybe I need to start doing serious drugs. When I first called the doctor's office to ask about this insomnia, the nurse suggested trying an over-the-counter sleep aid. These "sleep aids" turn out to be thinly disguised, remarketed antihistimines. Well, I tried one. It helped for a few nights, and then I stayed awake right through it, feeling those mysterious chemical villains prying my eyes open from behind again. I didn't sneeze even once, though!

So then I read about melatonin, the wonder hormone. My mother-in-law had some, so I tried that. What a disaster. It made me feel fidgety, hot, and no more sleepy than before. So now I've begged my father-in-law to prescribe a real sleeping pill. I suggested a new one that another of my doctor friends had mentioned, but Dad recommends an older one he knows and trusts. OK, fine.

Please let this work, God. I can't care for my kids, I can't work, I can't even pay attention when people talk to me.

I start to feel the effects of the first pill—relaxed limbs, eyelids drooping . . .

January 2

The prescription sleeping pills worked beautifully. Wow! On the fifth night, I took half a dose because I had read that if you stop cold turkey, you can have "rebound insomnia." Everyone is so worried about addiction to sleeping pills, I don't dare take them for more than a week. So I'm tapering off. The half dose left me floundering a little

to get to sleep, but following the sleep book's suggestions about routine and shortening the night seems to help.

January 9

Can't remember things from one minute to the next. Mind wanders when people talk to me. Can't cope with minor frustrations, the
kids fighting, a dish breaking, can't handle it. Small challenges are
beyond me, writing a check, finding a stamp, too hard. Tearful and
self-absorbed. Can't think a day ahead, don't care about anything except surviving till nighttime, then nighttime is the enemy.

I was doing fairly well without the sleeping pills. Then two nights
in a row I awoke far too early and couldn't get back to sleep. I don't
know what time because the books say not to look at clocks in the
middle of the night. It makes you more tense.

The second morning of this, I lie in bed awake till seven o'clock
when Ron stirs. "Are you OK?" "No." And then the tears break loose
and the trembling and repeating over and over again, "Please help me,
please help me, please help. It's too hard. I can't do this. I can't cope
with it."

"What is 'it'? What do you mean?" he pleads.

I don't know.

∽

What I want most: relief from consciousness. Strange how long the
days now seem. No more napping, no more hours of nursing, just too
much waking thought, spinning around and around, growing louder
and louder in my mind. The dimmer the light the longer the shadows.

All my little troubles seem huge in the darkness. I can't teach second semester, I tell myself over and over to the rhythm of the fan in our bedroom. I can't possibly finish the poem I've been commissioned to write. I can't go to the meeting, just can't bear it. Can't make that meal for church group. Can't do anything. Can't stand these thoughts over and over every night.

I want someone to knock me over the head with a board so I can black out.

~

Calvin's three-week January term has begun and thank God I had the foresight to ask for release time. I've hired a college student, Kim, to come each day while the kids are in school and watch Philip while I prepare for second semester. Who knows if I'll actually teach it? Most days I think I won't. I go through the motions of preparing just in case. I slump over my Shakespeare textbook, trying to read *Hamlet* again, and suddenly I *know* the melancholy Dane, understand him from the inside.

> *To die, to sleep—*
> *No more—and by a sleep to say we end*
> *The heartache and the thousand natural shocks*
> *That flesh is heir to. 'Tis a consummation*
> *Devoutly to be wished. To die, to sleep.*

Hamlet and I, both insomniacs, both feeling "how weary, stale, flat, and unprofitable/ Seem . . . all the uses of this world." No one is more painfully conscious than Hamlet. With him thought is almost a disease. Sinking into death sounds good to Hamlet merely as a way to get some rest. Then it occurs to him that in death there might still be consciousness, dreams, and what dreams may come? Ay, there's the rub. It's the blank he wants, the pure blackness.

~

Joie calls, a member of my small group at church. She heard in my words at our meeting last night, she said, some signs that I might be depressed, and had I ever considered that? I had, yes, I tell her. "I don't think I'm there yet," I say, "but if this goes on I could get there fast."

If I subscribed to a certain kind of piety, I would be looking for some purpose in this, as if it were part of God's little soul-redecorating scheme. Let's see: a little desperation here, accented with some light suffering there, and *voila:* a more compassionate person!

Nah. Maybe God will make something out of this, but in and of itself, it's just stupid.

"The Lord is my shepherd, I shall not want. He maketh me to lie down in green pastures; he leadeth me beside still waters. He restoreth my soul." Shepherds don't kick their sheep into holes to improve their stamina.

It's comforting to think that I am, on some basic level, merely a sheep, stupid and dependent. Jesus, please restore my soul. I don't know exactly what has happened to it, but now I know what it means to need it restored.

I've made an appointment to see my OB-GYN. Whatever it is, I have to get better.

January 11

My OB-GYN, after a good long discussion, says she thinks the problem might be low estrogen levels. I did get my period a month after weaning Philip, so at least that system is in gear. I'm taking the pill again, which elevates estrogen levels slightly. She also gives me a sample of estrogen supplements to try, thinking it will help especially during this week when I will get my period again and estrogen will be low. So I take one of the pills at eight in the evening. An hour later I start to feel unbearably hot. My body cooks and cooks for hours, and of course I cannot get to sleep. Finally, I resort to half of my last sleeping pill and fall asleep. Then I awaken too early and lay in bed for an hour before finally giving up, getting up.

Estrogen: not the answer.

With this last simple chemical explanation obviously ruled out, I have my worst day in a long time. I force myself to go into the office, even though in the lonely, crazy hours in the middle of the night, as my thoughts thud thud thud round and round in my mind, all I can think of is how hard it seems to do it all right now—the children, the marriage, the job. I can't get rid of the first two. Don't want to. But if only I could be relieved of my job stresses. Then I would feel better. Yes, that's it. I spend hours promising myself in the middle of the night: I'm not coming back next year. It's too hard. I'm not coming back. This is the only way I can relax enough to sleep.

But in the morning, I always think: Well, let's try for one more day. In case I change my mind.

So of course, the minute I stumble into the department suite today, my department chair pokes his head out of his office and says, "Deb, I really need that sheet listing the courses you want to teach next year. Can I have that today?" I must have looked stunned. What would I write?

I go into my office and close the door. Find the sheet. Fill it out. Then I write at the bottom: "Dean, it's hard for me to think about next year. I've really been struggling lately. I've been suffering from insomnia and I think it must be some sort of postpartum depression. I'm getting professional help. I'll keep you posted."

Immediately, relief. I feel better just having said it to someone. Depression. I might as well admit it.

Weirdly enough, I actually have a productive day, reading a whole play and consolidating my notes on it in preparation for class. But I sit there typing at my computer, barely holding back the tears. Later in the day, I notice a note from the chair in my box: "I'm sorry to hear of your recent struggles. . . . Take *care* of yourself. I'd be happy to talk anytime you like."

On my way home in the car, I think, "Is this sinful? Is it wrong for me to feel sad when I have such a great life?" But the thought comes back, No. This is not a matter of being a privileged, ungrateful, American spoiled brat. This is beyond my control.

When I get home I read about depression a little more. It all sounds familiar. The anxiety. Inability to concentrate. Feelings of hopelessness. Stomachaches, hot flashes, panicky feelings. This is it. This is my problem. It's depression.

I call the doctor and she offers to prescribe an antidepressant. No big deal to her. She makes it sound like this is a routine part of her practice, and I suppose it is. When I hang up, resigned to taking drugs for this, I wonder if I need to start thinking of myself as a PERSON WITH DEPRESSION. That would be a new thing for me. I've had my problems and struggles and even times of real grief. And hey, everyone feels down sometimes. But depression is not like the flu or the mumps. It's more like . . . I don't know. A state of being.

Then it occurs to me that many famous poets and artists have suffered from depression. I have just enough of my scant humor

supply left to wonder wryly if this situation might improve my poetry. I've always thought I was far too ordinary and middle-of-the-
road in every way to be a *real* poet. Well, it probably won't work.
And I don't really know anything about depression and art. I've
never read all those books by depressed women writers of the nine-
teenth and twentieth centuries, like Sylvia Plath's *The Bell Jar.* Never
read 'em. Too busy with my nose buried in the sixteenth century,
when melancholy states were blamed on bile, and despair was a serious sin. Besides, I'm not willing to slink around in a depressed state
for art's sake or anything else's sake. I just want to get better. Even
the stigma doesn't bother me. If I have to tell people as part of getting
better, fine. I don't care.

I start to feel more settled in the evening. At bedtime, I follow my
newly instituted prebed ritual: prepare the bed, turn on the little fan
for white noise, light a scented candle, sit with pillows on the floor in
a corner next to the bed, open the Bible, try to trace over the words
with my eyes and maybe catch a phrase or two, mumble a prayer, and
crawl into bed. I've been reading through the Psalms because that
was all I could think of to do, so I open to the place where I left off
the night before.

Psalm 30

I will exalt you, O Lord,
    for you lifted me out of the depths
    and did not let my enemies gloat over me.
O Lord, my God, I called to you for help
    and you healed me.
O Lord, you brought me up from the grave;
    you spared me from going down into the pit.

Yes, yes, here I am in the pit, in the depths. And it is God who heals and rescues. I believe this. I have seen it in a thousand ways.

> . . . weeping may remain for a night,
>> but rejoicing comes in the morning.

Weeping comes for me now in the night, in the unfriendly night. But in the morning there is no rejoicing; only a numb reprieve. When will the joy morning come?

> When I felt secure, I said,
>> "I will never be shaken."
> O Lord, when you favored me,
>> you made my mountain stand firm;
> but when you hid your face,
>> I was dismayed.

Yes, I am dismayed. The tears pour out and I am dismayed. You are here, I know, but your face is blank to me. You have favored me lavishly, beyond reason, all my life. I have always been strong. Now I am helpless and weak. I don't ask why. It doesn't matter. But I want it to end. I want to get through this shadow valley. Don't let me get stuck here forever.

> To you, O Lord, I called;
>> to the Lord I cried for mercy:
> What gain is there in my destruction,
>> in my going down into the pit?
> Will the dust praise you?
>> Will it proclaim your faithfulness?
> Hear, O Lord, and be merciful to me;
>> O Lord, be my help.

"*Will the dust praise you*"—*how arrogant of the dustling to challenge the Maker of the world! But I see now, this is not arrogance; it is desperation. God, I have nothing to bargain with, nothing to leverage. Whatever I am, I owe to you, even my very breath. You do not need my service, my praise. Yet your love for me is sturdy and constant. And isn't my wholeness better than a dusty powder of me in your sight? Isn't it worth salvaging me for whatever small service, whatever tiny piping of praise I can muster?*

> You turned my wailing into dancing;
> > you removed my sackcloth
> > and clothed me with joy,
> that my heart may sing to you and not be silent.
> > O Lord my God, I will give thanks to you forever.

The psalmist writes my future in the ancient past. In Hebrew, the perfect tense sometimes becomes the prophetic perfect, expressing God's action in the future or, more accurately, God's continous pattern of action beyond time. I will look back on this time, on this dark stumbling, and praise the faithfulness of God in bringing me onto firm ground and daylight. I know this; I have survived other, different pits. Rejoicing and dancing will come again. Jesus is here again, quiet and present, sitting beside me on the mourning bench. Gentle in the healing silence.

The tears come and come. Then, after a little while, I sleep. No drugs. I wake up too early again, but when daylight seeps in slits between the shades and the window frames, the morning's coming calms me, and I sleep again.

~

This isn't the first time God has spoken in reassurance from the place I happened to be reading. Augustine was finally converted when he opened the Bible at random, prompted by a neighborhood child at play chanting "Take and read." The verse he fell upon flooded him with conviction and altered his whole life's course. I imagine few fathers and mothers of the church would recommend opening the Bible at random, though, as if it were a Ouija board. Better to read according to some systematic scheme like the lectionary. Not every day will be inspiring, but the important thing is to keep your sails up. The wind blows where it will, and when it does, be ready.

From God's point of view, though, what's the difference? When the Spirit infuses the ancient words with immediate meaning, it's a miracle of intricate engineering.

Maybe the fever has broken now, and I can simply heal.

January 20

It's not over yet. This antidepressant is killing me. At first, it did indeed erase the anxiety, although it did nothing for the insomnia. I lay in bed awake at two in the morning, three, four—but I didn't care! Everything's fine! I'm fine, really I am!

Except for the shaking. Reducing to half a dose helped, but I still tremble constantly and feel as if half of me is quivering into some other dimension of space. The nurse says it takes four weeks for the side effects to go away blah blah blah keep taking the pills blah blah blah. I am losing ground, losing hold. Another night comes, I dread the night. My stomach hurts when I turn back the covers.

I can't sleep at all. I go down to the basement couch to avoid waking Ron. Hours pass, my whole body shakes with every breath, my teeth chatter. I have no thoughts, no conscious words. I hear myself crying out, Oh God, oh God, oh God, over and over again. Mind fraying and tearing, pieces pulling apart. Pray, pray for me. This is the pit, this is the mire. Pray for me now and in the hour of my death. Pray, for this is the practice of death.

It's still dark. Morning must have come. Ron appears at the top of the stairs with the still-pajamaed baby on his hip. I tell him I feel like I am having a nervous breakdown.

He orders me up to bed. I crawl, literally, upstairs to the bedroom, while Ron goes into crisis action. He calls his parents, who come right over from an hour away. (My "snowbird" parents are in Florida for the winter; he'll call them tonight.) When Kim appears for her usual day of Philip-watching, he sends her home and tells her we'll pay her anyway. He calls my doctor on the emergency line. As I lie upstairs in bed, I can hear him in the kitchen, palavering insistently with her, telling her that the antidepressant has left me in shreds and we had better come up with a better solution *now.*

By noon, my in-laws have comforted me with their soothing presence, and Ron has managed to procure the newest and best sleep drug from the pharmacy. I take the first pill and sleep for a couple hours. The doctor told Ron that I should definitely stay on the antidepressant, but I flatly refuse. Never again. My brain bucked that stuff off like a bronco.

By late afternoon, I start to feel a little better and emerge into the kitchen to eat something. I'm exhausted, but coherent and calm.

Ron goes to our regular Thursday night church house group, and they pray for me.

Pray for me. I need help. This is the pit, this is the mire. Pray for me.

January 21 - 24

The next day, the worst effects of the antidepressant have worn off, and the sleeping pill gave me a good night.

Something is happening, something I can't explain. It's a little like coming out of hibernation and, after blinking in the bright daylight, seeing someone coming—no, it's yourself—to greet you. As I sit on the floor in the corner next to the bed, trying to pray and think, I come to the curious realization that I have missed *myself.* We often speak about self-esteem and self-love, but that usually amounts to confidence and competent self-care and looking out for one's interests. It's a busy, practical basis for getting along in the world, a bland commodity. But I feel something different—a specific, clear-eyed, good-humored affection for the person that is me.

I have existed for so many months now in a state that can accurately be described as being beside myself. "I have of late lost all my mirth," as Hamlet says. Nothing left of me except the horrid parts, the whiny, self-pitying, resentful, and tearful-at-the-slightest provocation parts. Nothing unique about all that crap. Depressive states may lead later to profound art, but the condition itself is boring and generic. Very few people at their lowest points soliloquize like Hamlet. I suppose it's the upper orders of personality that make us unique. "Yes, I'm usually an enthusiastic and capable person!" I blurted out to Kim today, when she noted that I was looking better. I'm grateful to her; she entered our home and our family's life at a point of bewildering chaos, but she has handled it with grace and concern.

Thanks to Kim and my in-laws and most of all Ron, throughout all this the kids have been OK. Jacob has taken to praying every night, "Help Mama and Philip have a good sleep tonight." But other than that, they're going right on despite their mom's partial disappearance. I regret more than anything what Ron has been going through. I've been telling him constantly, I'm sorry, I'm sorry to be such a burden. But it's not the extra work he has minded so much as the temporary loss of *me*.

On Saturday, as part of a comprehensive stress-reduction plan, we decide to reinstitute a practice we've badly neglected: the Sabbath. But since Ron's main duties at the college are on Sunday, that day will always be a work day in our household. We decide to declare Friday evening to Saturday evening our rest day. Sort of doing this the Jewish way, I guess.

Now, by Monday, I feel better than I have in months. I can't say exactly what caused this distinct turnaround. The sleeping pills? Prayer? Letting go and giving up? Maybe it's just a standard-issue, garden-variety miracle.

I dress up, put on makeup, do my hair a different way, go into the office. Back at my computer my brain sparks with ideas for class and my fingers fly at the keyboard.

January 25

In one day, I see a counselor and a sleep doctor. The counselor asks about my family of origin and concludes the session with a serious summation: I have experienced *major depression*. That's the technical term. She seems not to trust my improvement. "You still have the antidepressant in your system, you know. Be careful. If the symptoms of depression come back, you need to get back on an antidepressant." Later she mentions that some experts think thirty minutes of exercise is equal to one dose of antidepressant. Well, I would rather run a mile a day—which would probably take thirty minutes and could possibly kill me—than go back on those drugs.

Then I see the sleep doctor, who turns out to be a jolly, encouraging fellow. He's impressed with the reading I've done on insomnia and with the sleep log I've been keeping. He examines me, asks lots of questions about my sleep behaviors and my emotional state, and then he looks me in the eye. "You're not depressed," he assures me. "Depression is much more constant. This is about sleep behaviors that got out of whack. Several things—chemical and emotional and behavioral—conspired against you and got you off track. And that sleep drug you're taking is the best one, but you're taking it in such a low dose it probably isn't even doing much. You're doing better on your own!"

When I ask about the research on mothers and sleep, he explains that sleep researchers, until recently, usually worked with male subjects. "It was simpler," he explains. "Men don't get pregnant in the middle of studies." Fortunately, he continues, major grant monies are now being awarded to studies on women and sleep. "There's so much we don't understand," he says with a combination of regret and excitement. "But one thing I can tell you: if you compare three people of the same age—a man, a woman who has never had children, and a woman who *has* had children—the woman with children will have the poorest quality sleep. And not even because the children are waking her. Something happens chemically and we have to find out what it is."

Amen, brother.

As I drive home, I try to add all this up. I've seen an OB-GYN, a counselor, and a sleep doctor. They all figured that my problem fell into their domain, that they could solve it with the techniques of their specialty. Isn't that interesting? If I went to a neurologist, he would tell me my problem was a tumor. God help me if I saw a proctologist.

I call up my father-in-law and ask him if he would like to remove my gallbladder. We laugh at the myth of medical science: doctors look at the evidence and find the right answer. The fact is, they don't *know* what's wrong with me. They make an educated guess and try something. Do no harm, but do *something*. If it doesn't work, the hypothesis wasn't correct. Trial and error. Meanwhile, guess who suffers from the errors.

I decide to take into consideration all their professional opinions, but make up my own mind. No one has been more observant of my symptoms than me. So I'll write my own diagnosis:

Sleep deprivation from Philip's night wakings left my brain chemistry depleted and my sleep habits in a shambles. Hormonal shifts caused by weaning along with the intense stress of trying to do too much sent me over the edge, causing insomnia. Insomnia further depleted my brain and spirit, allowing me to dip toward depression then bob back up again after decent nights. Finally, the dips got low enough to get out of control.

Now, I'll write my own prescription, too:

· Weekly Sabbath from Friday sundown to Saturday sundown— for Ron, too. No housework. No schoolwork. No errands. Rest and fun with the family.
· Exercise. Thirty minutes every other day. Let's test that exercise-equals-antidepressant theory.
· Good diet. Vitamins.

- Sleep restriction therapy, supplemented with the sleeping pill when needed.
- Stimulus control therapy. Follow all the proper rules about getting out of bed when I can't sleep, practicing my before-bed ritual, and so on.
- Laughter therapy. Read something funny before bed.
- Refusal to let anything get to me. If stress comes, run in the other direction until rested. Repeat as needed.

February 21

Nearly four weeks have passed. I haven't felt this good in a long time. Years, I think. For the first week I was on a kind of high—a healing high, I guess. Since then, I've had crabby days, some persistent sadness. I'm not altogether well yet, still working with minimal reserves. Won't be able to build those up, probably, until summer comes. But overall I seem to have found a new rhythm.

April 27

I was taught as a child that salvation was about clouds and the heavenly city and shining and singing and gold for eternity. "I've got a home in glory land that outshines the sun," we sang in Sunday school. I still believe this, and not in a much more sophisticated way. I'm definitely planning on a mansion, preferably with maid service.

What about the meantime, though, the troubles and disasters of the here and now? My Shakespeare students—who have turned out to be the world's smartest and most delightful students—just finished reading *King Lear,* Shakespeare's excursion to the very precipice of nihilism. To help us think about how the dark world of this play compares with other views of the world, I read to them a passage from a recent, Pulitzer Prize–winning novel. The novel concludes with this summary musing on the characters' sundry disasters:

> We live our lives, do whatever we do, and then we sleep—it's as simple and ordinary as that. . . . There's just this for consolation: an hour here or there when our lives seem, against all odds and expectations, to burst open and give us everything we've ever imagined, though everyone but children (and perhaps even they) knows these hours will inevitably be followed by others, far darker and more difficult.

Just this? Just this fashionable, agnostic, literary affirmation of the now in the face of an eternal emptiness we can only wish held more? I stand there and look at my class and say: For me, that is *not enough.* If that's all there is, forget the whole thing. I can only be bothered with the heartache if there's a divinity that shapes our ends, and they become a beginning.

The end is where we start from. That's T. S. Eliot, but those Hebrew verb tenses say it, too. They suggest that the future is not the result but the source, the fountain that flows toward us in the present and then floods into the past. Salvation is not all in the blue-sky hereafter. Nor is it merely a few tender, epiphanic moments—though those may come, too. Salvation flows into the here and now mostly as a matter of practical, nonmetaphorical, fits-and-starts rescues. It was bad, but God made it better. It was broken, but it healed. I made mistakes, but God made some good come out of it. I was lost, but now am found.

1 9) attention

"Miriam, you *have* to have some vegetables."

"How much do I have to eat?"

"Mama, can I be excused to get the . . ."

"Just eat some."

"Ron, can you pass the rice? Yes, Jacob."

". . . ketchup?"

"Philip, no no! Sit down! Deb, can you cut up

some more . . ."

"Mama, Jacob's hitting me!"

". . . meat for Philip."

"Squaaaaawk!"

"No, he's not, Miriam. He's just—he ate all that meat already?—trying to go around."

"So at this meeting today, I was telling John that . . ."

"Daddy, I don't like these carrots. They're squishy."

"Squaaaaawk!"

"Miriam, you interrupted me."

"Where's the ketchup? I can't find it."

"But I don't like the . . ."

"Squaaaawk!"

"You interrupted me!"

"Okay, okay, okay!"

"What do you *say,* Miriam?"

"Jacob, it's got to be in the door of the fridge."

"Sorry, Daddy."

"So I told John that . . ."

"Ron, the baby is crawling out."

[fifteen minutes later]

"OK, who wants ice cream?"

"Memememememememememe!"

"Oh, *somebody* has his own special super *duper* ice cream."

"Come on, *you're* all getting chocolate."

"I want a huuuuuge scoop."

"I want vanilla. Don't we have vanilla?"

"You'll all get a *reasonable* scoop."

"Hey, Philip's got the cover . . . oh—my—gosh, *look* at his *face!*"

Philip pulls the cover of the ice cream tub down from his face, which is now entirely smeared with chocolate ice-cream soup. He looks at us as if to say: "What? What are you all looking at?"

Baby Boo-bah

We call him "Boo-bah." Miriam came up with this, my little Garden-of-Eden girl. She loves to go barefoot, she wears her hair long and tousled, and she names things. She named herself when she was about eighteen months old. She couldn't say "Miriam," so she called herself "Mini." We repeated this back to her, as parents do ("Does Mini need a bankie for nigh-night?"), and soon we were calling her "Mini" all the time. It fit her so well we never stopped. Then Jacob came along, whom we had planned to call "Jack." But within months of his birth, Miriam dubbed him "Jakey" and that was the end of it. So here we go again with Philip. All that agonizing over our children's names, all that trial and error before their births to wed mellifluous sounds to appropriate meanings, and we wind up with Mini, Jakey, and Boo-bah.

Baby Boo-bah has reached the happy-baby stage, when his world is a fabulous, fascinating amusement park. He knows what he wants and will devise a means to get it, but if we take it away or pick him up, he's quite happy to move on to the next swell thing. His legs look like a miniature sumo wrestler's, but the rest of him has slendered from the potato-sack look to a taut paunchiness. All of our babies have wasted no time in getting mobile, and Philip was already shocking onlookers at four months by torquing up his little legs, reaching forward with his arms, and dragging himself about two feet in one mighty heave. The butterfly stroke on carpet. Now, at ten months, he pulls up on anything, even bare walls. Then he bobs up and down on his toes, as if testing the floor at that particular spot. Sometimes he'll stand there and squawk, like a tiny but very loud coach shouting out orders to an imaginary, inept basketball team. Then he's off, sidestepping along on his toes, or bending down to check out whatever interesting items might be found at chubby-knee level.

I've fallen completely in love with each of my babies at this age. Not that I didn't love them before, but at eight or nine months the clouds of the first months part, and we become the stars in each other's firmaments. Philip, with all his focus on action, action, action, is not what I would call an adoring baby, not the kind you can coo with face to face for ten minutes at a stretch. He's happy among his special people, and he often wants to be picked up and hugged—but just for a minute. He yells in his high chair or playpen, so I grab him out and enjoy his weight against my chest, enjoy being his default state, the home from which he ventures, the return. This lasts about five seconds. Then he twists his upper body around like a spring and scans the room for the next order of business. "Hey, thanks for bailing me out!" he seems to say. "Love ya! OK! Gotta go! Work to do!" Then he wants down so he can crawl straight for the electrical outlets, or pull up on the china cabinet, or knock all the shampoos off the tub-edge and into that cool, slippery, white expanse below. Or make an attempt on the toilet paper roller. He would love to have his way with that thing.

He's saying his first word now, too. It's "WHAAUUUUGH—aaaaaahhhhhh." That is to say: "uh-oh." It does sound like "uh-oh," but he's so excited about it that he overdramatizes a little. He's been babbling mama and dada for weeks without very exact aim. "Uh-oh" is the term he has first connected consistently to an action or thing. He knows that when something drops, it's "uh-oh." In his thoughtful little way, sitting bent over a pile of blocks, he sometimes says his word over and over just for fun, practicing quietly to himself as if he's contemplating all the subtle connotations.

Back on the Beam

It's good to be able to enjoy him again. Of all the lousy things about the insomnia adventure, probably the worst is that I seem to have missed a few months of Philip's life. They're gone; that's all there is to it. I try to make up for the loss by enjoying him as intensely as I can now.

I don't know what to think about what happened to me last winter. Is my sanity really that fragile? Some chemical weirdness sent me sliding downward, I'm convinced. But "those women and their crazy hormones" is never the full explanation. I can only humbly attest to the complexity of interaction between our minds and bodies.

Sanity is a fragile, intricate balance. Sanity is like a beam that most people walk along quite solidly most of the time. Others have a tendency to teeter here and there, and still others fall off repeatedly. Now I know what it feels like to teeter, and how little it takes to mess up the balance.

I've also come to understand that while depressed or anxious states do sometimes offer a clearer view of the scary things in life, they can also tell lies. My mental tempests showed me that I was trying to do too much. But the anxiety also distorted the situation; small, manageable problems seemed like monsters.

I'm frightened by all this. I'm pretty sure now that I'm going to heal completely. But what if I had not come out of it? And what about other people who never do? The helplessness is the worst part; when you fall off the beam, the swampy places below drag and drag on you, and you feel yourself sinking. I never want to get near those distorted, devouring places again.

The only way out is for someone to grab you and pull. Some

people need family and friends, some people also need doctors and pharmaceuticals to get a foothold again. We all need some divine help. I was surprised to find that divine help comes partly through an amazing resilience built into our minds and bodies. Some survival mechanism kicked in for me, even when I felt I had no strength left. I could feel it happening. The sleep medication helped, but most of the healing has come from simple things: the brain's natural healing powers, hope, love—apparently it all mingles together. We grab hold of God and the people who care for us, and that helps get us steadied. And by grace, maybe limping a little, we get back on the beam and slowly start walking again.

Fragments and Obstacles

I continue to feel a little stronger each week. My sleep is still not as deep or calm as it used to be, but it seems to suffice. I work through most days cheerfully and have enough energy, usually, to get by. The days are very full. I hit the ground running when Philip wakes us up in the morning, and I rarely sit down all day. Even late at night, I'm still switching laundry loads or grading papers for class. I seem to have forgotten how to relax.

I'm used to this chaotic life, having been a mother now for seven years. But I must say, where two kids was manageable, three is crazy. Often it's downright comical. Sometimes when we are all at cross-purposes in our small kitchen—one of us grabbing a spoon from a drawer, someone else opening the fridge, someone else setting the table—we'll make a game out of it and crowd into a little knot of jostling people, banging into each other purposely and saying "Excuse me! Oh, pardon me! Excuse me!" Or Ron and I will be attempting to say one complete sentence to each other, but this will be interrupted when Jacob runs bawling into our presence, protesting one of Miriam's many injustices, and Philip is meanwhile yelling out his immediate need for, say, a cracker, and Ron and I will look at each other knowingly and simply continue the conversation EXCEPT AT THE TOPS OF OUR VOICES SO AS TO BE HEARD ABOVE THE DIN. HA HA.

The other day I had one of those parental moments that almost seems as if it was orchestrated by a sitcom writer. Early in the afternoon, I thought to myself, "The evening should go pretty smoothly tonight. None of the kids needs a bath." Then Miriam showed up after school, covered with mud from her hair to her sneakers. "We played in the mud today," she announced. "Up to the tub with you," I replied, insisting that she strip off her crusty clothes right inside the back door. An hour or so later, all the neighborhood kids were outdoors running from yard to yard and I was inside with Philip. Miriam came to the door: "Jacob *needs* you," she reported, looking worried and urgent. I found him outside, hiding near some bushes and looking upset. He had apparently eaten something that didn't agree with him and suffered the consequences in his, uh, southerly regions. So I trundled him into the house, up the stairs, into the bathroom, where we stripped off his clothes—an unpleasant and delicate procedure. I stood him up in the tub to wash off his bottom, then put some sudsy water in the tub for a good sitdown soak. While Jacob was in the tub and I was attempting to fold up the scary clothes for transport to the washer downstairs, Philip, standing on one extreme tiptoe, managed to get the other sumo leg over the edge of the tub and give himself a good heave. Splash! In his clothes, face first. I fished him out, hugged him to me (getting myself soaked, of course), and realized that at this point we had *all* taken a bath.

It's a good thing I was in good spirits. As with all comedies, one slight alteration in mood can veer the whole thing toward tragic.

"Go with the flow!" people cheerfully advise busy mothers. Yeah, sure. Even after all these hundreds of days filled with interruptions and deferrals, I still can't settle to it completely. I get so tired of never finishing a task. Time is always up. Either baby wakes from his nap or the kids get home from school or Ron gets home from rehearsal or it's time for me to leave the office to get home at the time I promised. I get tired of the persistent demands of "Mama, Mama!" sometimes from three different rooms simultaneously. I get tired of rarely completing a sentence with Ron, let alone having a conversation. I get very, very tired of stepping over toys and socks and books and papers all over the house. My life is a pastiche of fragments and tiny obstacles.

The Lineup

It's difficult these days to give each other that most rare and precious gift: attention. I'm so busy taking care of material needs and keeping the forces of chaos at bay that I forget to show affection to or enjoy or even look at these people I love. Sometimes I drop the older kids off at school and just as they're about to crawl out of the car, I realize Jacob has a milk mustache. As we shuffled around the house getting ready for school, I never even looked at his face! And when was the last time I looked Ron in the eyes as lovers do in their first passions for each other? My friend Karen, who had her third baby two months after Philip was born, remarked to me, "One thing I've noticed now is that it's very hard for Mark and me to focus on each other." "Yes," I replied, raising my voice slightly to be heard over

Jacob, who was whining piteously about something he wanted. "Unless the husband is whining louder than the others, he's *fourth* in line."

It was a vulgar way to put it, but it's true. It often feels like they're all lining up to demand something from me. Even though Ron does his full share of the parenting, they don't seem to line up for him in quite the same way. I find myself, in response to this, constantly staking and restaking my own territory. It feels like a perpetual wrestling match. The women's magazines that remind us gravely how important it is to "Take time for yourself" make it sound so simple, as if it's a matter of pencilling in a luncheon on your calendar and that's that. Problem solved. They never add, "And you're going to have to fight for it." Sure, you can take a bath and lock the door, but one of the kids will probably pound on it to ask if he can have some ice cream. Sure you can schedule that lunch with friends, but you'll have to wrench yourself away from an abject baby, wailing in the arms of a chagrined babysitter. Sure, you can start reading a novel, but try to choose one with very short chapters. In fact, sentence fragments might be best.

Sometimes I wonder if it's worth the effort to defend my territory. Maybe it would be easier to be everyone's servant and be done with it. Still, I fight because it seems like a matter of survival. I've claimed my little corner of actual space in the bedroom, although Philip has gotten in there and pulled my books off the bookshelf more than once. But mostly I mean that I have to defend a little bounded space for myself on the fields of time and attention. I embrace my family because I love them, but I'm always resisting, too, because I fear that if I don't, I'll lose myself completely. They'll swallow me because their demands are deeper than I am.

The scary thing is, it's not going to get better any time soon. The fragments, the deferrals, the obstacles, the tussle of wills, the children literally crawling all over me, especially when I've just made myself a cup of tea, and after all that, the sheer noise—this is the way it's going to be for many years.

～

And yet, and yet. Scattered as I am these days, Philip can stop me short with his charms and lure me into sustained attention and delight. There's something about our small children that teaches us all over again how to love one another. They draw us toward ideal love: fierce, tough, and elastic, fully particular, fully attentive to the individuality of the other. I remember the rapture of gazing on our newborn babies, falling into that state of reverie irresistibly and without measuring time. And even now, how I love Philip's soft body, the curls on the scooped nape of his neck, his wet eyelashes like dark, delicate stars. And I know he delights in me, too. When we're reunited after a night's sleep or a day's work, what sweetness! He snuggles against me, filling that hollow spot in the chest that we all feel. He fits right into it. And there's something about the way he grabs his little arms around my neck and lays his head against my shoulder and clamps his legs around my side that tells me he feels that longing, the longing that comes from being a discrete being, discrete in physical form, but so connected in spirit, the basic paradox of our nature, that out of which all our deep longings come. All that we love, all that we ache to keep.

The Imperative of Intimacy

Feminists of the last generations warned us: Beware! Beware of enmeshment, it can drown you! Beware of defining yourself through others, you can lose yourself! Beware of those tangled boundaries between you and others, they can strangle! After giving birth to three children and dipping into a brief depression, I'm forced to concede a few inches concerning the vulnerability of women's mental states. I can no longer recoil in pure indignation when I read misogynist treatises from centuries of yore claiming that women are crazy and unreliable. Women who spent their lives pregnant or nursing, from the early teen years to their early deaths (often from childbirth complications)—how could they not have been a little crazy? It's the hormones, it's the sleep deprivation, but it's also the relentless demands and the shrinking territory of a woman's self. I can make out the shadows of cages that held other women, closed them in till some either disappeared, went mad, or turned monster.

But after a generation of scholarship and popular discourse obsessed with unmasking the power dynamics in every relationship in history, we are in danger of becoming ossified in our cynicism, constantly on guard, preoccupied with analyzing who's getting what from whom in our economic-exchange relationships. We seem to have forgotten how to enjoy each other at all. A book I read recently by poet Alicia Ostriker suggests that American women's poetry of the twentieth century, for all its rage and cheerful irony and devastating critique, also holds out hope for a renewal of genuine intimacy. Historically women's pleasure in relationship has been embedded in hierarchies—with the woman always on the bottom—so that "female ardor has been chained to submissiveness" and "[t]o love has meant to yield." But what women long for and are beginning to imagine, proposes Ostriker, is "relationships defined by mutuality and interpenetration rather than by the culturally privileged grid of dominance and subordination." She perceives in contemporary women's writing an "imperative of intimacy."

Perhaps for most women most of the time, the main task is still to keep from being submerged in relationship, to guard those boundaries of the self. So much of public feminist discourse, feminist theory, and psychological development study continues to bolster the defenses of women's autonomy and selfhood. Good thing, too, as the news is still full of women who get run over by forces happy to crush and discard them. But for some of us, some of the time, it has become safe to relish the fluidity of boundaries, even to celebrate it as a location of transcendent experience. After all, autonomy cannot be an end in itself. If we were all to become perfectly autonomous individuals, bristling with freedoms and choices at every turn in our lives— well, then what? What would we be choosing *for?* What would be the final result of our hard-won autonomy? The Preacher of Ecclesiastes, one of the many voices of dissent embedded in the Scriptures, embarks on an earnest search for wisdom and meaning, but finally concludes:

> *"The fate of the fool will overtake me also.*
> *What then do I gain by being wise?"*
> *I said in my heart, "This too is meaningless."*
> *For the wise [woman], like the fool, will not be long remembered;*
> *in days to come both will be forgotten.*
> *Like the fool, the wise [woman] too must die!*

A thousand other poets remind us that at the end of our lives, we face death no matter what—no matter how self-actualized we have been. If we are only ourselves, then we are but a "poor, bare, forked animal," as Shakespeare's King Lear puts it. In this light, our interconnectedness is good news. Love, caring, serving others, interconnections, and all those mushy, treacherous things women are supposed to be good at—these turn out to be a shield against vanity for all humans, a rescue from the autonomous self and its blinkered tyranny.

Many women seek connection and intimacy with a lover. For the lucky ones, it works and they get to experience the delightful union of free equals. It requires enormous effort and concentration to maintain this, however, as lovers so easily take each other for granted or become rivals—or traitors. But the intimate knowledge, the deep attentiveness that leads to delight in our children seems to come more naturally, even arrests us with surprise. Mutuality and interpenetration. Fluid boundaries. A sense of self merged with others. What mother does not feel these sensations wash over her without her conscious effort? It begins in the body, with the experience of the child within. Another being, but completely integrated into oneself. Even after the traumatic separation of birth, the fierce desires of breastfeeding; even beyond that, the precious sensation of holding the child; even beyond that, the reshaped soul where the child always remains.

Women of my generation experience these fluid boundaries, physical and spiritual, under new circumstances. We have a much better chance of surviving motherhood with both our physical health and our sanity. We have choices and opportunities that enable us to protect our bodies, train our minds, and direct our lives. Where our grandmothers survived the difficulties of their lives by saying "this is obedience" or "this is my nature," we can more often say "I've chosen this." There will always be further frontiers, but many of us are now in a position to realize, some of the time anyway, the hopeful vision Adrienne Rich presented at the end of her lengthy treatise on the ideologies and histories of motherhood:

We need to imagine a world in which every woman is the presiding genius of her own body. In such a world women will truly create new life, bringing forth not only children (if and as we choose) but the visions, and the thinking, necessary to sustain, console, and alter human existence—a new relationship to the universe. Sexuality, politics, intelligence, power, motherhood, work, community, intimacy will develop new meanings; thinking itself will be transformed.

By "genius," Rich does not mean an exceptional intellect. She's using the word, I'm quite sure, in the sense of "animating spirit." Rich hoped that women's bodies would no longer be detested or ignored, but appreciated as a significant part of our experience as women. Biology is not destiny, late-twentieth-century feminists insisted. No, but it is not nothing, either. Women of my generation, those who have been able, more or less consistently, to be the presiding geniuses of their bodies, have the opportunity to discover in our embodied experience ways to sustain, console, and alter existence for everyone—ourselves, our men and fellow women, and our children.

Perhaps women of my generation can work on living out the dynamic tension between guarding our individuality and surrendering to this blissful merger. If we can reach some new wisdom about this, it would make a lovely gift for our daughters and sons. I think one thing that we must especially draw from our embodied experience is that a balance between boundaries and merger is not merely the path to health for women's lives, but an essentially human task. We are individuals; we are interconnected. We need to fulfill both dimensions of our nature. It is possible for us to attend to one another in respect and delight, in the particularity of body and soul. Yes, there are a thousand pitfalls—jealousy, insecurity, lust, apathy, old conventions, bad models—but when the connection works, it seems certain that this is the way it's supposed to be.

One way for mothers of my generation to work on this balance between boundaries and merger is to urge the fathers of our children to ease a little toward the merger side of things. It has been easy for men to conceive of their lives as a solo quest, with women and children as either decoration or support staff. But when more men surrender to relationship and the blurred boundaries of self, all of us will benefit. It's easy to imagine how this can work for fathers, as day-to-day child care is a veritable boot camp for ego-tempering. Could more fathers choose to resist the god of work and upward mobility and achievement (among our chief idolatries as Americans) and stay home part-time for fifteen years, fully sharing in the raising of the children? Could we alter our work and economic structures on all levels to permit this? What would happen if it became routine for fathers and mothers alike to fold snap-crotch T-shirts and cut food into tiny pieces and stir supper on the stove while a toddler wailed and clung to their legs? These tiny ministrations can drive one crazy, but they are acts of mundane generosity that can also train the soul to love. So why not share the craziness more? It would keep us all sane. It would rescue women from drowning and it would rescue men from the tyranny of the self.

I would like to warn my daughter and my sons, too. I would like to say, Beware! But believe in the delight. Defend your autonomy where you need to, but seek out the communion. You'll never get it all the time; you can't. But remember the way it's supposed to be: offering unhurried attention, respecting individuality, connecting deeply, reveling in delight.

Silly Songs

The focused attention that leads to delight requires extraordinary trust. I think one of the reasons delight comes naturally and powerfully with our children is that they offer us unilateral trust. With other people, potential colleagues or friends or (especially) lovers, there's always the dance of suspicion before trust can settle in for a fidgety stay. But babies are not born worried about power differentials. I remember giving Jacob his first bath at the hospital, resting his floppy body on my forearm and cradling his head in the palm of my hand. With my other hand I poured warm water over his hair from a plastic pitcher and then rubbed in a little drop of shampoo. A gently sacramental moment, somehow. The nurse looked over my shoulder and noticed how Jacob stared up at my face with his lively eyes. "Look how he trusts you," she said.

When I see my children's trust in me and feel the powerful undertow of my love for them, I want to smack my forehead and say, "*Now* I get it! *Now* I understand, God, what you've been trying to tell me all this time!" In loving my children, I've found it much easier to trust God.

For one thing, I can imagine from the inside a persistent, patient love willing to set aside the costs. I know that even when Philip was getting me up twice a night to nurse and I could barely stand or think, even at four o'clock in the morning I loved reaching into the crib to lift him to me, recognizing his particular shape and smell. Even when bedtime goes badly because Miriam and Jacob are hitting each other over the toothpaste and we have to wrestle Philip down to get his pajamas on and I can't believe I put up with all this and why can't they simply cooperate for once?—I get over it, and I still love them.

My lapses into frustration or resentment are the result of my finitude; I get tired, I have work to do, the hours are running out. Happily, God isn't limited by all that. So if *I* can forgive my children a million times for the exasperation and the inconvenience because it seems like *nothing,* really, compared to the deep connection between us, then I know God—who is much more patient and much less tired—can deeply love me. "For as the heavens are high above the earth," says the psalmist, "so great is his steadfast love toward those who fear him." The Hebrew word for God's love is *hesed*—unfailing, untarnished love, like steel. Now I know, at least a little, how that feels.

And I'm not so afraid anymore, either of God's anger or power. Many of us struggle with the image of God as the peevish taskmaster, the stern disciplinarian that we would just as soon defy or escape. Divine anger is a serious matter, one I suspect I'll understand better when my children are teenagers. But already I can see that sometimes when I'm angry at Miriam or Jacob, I am definitely in the right. It really *is* stupid and wrong for them to fight over who gets the bigger brownie. And I can see that what they sometimes perceive as cruel and random tyranny—"Yes, you *have* to come in and get to bed"—is really for their well-being. So I can't resent a God who has rules and gets angry. We need the rules and sometimes we well deserve the anger. But we're very mixed up about this. Some of us have taken to cowering and ranting, even attributing abusive vindictiveness to God, when all we're seeing is a mistaken projection, the kind of wounded vision we're left with because of the worst in human cruelty. The psalmist offers a corrective: "The LORD is merciful and gracious, slow to anger and abounding in steadfast love." God begins and ends with mercy.

In recent decades, some feminist theologians have objected to the whole idea of submitting in obedience to an all-powerful being or merging into "unity with Christ" or "turning the other cheek." Oh yeah, *that's* what we need from religion: more subsuming of women's identities, more of that domination grid, more enforced humility. People run from God to maintain those same boundaries of the self; they run for fear of being squashed. Adrienne Rich did not mention religion among the institutions she hoped women's ways of thinking might reform. Like so many others, she considered Christianity and Judaism hopelessly patriarchal. Other theologians have rescued the idea of God only as a wholly immanent spirit—the god or goddess within. This, too, is a reaction of fear rather than hope, although perhaps a necessary stage. But in my best moments as a mother, I see so clearly that God does not wish either to squash us into generic slaves or dissolve inside us, but to bring us to maturity. What astounds me the most about my children is that they are so clearly individuals—complex personalities, unique bodies, new souls on the earth. That is the greatest miracle of all, the very thing I want to treasure most tenderly. Why would God create us all unique if the goal is to flatten us into nothings?

C. S. Lewis wrote a series of letters to his friend Malcolm in which they discussed prayer, and one problem they puzzled over was why God would want us to pray if he already knows everything about us and what we want and what's best for us. Lewis concludes that the reason God invites us to pray is that by "unveiling, by confessing our sins and 'making known' our requests, we assume the high rank of persons before Him." The relationship is supposed to be one of intimate knowledge, person-to-person exchange. The difference in power between us and God does not have to mean oppression and disaster. Differentials are sometimes precisely what sends energy flowing through the system, moving us toward mutual flourishing.

Even more, God is willing to wait with us as we grow, consider our capabilities, and delight in us along the way. "God knows our frame, remembers that we are dust." This is reassuring at those times when I act like God's little toddler. I'm capable of independent action and thought, but full of roaring conflicts and ready to run to the Big Provider with a tantrum when things don't go my way. Or sometimes I'm more like my older children. Jacob, especially, will ask me for, say, a bagel, and even though I don't respond because I'm busy doing something else, I'll start getting the thing ready for him. But instead of noticing what I'm doing, he'll keep asking and asking until it arrives in front of his nose: "Can I have a bagel? Mama, can I have a bagel? Can I have it now? I'm really hungry!" He's unable to perceive that I heard the first request and the bagel is already in the toaster.

No matter how taxing some days can be, at every stage of their growth our children surprise us with their particular charms, their invented phrases, their delighted smiles—and we can't help but pay attention. That's what we remember. We try to forget the nasty parts because we know the delight is what takes us forward toward where we're meant to be. "As far as the east is from the west, so far does [God] remove our transgressions from us." Delight is what God wants most, too. Not, I think, delight in elegant repose, as when one contemplates a lovely painting. But raucous, celebrative delight, as in those times when we are downright silly with our children, when we grip them under the arms and fly them overhead like planes and say "Suuu-per Ba-byyyyyyy!" and they squeal and laugh, lit up from the inside. Or when we carry on entire conversations consisting of variations on the tongue-raspberry. Or when I sing Philip ridiculous songs, like the toreador march from the opera *Carmen,* except with boo-bah syllables: Boo bah, ba-do bah, ba-do, ba-do, boo baaaaaah. Boo bah ba-dooooo, boo bah ba-dooo. And Miriam and Jacob say, "Sing it again!"

My pastor, Jack, once preached a sermon with a kind of refrain: "The best in us is not foreign to God." It was a serious sermon about the Resurrection, but the basic idea was that the best parts of our nature don't come out of nowhere. They are reflections of qualities perfectly originated in the Creator's nature. Why think of God as a terrible, nasty oppressor in the sky? Why not think of God more like the mother singing silly nonsense songs or the father dancing the baby around the room in a whirling, ecstatic waltz?

The best in us is not foreign to God. What I want for my children, in my own imperfect, messy, distracted way, is that they flourish as individuals and delight in their world and connect deeply with others. I believe that's what God wants for us. To grow up into beings capable of returning God's delight in us with our own trusting delight in God. Jesus says to his disciples before his crucifixion, "I have called you friends." They were rather bumbling friends, obtuse and disloyal, but Jesus offered them friendship as a rendezvous point where he would wait for them—and us.

~

Jack preached this morning on Mark 9, the peculiar story of Jesus' transfiguration in the presence of his disciples. He spoke about "thin places," where the veil that separates us from full perception of God is shimmery thin, and about "wrinkles in time," where the future glory enters the present. I kept thinking, "That's what I want. I want to be radiant. I want to reflect God's glory." As one of his illustrations, Jack said he remembered a baptism in our church during which a mother stood "right there" (he pointed to the space around the font) and held her baby while the congregation sang a hymn, and he watched this mother gaze at the new baby, and her face was radiant.

Ron turned to me and whispered, "Jack told me about this illustration when we had lunch together this week. He's talking about *you.*"

We are, most of the time, so dull and lightless. Could it be that our love for little ones, even when we are hardly aware, can draw back the veil for a moment and reveal the attentive delight meant to be ours, if only we will both rise and surrender to it?

20) little man

I stride along the road that runs across the top of the dune bluff, high above Lake Michigan. I look out at that broad horizon, soft and beautiful like a silk thread edging the slate blue satin, the living waters of the lake. The horizon curves far to the south and north, and I see the greatness of the earth, the vastness of time. It feels cozy and safe, somehow, to be so small against it.

Perspective is what I need most right now. The days have been going by so fast. Events come zinging at me and then they're past, wave after wave. My feet pound the asphalt, my arms swing, and I think how strong I feel again, how streamlined and agile. Then I wonder if this new strength isn't quite as rich as the weaknesses of the past two years. Can I feel as deeply now? Am I still cracked open enough for life-water to seep in?

When I was a teenager and a younger woman, I used to walk several miles a day and spend the time in fairly concentrated meditation. These days, a walk is a rare treat and sustained prayer beyond my capability. Well, I have learned that a robust prayer life may be a fine and desirable thing, but a lousy prayer life works for a while, too, in a pinch. Making sense of things in snatches while waiting for the tea water to boil or driving to the office or helping Philip down the slide for the fortieth time—it's all right. God can build things with pitiful dribbles of thought, too. Anyway, I think experience might have advantages over prayer. Chattering away at God we can block out what we need to hear. But when we're busy in the middle of things and our guard is down, sometimes whatever astonishing truth God needs us to recognize can take us by surprise.

Maybe I'm not as cracked open as I have been. But whatever slipped into me these last few years still burns there. Everything burns more now, more painfully and more energetically. I'm angrier, more passionate, tougher, and softer, too. Maybe becoming a mother has invested me deeper in the world and in the eternal, for good. It's put me in view of the horizon and set me walking with the fiercer winds.

First Birthday

In his twelfth month, Philip is getting around with impressive efficiency considering he hasn't yet taken his official first step. He loves to snoop around in the pantry cupboard and dig his hand in the boxes. Once we caught him stuffing raw oats right into his mouth—we couldn't resist neighing and making horse jokes. Or he likes to open the fridge, fish around in the fruit drawer, pick out an apple or nectarine, and then perch himself on the open dishwasher door where he swings his plump legs and nibbles. He can't get very far with his tiny front teeth, so then he puts the apple back. We're always finding little nibble marks on our fruit.

He's clearly a person who enjoys life. He loves being outdoors, probably because it's the one place we're not constantly telling him "No no!" He loves climbing and finds his way into the bathroom sink at least a couple times a day. He especially loves eating. We can hardly eat our own food because we're so busy keeping his plate stocked with carefully chopped morsels. Anything at all will do—he's not the least picky—but keep up with his appetite or he'll demon-strate exactly how loud he can yell. At the end of the day, he even seems to enjoy going to sleep. Our little pop-up baby is now our best sleeper.

Two days before Philip's birthday, our friends Trevor and Linda arrive from New Jersey with their six-month-old daughter, Michal. I'm secretly amused, in a thoroughly affectionate way, by Linda as the classic new mother, fussing over Michal and anxious about every detail. *Go get her blanket from the car—and should we put the crib there, or there? It's time for her cereal right now. If we leave in an hour she can nap on the way and then it will be time for a feeding and we really should be back by seven-thirty.* I'm completely enjoying this, helping Linda in every way I can think of, because I know I was *exactly* this particular about things, even with my *third* baby.

Michal is an especially beautiful, dark-eyed, sweet baby. I like holding her, but it feels a little uncomfortable, too. When other people offer to let me hold their babies, I always think for a minute that it's going to bring all these feelings and memories flooding back. But it never does, because it's some *other* baby. Nothing can bring back the feel of my own babies, their perfect fit, the perfect understanding between us about when to shift to the shoulder or turn around to face front.

Nothing can bring it all back. Even the photos and videos, as much as we love them, are thin little reminders. Trevor and Linda, still the intimate family trio, tell us they are impressed with our aplomb among our boisterous brood. It's a generous comment, and it makes me proud and sheepish at once. Do we know what we're doing? It feels like we simply manage day to day, make up a new rough-and-ready system whenever the old one falls apart, get by more or less. When we look back, we can never remember every turn, but we can see, to our amazement, how long a road it's been.

I'd like Philip's birthday party to be a lovely occasion for reflection on the past year, for tender memories of his birth hour and dreamy strolls through photo albums. Instead, my mind is full of profound thoughts such as "We have no paper plates. I'll have to get some nice paper plates" and "I'm going to *buy* lasagnes—there is no way I'm going to try to make them."

We're surely looking at another of those classic contrasts between the first kid and the later kids. Miriam's first birthday was a quiet day with just the three of us. I made the world's most ridiculously conscientious cake, which contained not a speck of sugar, weighed about fourteen pounds, and no one liked, not even Miriam. We bought her a cute outfit that turned out to be way too big. I cried because my baby (and I) had made it through one year. On Jacob's first birthday, we staged a more conventional party. The four grandparents were there, and we all sat around the table in the dining room and wore birthday hats. There were quite a few presents, and we took lots of pictures.

This time, we have Trevor and Linda and Michal, plus our five people, plus grandparents, and my brother has stopped by for a while. Poor Philip seems very small as we all mill around the house, bumping into each other, trying to get the meal ready. I'm serving the store-bought lasagnes buffet style, and my mom brought a salad. I did manage to put together a homemade chocolate cake. We all grab a plateful and then sit on various perches in the living room with the plates on our laps. I drag Philip's high chair in there and he presides. Once everyone has served themselves I realize I haven't even thought what to feed him. I pull some leftover pasta out of the fridge.

Later we stand around and sing "Happy Birthday," try to video-tape it, but we have to do it all over again because during the first performance, Ron was up in Miriam's room talking her down from a pout session. Ron's folks brought a present—an outfit that won't fit him until next spring. My parents forgot their present, but remembered the card and the check. Philip gets one other present from us, a neat musical stacking toy I bought only hours before. That's it. The storm blows in, blows out. We do the dishes. It's over. He's one year old. Life flows right on.

If there were more time to reflect, if I could sort out the images, if I could gather together the thoughts, if I could feel it all again. But nothing can bring it all back. How long a road it's been.

Benediction

Little Man, you are launched. You are mine and not mine, you are a new thing. Glide with me a while still, and I will love you.

My treasure, my abundance, I put all the books away now. You must tell me what comes next. Let your story overtake my words, let it fly, let it sing.

For you is the mystery waiting, for you it was hidden for ages in God who created all things. Be rooted and grounded in love. Comprehend the breadth and length and height and depth. Know those things that surpass all knowledge. Be filled to the measure, my little one, with the fullness of God.

afterword

"The imagination that entertains a God has much
to accommodate."

—STEPHEN DUNN

"You wrote this book during your third pregnancy and then during
the baby's first year? Are you crazy? I haven't even been able to write
up a decent grocery list since my first baby was born!"

I know you are going to wonder how the heck I did it. And the
answer is: I'm not exactly sure.

I do know that I *had* to do it. I felt absolutely driven. This third
baby was going to be our last, and I wanted to savor every moment
of the experience. Writing about it was a way I could do that.

Also, I wanted something new to read, for heaven's sake. I got
tired—maybe you have, too—of all the books that treat pregnancy
and birth as a merely medical event, an assortment of physical changes
and fetal developments. Giving life to a child seemed to irradiate my
thoughts about everything else—the body, womanhood, work, culture, God—everything. I wanted to read something that treated motherhood in the fullness of its dimensions, social and personal, body,
mind, and soul.

Sometimes, as all mothers know, if something must get done you
have to do it yourself. So I started writing. I started out simply

recording events and feelings, and then I let those experiences take me anywhere they led in my cluttered, possibly overeducated mind. This explains why the book leaves funny little tracks through all kinds of seemingly unrelated territory: Shakespeare, the Bible, popular sociology, Sesame Street, medieval art. I kept finding that there really weren't any dead ends: everything seemed relevant. I was bringing a new person into the world, so the whole world was fair game.

I also found that I was continually connecting my own body to spiritual matters in a way I hadn't often found in other books. I couldn't help it. It turns out that pregnancy and early motherhood are periods of intense body-consciousness as well as a crucible for spiritual growth. So I let it all mix together. Only later on did I realize that I was working in a genre I'd never heard of before: embodied feminine spirituality. Now I'm convinced that spirituality *must* be embodied, and why haven't we always known this?

None of that answers the question, though, of *how* I actually got the writing done. I'm always envious when I read acknowledgments pages and an author says, "And thank you so much to the such-and-such foundation for funding a year at the Motley Memorial Library to research this book, and thank you to my dear friend so-and-so for loaning her beautiful flat in the city so I could write in peace." A year with nothing to do but write? A room of one's own? Unbelievable.

This book was written mostly in a corner of my bedroom in snatches of time, mostly between ten and eleven at night, over the course of three years. Many nights all I could do was slump over the keyboard for fifteen minutes after the kids were in bed and tap out a few sentence fragments. What you read in this book is all true, but please realize there has been *lots* of revision. The original drafts were truly horrible.

There were a few blessed twenty-four–hour periods here and

there when I did actually go away and write at my parents-in-law's great little house on the lake. And in the last stages of revision, especially during the last month of the process, I was able to work full days in my office or in the library.

But even with those more consolidated periods, this is a book rescued from fragments—fragments of time, energy, and space that mothers of young children stitch together to accomplish anything. As T. S. Eliot said, "These fragments I have shored against my ruins." He was speaking of vast cultural movements. I'm just thinking of sleep deprivation. Anyway, if this book wound up with any coherence at all, it is a miracle.

So whatever eccentricities, blatant inconsistencies, contradictions, errors, and foolishness you find here, let them stand as the appropriate literary representation of a state of mind a little frayed around the edges. What literary style best captures the life of an expectant or new mother? Until recently, no one has known. New mothers, especially, have rarely written. They still don't do it very often. It's just too hard. One must be really quite nutty or desperate to try it.

In my case, I would probably have gotten nuttier if I hadn't. There was an element here of avoiding ruin. I went to the writing place—in my mind, I mean, as the actual physical location varied—because I desperately needed a place of retreat. While writing is definitely work, it is also release, and that leads to a kind of peace. As my late colleague Lionel Basney wrote: "A gift is not an ore . . . it is a need." This book came from a need to understand this passage of life more fully, and I hope that out of the space this need opened up in me, a gift for others might emerge.

One other note by way of explanation: my experience of motherhood is very ordinary. I'm married, my babies are all homegrown, we're all healthy, I go to church regularly, I have a teaching job. While I was writing, I often thought: What about adoptive mothers? What about babies born with disabilities or who are ill? What about mothers who never breastfed? What about lesbian women? What about women who have suffered the pain of infertility?

My small circle of faithful draft readers represented some of these concerns for me, and I tried to think outward toward other women's lives as much as I could. But I figured out right away that I could never try to account for other people's experiences, and certainly ought to keep quiet about things I know nothing about (although I certainly stretched *that* rule frequently enough!). I concluded that the best way to respect the variety of women's experiences, particularly women's pain and grief, is to cherish my own experience and describe it truly and well.

~

As I write this, my baby Philip is almost two years old. Meanwhile, Ron and I have just received the news that Ron's brother and his wife have welcomed their long-awaited first baby, Gabriel John. I feel a kind of greediness come over me: I want to see him and hold him and get a piece of him for myself. I miss the incredible intensity surrounding a baby's birth, and I'm quickly forgetting what it was like. Even in the process of writing about my own babies, I sometimes despaired that the intensity I wanted to capture for readers was fading fast. I know I missed important things. I couldn't say it all!

I hope that by telling my own thoughts and feelings, I have recaptured or perhaps amplified for you some of what is most amazing and transformative about your own experiences. At any rate, I have to stand back now. Gabriel is their baby, other stories need to be told.

acknowledgments

I'm honored to thank the many people who supported the writing of this book. My husband, Ron, makes everything possible and is clearly the pinnacle of civilized manhood. Jana Riess launched the whole thing with her encouragement and advice. My agent, Lorraine Kisly, believed from the start and lent her editorial and business savvy as well as her personal wisdom at every stage. My editor, Sara Carder, fell in love at just the right moment, then made the publication process fun.

My beta-readers improved this book immensely. Jay Robinson kindly put up with some early chapters. Beth Steenwyk rescued readers from many horribly tangled sentences. Elizabeth Vander Lei, Jennifer Sacher-Wiley, Susan Van Winkle, and Charlotte and John Witvliet made numerous wise suggestions based on their experiences as mothers (or fathers, in John's case) and professionals. Linda Rubingh also challenged me theologically when I needed it and offered many mighty prayers. All of these people kept me going with their generous encouragement.

Marchiene Vroon-Rienstra also read parts of the manuscript and came to the rescue in several emergencies. My mother, Dorothy Shreve, as always, prayed for me. And she waited a long time to read this because I was too scared she might not like certain parts. Thanks to all my parents and friends for encouragement and for forgiving me wherever necessary.

My colleagues at Calvin College, especially in the English Department, contributed their enthusiasm for the project and patiently answered many strange questions out of the blue about Hebrew verb tenses, implantation times, Indo-European etymologies, etc. Dr. David Van Winkle kindly tracked down several matters of medical fact. Kim Huizinga provided much loving care for the children so that I could find time to write.

Miriam and Jacob thought the whole thing was pretty cool. I hope they don't change their minds someday and get embarrassed. This book is dedicated to Philip, *sine qua non*.

suggested reading

The following are a few of the books mentioned in *Great with Child* or used for background research. I thought readers might like having the full reference for these and a word or two of description.

Blum, Linda. *At the Breast: Ideologies of Breastfeeding and Motherhood in the Contemporary United States.* Boston: Beacon, 1999.

  It's a work of sociology, but it's so well written you won't mind. I didn't
  realize how confused I was about breastfeeding till I read this book. Blum
  has done modern moms and future historians a service.

Borysenko, Joan. *A Woman's Book of Life: The Biology, Psychology, and Spirituality of the Feminine Life Cycle.* New York: Riverhead Books, 1996.

  Borysenko is a Harvard-trained physician who has made her life's work
  out of exploring the mind-body connection. This examination of women's
  physical and psychological development is organized in seven-year incre-
  ments from birth to old age.

Chicago, Judy. *The Birth Project.* New York: Doubleday, 1985.

This one is out of print, but you might be able to find it at your library. The book documents the complex process of researching, designing, and producing, in needlework and other media, Chicago's images of giving birth.

Clifton, Lucille. *Good Woman: Poems and a Memoir, 1969–1980.* American Poets Continuum Series, vol. 14. Boa Editions, 1989.

Clifton is one of those poets whose language seems simple and unstudied until you realize that her mastery of sound and image has just startled you into new insights.

Dement, William C. and Christopher Vaughan. *The Promise of Sleep.* New York: Dell, 1999.

Dement is one of the founders of sleep medicine, and the book manages to do two things at once: give an interesting account of the rise of sleep medicine and provide plenty of solid knowledge for the general reader about promoting healthy sleep. It has a good reference section and is highly readable, too.

Doyle, Brendan, ed. *Meditations with Julian of Norwich.* Santa Fe, N.M.: Bear & Co., 1984.

There are many good editions of Julian's full text available these days, but this *Meditations with* series is a nice place to start for newcomers to Christian mysticism. There are other titles in the series, too.

Frankel, Ellen. *The Five Books of Miriam: A Woman's Commentary on the Torah.* San Francisco: HarperSanFrancisco, 1996.

Frankel enters the midrashic tradition armed with immense scholarship, humor, and panache. Rather than writing in her own voice, she creates a cast of characters who engage in lively dialogue about each section of the Torah. A brilliant and illuminating strategy all lovers of Scripture might appreciate.

Lamott, Anne. *Operating Instructions: A Journal of My Son's First Year*. New York: Fawcett, 1993.

> Another book about surviving the first year of motherhood. I find Lamott's candid humor irresistible. Her loving portrait of her friend Pammy is in some ways the richest treasure of the book.

Lewis, C. S. *Till We Have Faces: A Myth Retold*. Eugene, Ore.: Harvest/Harcourt Brace, 1985.

> Lewis considered this his best book. It's surely one of the most profound books I've ever read. You think you're merely reading a great story and then . . . well, you'll see.

Mum.org

> A classy, well-researched but friendly site dedicated to the history of menstruation and contemporary women's health issues.

Nilsson, Lennart. *A Child Is Born*. New York: Bantam/Doubleday/Dell, 1990.

> Nilsson, a Swedish photographer, gathers many of his incredible photographs of conception, fetal development, and birth in this book. There are several good pregnancy reference books out there, but this gorgeous book is unique. I found it indispensable.

Otten, Charlotte, ed. *The Book of Birth Poetry*. New York: Bantam, 1995.

> A well-organized, wisely chosen collection of poems about all things birth-related.

Rich, Adrienne. *Of Woman Born.* New York: Norton, 1976.

I found this scholarly, sprawling, feminist classic occasionally tiresome in its polemic, but it's still worth reading for its interesting histories and important prophetic insights.

Roberts, Cokie and Steve. *From this Day Forward.* New York: William Morrow, 2000.

Half of the book is a memoir of the Robertses' marriage, with a focus on how they managed to merge his Jewish faith with her Catholicism. Alternating with chapters on the Robertses are fascinating chapters about the history of marriage in America.

Shalit, Wendy. *A Return to Modesty: Discovering the Lost Virtue.* New York: Free Press/Simon & Schuster, 1999.

A scary book, because it's so convincing in its exposure of America's moral poverty when it comes to sex—and the cost of this for women. Shalit draws upon philosophy, history, popular culture, and her own lively spirit to call for something better.

Weissbluth, Marc. *Healthy Sleep Habits, Happy Child.* New York: Fawcett, 1999.

A well-researched, sane, sensible book on children and sleep. That combination is not easy to find, despite the bulging shelves in the parenting section of the bookstore.

Zammit, Gary K., Jane A. Zanca, Gary Zammit, M.D., and Jean Zevnik. *Good Nights: How to Stop Sleep Deprivation, Overcome Insomnia, and Get the Sleep You Need.* Kansas City, Mo.: Andrews and McMeel, 1998.

You can imagine why I found this title appealing. The book is clear and readable without being patronizing. There are other good ones, but this is the one that helped me.

permissions

discussion questions

The questions below aim at those underlying spiritual issues that so fascinated me during this passage of life, and I hope they will spark discussion both for mothers and women who are not mothers. They correspond roughly to the chapters.

1. In what ways do you experience or claim the "reckless yes"?

2. How might we find power and wisdom in our monthly cycles?

3. What things have you desired but had to learn to live without? How does God fit into this sense of loss for you?

4. When has God said yes to you? How might we hold to those times during passages of life when God seems to say no?

5. How have you experienced the cost of pregnancy, motherhood, or serving others?

6. How might women convey the wisdom of attentive waiting to the rest of humanity?

7. Motherly fears are legendary in their power. How can we cope with them in faith?

8. Do we hate our bodies? How can we love them, and teach our daughters to love their bodies?

9. Do you tend to regard God's will for you and those you love as "destiny" or "ordination"? What difference does it make?

10. Does the myth of Psyche offer any insight on your own life, work, and struggles?

11. Why is pregnancy often a difficult time in a marriage?

12. How can we celebrate the pregnant woman and her body without patronizing her?

13. In contemporary American culture, have we lost the spiritual dimension of the birth process? How could we claim it back?

14. How can we make a place to listen to one another's birth stories?

15. How can we be more truthful and accepting both of the difficulties and euphoria of the first few weeks after birth and of breastfeeding?

16. Feeling fragmented and foggy is a common state for mothers. Is there any way to make friends with this condition? Can anything good come of it? What ways can we care for ourselves and others during these foggy times?

17. When have you felt rescued or healed? What contributed to that rescue or healing?

18. Do you experience a "dynamic tension between guarding our individuality and surrendering to this blissful merger" (p. 272)? How can we help our daughters and sons live that tension better than our generations have?

19. If you are a mother, what has motherhood taught you about the nature of God?

20. What, most of all, has the book recaptured or amplified about your own experience?